CORPORATISM AND ACCOUNTABILITY

CORPORATISM
AND
ACCOUNTABILITY

Organized Interests
in
British Public Life

EDITED BY
COLIN CROUCH
AND
RONALD DORE

CLARENDON PRESS · OXFORD
1990

Oxford University Press, Walton Street, Oxford OX2 6DP

Oxford New York Toronto
Delhi Bombay Calcutta Madras Karachi
Petaling Jaya Singapore Hong Kong Tokyo
Nairobi Dar es Salaam Cape Town
Melbourne Auckland
and associated companies in
Berlin Ibadan

Oxford is a trade mark of Oxford University Press

Published in the United States
by Oxford University Press, New York

British Library Cataloguing in Publication Data
Corporatism and accountability: organized interests
in British public life.
1. Great Britain, Corporatism
I. Crouch, Colin, 1944–   II. Dore, Ronald, 1925–
321.9
ISBN 0–19–827590–0

Library of Congress Cataloging in Publication Data
Corporatism and accountability: organized interests in
British public life / edited by Colin Crouch and Ronald Dore.
1. Pressure groups—Great Britain.   2. Lobbying—Great Britain.
3. Trade regulation—Great Britain.   4. Pluralism (Social sciences)—
Great Britain.   5. Great Britain—Politics and government—1945–
I. Crouch, Colin.   II. Dore, Ronald Philip.
JN329.P7C67 1990   306.3'0941—dc10   89–39533
ISBN 0–19–827590–0

Set by Hope Services (Abingdon) Ltd
Printed in Great Britain by
Courier International
Tiptree, Essex

Preface

THE research reported in this volume was supported by the Economic and Social Research Council. Its origins go back over a decade. The mid-1970s saw much talk in the public prints about Britain's 'ungovernability' and 'creeping corporatism'. Academic journals frequently carried discussion of corporatism as a concept: whether its association with fascism said something about its 'essential' character; whether there could be social democratic as well as authoritarian versions; whether it was just a plot to incorporate the working class in subordination to capitalists.

Imprecisely conceived and ridden with posturing as much of this debate was, it seemed to some members of the Sociology and Social Anthropology Committee that there were real issues involved—factual issues which required understanding, and policy issues which required informed judgement. Undoubtedly there were areas of public life—areas of great importance both for the nation's economic efficiency and for the distribution of income, wealth, power, and personal liberty—which were not left to market forces to sort out, were not, either, directly subject to administration, but nevertheless *were* part of public life. Government agencies in some shape or form *were* involved, but operated by persuasion, by bargaining, by compromise, by delegation.

And in those areas, what prevented the abuse of power, either governmental power or monopoly market power? Where matters were left to direct administration, the agencies involved were subject to the scrutiny of Parliament. Where they were left to the market, the consumer was sovereign (though, as A. O. Hirschman (*Exit, Voice and Loyalty* (Cambridge, Mass.: Harvard University Press, 1970)) had eloquently pointed out, in a lot of oligopolistic markets he had to use protest and not just the traditional option of withdrawing custom). But in the grey areas, who was accountable to whom?

It looked like both an intellectually challenging question and one that was amenable to empirical research. It was also manifestly a problem that had some bearing on how decent a society we were going, in future, to be able to live in.

And this was a time when the committees of the Social Science Research Council, as it then was, were actively casting around for challenging and important questions amenable to empirical research. For it was a time when the grey areas were invading the field of research funding too.

Hitherto, the Council had operated almost exclusively in a quasi-market mode. Research projects devised by academics under the inspiration of their own demiurges competed for limited funds. Peer review provided the analogue of consumer sovereignty. Peers were supposed to be interested in the 'intellectual quality' of the research and its 'contribution to the discipline' rather than in any questions of usefulness for public policy ('relevance' in the jargon of the time.)

Two things changed this. One was the spread of proactivism in government—the corporatist habit of looking for opportunities to take ameliorative initiatives, and to take them in co-operation with private interests rather than by direct administrative action. The other was increasing public scepticism as to whether the universities were giving value for money—an acceleration of the trend which resulted in the cuts of the 1980s. As real revenue growth stagnated, as constraints on public spending tightened and the then Chancellor of the Exchequer, Mr Denis Healey, began the process of selling off the family silver with the BP share issue, many, and not only Opposition MPs, began to wonder just *how* much the taxpayer ought to be subsidizing the demiurges of social science researchers. How much—to the tune of how many million—did the social need to affirm and sustain the value of scholarly curiosity and social-scientific rigour (together with, perhaps, occasional serendipitous 'relevance' to policy) justify paying for academics to study cross-cousin marriage in southern Poland or initiation rites among Californian ranchers?

It was a question which the Research Councils had to answer if they were to continue to demand expanding budgets. They did so by assuming the right and the responsibility of seeking to direct research into areas of social importance. A steadily increasing part of the SSRC's budget was earmarked for spending in the 'initiative mode' as opposed to the traditional 'responsive mode'. In classical corporatist fashion, groups of academics were to be given the privilege of having their research bills settled out of public funds and in return agreed to shape their research in ways deemed to be in the public interest— that agreement often being a bargained compromise between what fascinated academics and what committees thought 'important'.

The 'Corporatism and Accountability Initiative' was one such exercise. It was shaped, first, in a conference sponsored by the Sociology and Social Anthropology Committee of the SSRC and held at the Institute of Development Studies in 1978. Out of that emerged the decision to set up an 'exploratory panel', chaired by Dore. One of its members, Crouch, was appointed as Convenor, a half-time post for twelve months, during which time he met nearly everyone in Britain who was working on issues related to corporatism and wrote a comprehensive account of research in progress and where the gaps were. This, together with ideas arising from a second conference organized at the University of Kent in 1981, was incorporated into a final report of the panel (published by the ESRC). This recommended support of research in four areas, viz.: the balance between self-regulation and external legal regulation; the trade-off between delegated responsibility and internal democracy in internal accountability; the effect on internal industrial relations of enterprise bargaining with government; and the external monitoring of internal self-regulation. All except the third of these are represented in various of the papers produced here.

The recommendations were accepted, a budget of £0.25m. allotted, and a successor 'executive panel' set up in 1983. There were some eighty initial bids for funds when the panel advertised its existence and it finally chose teams of researchers.

Members of the panel acted as monitors, keeping in touch with the researchers and reading their interim reports. As a means of promoting the exchange of ideas between researchers, a one-day conference was held a few months after the awards were made, and there was a Corporatism and Accountability newsletter which ran to three issues. Two one-day conferences have been held to report research findings, one on vocational training and one on the professions and how far the corporatist arrangements to which they are subjected have been altered by new concerns for national 'competitiveness'. Both conferences were for 'practitioners' as well as researchers.

The chapter by King and Schnack was first published in the *Political Quarterly*. We are grateful to the editors and publishers (Basil Blackwell) for permission to reproduce it here.

October 1989

C.C.
R.P.D.

Contents

Figures

Tables

1. Whatever Happened to Corporatism?

Colin Crouch and Ronald Dore

'Ism' words and their equivalents in other languages, like 'shugi' words in Japanese, always give difficulties. Most of them can stand both for *ideology*—for some ideal actively advocated by political partisans—and also for a *category of analysis*—a description (used either in common everyday talk or in specialist social-science discourse, or in both) of some actual social reality. Thus 'nationalism' can mean both 'a doctrine that all groups of people who feel themselves to be members of a nation *ought* to have their own nation-state' and also 'a sentiment of identification with a group which defines itself as a nation'.

'Capitalism' and 'feudalism' are rather less dual-purpose words in that sense, much more specialized to the description of social forms. (Hence, one usually says 'capitalist ideology', not just 'capitalism', if one wants to refer to the doctrine that capitalist forms of organization are a good thing.) But 'corporatism' is pre-eminent among the ambiguous 'isms'. It started life, after all, very much as doctrine—as a reaction, in its early, post-1870, German and French phases, to *laissez-faire* individualism, and later to Marxian socialism. It was the name which certain thinkers gave to their ideal form of society—one which would be organized in such a way as to eliminate conflict and accord to everyone rights and duties proportionate to the functional importance of their role in society.

As an ideal, corporatism has traditionally been an enemy both of liberalism and of class-conscious socialism. And the twentieth-century states which have claimed to embody that corporatist ideal—Italy, Portugal, Austria, Spain, Brazil—have shown that enmity to be fully justified. For the liberal, or the socialist, therefore, so salient are the evaluative overtones of the

A version of this chapter was presented by C.C. at the Sociology section of the 150th annual meeting of the British Association for the Advancement of Science, Oxford, Sept. 1988.

word 'corporatism' that it is difficult to use it simply as a tool of analysis, to ask whether, empirically, a society has become more or less corporatist without seeming to ask whether or not it is on the road to perdition.

So there is a special value-purging problem about dealing with the concept of corporatism. But there are also the general problems which 'corporatism' shares with 'capitalism' and 'feudalism'—how can one characterize the structure of a whole society in such a way that the definition (1) can apply to more than one society, and (2) is not vacuous and offers clear empirical criteria for deciding whether a society fits the definition or not. That is difficult enough when one is dealing with a relatively simple agrarian form of society, as is apparent from the attempts to define feudalism in ways which definitively include or exclude Mogul India or Tokugawa Japan. It is apparent, too, in the endless attempts by Marxist historians to pinpoint the point of transition from feudalism to capitalism in Europe or Japan. How much more difficult to reach all-embracing characterizations of the structure of modern societies.

Hence it is not surprising that a lot of the writing about corporatism is bedevilled by definitional problems, or that some of the attempts at definition should turn out to be so cumbersome. Take one of the subtlest and most often quoted of definitions, Philippe Schmitter's (1974):

a system of interest representation in which the constituent units are organised into a limited number of singular, compulsory, non-competitive, hierarchically ordered and functionally differentiated categories, recognised or licensed, (if not created) by the state and granted a deliberate representational monopoly within their respective categories in exchange for observing certain controls on their selection of leaders and articulation of demands and support.

The trouble with such macro-level definitions is that they do not leave very much room for the more and the less. Marxists are used to knowing when one 'social formation' gives way to another, because the event is classically punctuated by revolution. But corporatism is interesting precisely because there is a widespread impression, fostered by political sloganeering and journalistic analysis, that what we are witnessing in most capitalist democracies is 'creeping corporatism', a slow transition *towards* corporatism—certainly not any conscious creation of a

Schmitterite regime, much less the creation of such a regime under the avowed banner of corporatism.

One way to tackle that question is to disaggregate, to move from the macro to the micro. One viable way of trying to define 'feudalism', for instance, is by starting with a definition of a 'feudal relation' (in terms, say, of the exchange of protection and service) and to call a society more or less feudal depending on the density of such relationships in the total economic system. 'Capitalism' can be defined in terms of the density, within the total volume of work arrangements, of free-contract wage relationships between owners of property and owners of skill or labour power (as opposed to individual or family enterprise, or co-operative arrangements where owner and worker coincide, or coercion-using slavery). In the same way, if one starts off with a clear definition of a 'corporatist arrangement', one can then get at the question which is really bothering people—the question about 'creeping corporatism'—by asking, 'is there evidence of an increasing density of corporatist arrangements in the socio-economic structure?'[1]

So let us offer a definition not of 'corporatism', but of a 'corporatist arrangement':

> An institutionalized pattern which involves an explicit or implicit bargain (or recurring bargaining) between some organ of government and private interest groups (including those promoting 'ideal interests'—'causes'), one element in the bargain being that the groups receive certain institutionalized or *ad hoc* benefits in return for guarantees by the groups' representatives that their members will behave in certain ways considered to be in the public interest.

The archetypal examples of such arrangements, of course, are the old medieval corporations. The doctors and the lawyers of medieval England—as well as the civil engineers and all the other professional groups which got their charters in the nineteenth century—were granted monopoly privileges (the right to decide who should and who should not be allowed to sell

---

[1] Philippe Schmitter, together with Wolfgang Streeck (Streeck and Schmitter 1985*a*: 28), has also concluded recently that 'the idea of a comprehensive corporative–associative social or political "system" is fundamentally misleading', and that elements of 'private interest government' (much like the notion of 'corporatist arrangement' here presented) are better worth pursuing.

certain kinds of services) in exchange for promises to make sure that the professional standards of those who did sell those services—their skills and their morals—were what the public had a right to expect. More modern forms—this time the granting by the state of an *ad hoc* concession rather than an institutionalized privilege—include, for instance, the bargains sometimes struck in the 1960s and 1970s in Britain between the British Rail management, the railway unions, and the government: more state funds for railway modernization provided that the unions would agree to get their members to accept productivity improvements and changes in work practice.

Our definition, to drive the point home, has, as its main constituent elements: first, the idea of a bargain; secondly, the idea of a distinction between a group interest and a wider public interest; and thirdly the notion of a discipline exercised over group members.

The discipline groups exercise over their members, of course, is not confined to corporatist arrangements. Groups constrain the behaviour of their members for their *own* good as well as for a wider public interest. The Football Association, for example, lays down rules as to how football is to be played in order to have the universality and continuity necessary to a national and international structure of competitions—a shared interest of the clubs themselves. (Where, as in Australian cricket, the search for gate-returns produced new Packerite market-orientated forms, there still had to be a parallel rule-bound system, not *ad hoc* anarchy.) We would not speak of those as corporatist arrangements. But we do use the word corporatist when the Football Association requires its members to spend a lot of money and introduce new admissions practices, in order to stop hooliganism *in a wider public interest* (getting in return the right to continued police services, freedom from even more draconian statutory restrictions, and so on).

Of course, the distinction between the group's *own* interest and a wider public interest is often somewhat artificial, or at least a matter of more and less. The ethical disciplinary committees of the doctors and the lawyers, for example, are not only a means of protecting the public; they are also a means of being seen to protect the public, of raising the profession's reputation and so its ability to charge higher fees. Football clubs and their members would *also* benefit from a general *long-run* decline in hooliganism in society. The control of inflation, which is the major public, society-wide, interest which an incomes policy is intended to achieve, may be expected to produce faster growth and hence ultimately higher incomes. That can be argued to provide a motive for wage restraint even for powerful unions which could be fairly sure of keeping ahead of inflation if they used their bargaining power to the full. But the longer-term gains in question often, first, are a long way off; second, require acceptance of a complex chain of reasoning if one is to believe that they will be achieved; and third, require acceptance that *one's own* co-operation is necessary for the benefit outcome and that the 'free rider' option does not exist. There is thus—to stick with the incomes policy example—a triple discount to be applied to long-term private benefits when they are compared with 15 per cent extra in your pay packet next week. Corporatist arrangements are designed for just such situations—where the collective good does require a restraint, an exercise of discipline, which private benefit calculations would not themselves produce.

WHY RESEARCH ON CORPORATISM?

The 'growth of corporatism', then, can be rephrased in micro-level terms[2] as 'growing density of corporatist arrangements in society'. That at least offers some criteria for specifying what one means by 'growth'. But why should it be a matter of some interest for academics to address their research to the question whether there really is a growing density of such arrangements,

---

[2] Macro-, meso-, and micro- have become popular in the corporatism literature of late. Alan Cawson (1986) uses the terms to refer primarily to the size of the unit to which the arrangement applies—the whole economy, an industrial sector or region, the inside of a single corporation. We use 'micro-level' in a different sense here, distinguishing it from a 'macro-level' holistic characterization of a national political structure. Hence, an incomes policy, or some other kind of bargain concerning the management of the macro-economy, would be just as much *a discrete* corporatist arrangement—to be analysed in terms of who talks to whom, what public interest the arrangement is supposed to serve, what are the interests and weapons of the parties, how are their representatives accountable to them, etc.—as a union, local health authority, hospital management bargain over private pay-beds or working conditions in a particular hospital.

what form they take, and what their consequences are? Clearly because it is—or was during the 1970s Britain in which the research reported in this book was first planned—a matter of public concern. And how had it become so? Very largely because corporatist arrangements are thought often to involve the granting of privileges without clear accountability. They were seen as inadmissibly circumventing established procedures by which the public interest—in getting good service, in maintaining market competition, in preventing diversion of public funds, etc., etc.—can be protected, and seen to be protected. One notable incident in the mid-1970s evoked a full expression of these concerns. It involved incomes policies. The Chancellor of the Exchequer reached a formal understanding with the Trades Union Congress (TUC) that he would reduce income taxes if the TUC would promise to persuade its members to restrain wage increases within a given percentage norm. Apart from the problem that the TUC was unable to deliver the compliance of its members anyway, criticism—indeed, outrage—centred on the fact that the setting of tax levels was the proper business of Parliament and it was inadmissible that Parliament's functions should be thus usurped.

There was a widespread assumption that corporatist arrangements *were* on the increase. But there was a difference of opinion as to whether this was inevitable or not. There was also a sharp division of opinion as to whether it was a good thing or not.

Those who assumed that corporatist arrangements were on the increase did so for two reasons. First, because corporatist arrangements were often a response to market failure, and for a variety of reasons market failure was becoming more common. Secondly, they were also seen as a response to political failure— a means of reinforcing inadequate political authority—and failures of authority were also seen to be increasing.

In fact, we might usefully add to our definition of a corporatist arrangement the following:

and that arrangement, as a feasible alternative, can be seen as a substitute for either:

1. leaving things to the market, or
2. leaving them to the decision of some conventional organ (legal, executive, or judicial) of government.

The increases in market failure and political failure were seen by some observers to be, not just the product of mismanagement or failure of will, or historical happenstance, but the result, rather, of evolutionary structural changes in society. As for *market failure*, the reasons why corporatist arrangements might be expected to increase are basically the same as all the reasons—of increasing technical and organizational complexity accompanying the development of technology—which prompted Hilferding (1910) to talk about 'organised capitalism' and Schumpeter (1942) to speak of capitalism, by its very success, inevitably leading to socialism. They are the reasons which caused Keynes to write the 1926 pamphlet to which Schmitter has drawn attention (*The End of Laissez-faire*) and Churchill, in his famous Romanes lecture a few years later, to talk about the need for a parliament of industry with functional representation to supplement the territorially representational existing Parliament.

The depression of the 1930s was one factor which intensified the involvement of the state in the economy and hence the search for organizational forms which could balance the interests of sectional (producer) groups against those of the nation—the consumers—as a whole. It produced one of the earliest and longest-lived corporatist arrangements in Britain, the Milk Marketing Board. Since the war, the rise in welfare expectations, the political imperatives, first of maintaining full employment, then of containing the inflationary pressures which growing union power in a full employment world made inevitable (to simplify a much more complex chain of causation), vastly increased the load on government. (The steady rise in the tax take to over 40 per cent of GNP in most industrial societies being the most obvious symptom thereof.) The need to find methods other than direct administration to substitute for failing markets was a powerful source of new corporatist arrangements.

If affluence and rising expectations were one consequence of technological development which increased the role of the state, another path of causation was via the intensification of international trade competition, a consequence, in turn, of the rapid cheapening of transport and communication. Late-developing countries like Japan have long given great importance to the role of the state in promoting the nation's ability to compete internationally—in accelerating investments in infrastructure, in long-term R. & D., in vocational training;

expenditures in the benefits from which externalities are so important that markets dominated by calculations of short-term rates of return would always neglect them. In the pioneer industrial countries it is only in recent decades that the need for 'industrial policies', the need for government action to enhance 'competitiveness' (a word hardly heard a decade ago), has come to be a staple theme of political discourse.

As for *political failure*, the belief that it was becoming more endemic a problem, and that corporatist arrangements represented a sensible/misguided attempt by public authorities to try to supplement their own store of authority by co-opting that of representative groups, was made overt in the debate sparked off in the mid-1970s by signs of what journalists called Britain's 'ungovernability'.

Again, this was seen as a trend phenomenon affecting all modern societies, not a purely British failing. Modern societies were seen to have become ungovernable because of the plethora of interest groups that were able to lobby, pressurize, or even (and here corporatism became relevant) take over some functions of government (for examples and discussions see, *inter alia*, von Beyme 1984; Dahrendorf 1980; Hennis *et al.* 1977, 1979; Rose 1979). The result was said to be that governments tried to please everyone and, in so doing, relinquished authority. This meant increasing government expenditure, and either excessive consequent taxation or increasing public deficits, or both; all routes seemed to lead to inflation. The rich, pluralistic interest group activity that had been applauded as the flower of democracy in the 1950s was now derided as the weed that was choking it—sometimes by the same authors (compare Beer 1965 and 1982). Again, the interest groups most often cited were trade unions, though a few authors were bold enough to identify democracy itself as the problem (e.g. Brittan 1975).

It was not just that corporatist arrangements among producer groups impeded market forces; they also impeded the proper exercise of state power, a power which was needed to safeguard the market order and law-abiding behaviour in general. On the other hand, of course, corporatist arrangements could be used as precisely the means by which the unruliness of pluralism— or, indeed, of a fragmented, individualized modern society— could be tamed and disciplined. Comparative research tried to address this issue, and adduced considerable evidence that societies that made wide use of corporatist arrangements, particularly at the macro-economic level, were in fact more orderly than other liberal democracies (see especially Schmitter, 1981; also Crouch 1985; several of the studies in Goldthorpe, 1984; Schott 1984). Even the main work to appear that attacked the impact of organized interests on economic efficiency (Olson 1982) allowed a structure that captured much of corporatism (encompassingness) to stand as a solution second best to the free market and preferable to pluralism.

This, however, left the question of what kind of social order was produced by a wide range of corporatist arrangements. A major problem of corporatist research was that dubious history to which we have referred. Several analysts, ideologically from the left and right alike, who described certain institutions as corporatist deliberately intended such echoes. Initially most were from the left and denounced corporatism as a means of incorporating and emasculating the working class (e.g. Panitch 1976; 1980). Also, one of the main seminal articles of 1974, the year when the international corporatist debate was really under way (Schmitter 1974), emerged directly from the context of Latin American research, though it was immediately applied to Western Europe.

However, as the decade progressed and comparative studies emerged, some authors changed their view. Corporatist arrangements seemed to correlate most obviously with social democracy, hardly a fascist political form. Some authors who, earlier in the 1970s, had been sharply critical of corporatist arrangements ended by advocating them as the form of politics most able to combine widespread interest representation with economic efficiency, perhaps as social democracy's only stable form (Cameron 1985; Crouch 1977, 1985; several of the papers in Goldthorpe 1984; Lange and Garrett 1985; Schott 1984). Concomitantly, by 1988 the Conservative government had officially condemned corporatism as having 'limited competition and the birth of new firms whilst, at the same time, encouraging protectionism and restrictions designed to help existing firms' (Department of Trade and Industry 1988: 1).

One central focus of the 'evaluation' debate was whether corporatist structures aided or obscured accountability. According to one account, by involving organized interests in government, by placing on them the burden of restraining as well as representing their clients, corporatist arrangements aided accountability in a world where parliamentary scrutiny was clearly too blunt an instrument. But other voices drew attention to the secretive nature of most corporatist activity, and its unofficial, semi-legitimate nature. Parliament might be a blunt, executive-dominated tool, but at least it was elected on a more or less transparent basis, published its proceedings, and acted through widely understood and regular procedures. How did the apparently charmed circle of corporatist actors achieve their positions? What did they say to each other? What rules governed their action? (See several of the papers in CSSP 1976; and for an account of Austrian arrangements which raises similar questions concerning that doyen of corporatist cases, see Marin 1982.)

While academic research and political debate interacted throughout this time, the former eventually left the polemics behind. While nearly all discussion concerned activity at the level of the nation-state, some researchers looked at relations at the level of the firm and spoke of micro-corporatism. Others explored a meso-corporatism, meaning two separate but equally interesting phenomena: on the one hand activity at the level of industrial sectors; on the other, geographical regions. The former became particularly prominent as the 1970s macro-economic issues of inflation control were succeeded by the sector-specific issue of restructuring (e.g. Cawson 1985). Much of this work centred on Germany, with meso- running into micro- in the 'crisis cartels' established by various public authorities, companies, works councils, and unions around the beleaguered steel industry of the Ruhr and Saarland (Esser *et al.* 1983).

Regional corporatism also has its main application in Germany (Sabel *et al.* 1987), where a regional (*Land*) tier of government makes available the public authority central to corporatist relations, and at a scale similar to the size of the small nation-states usually cited as the main corporatist cases. Regional corporatism has also emerged in Italian (Weiss 1988) and British (Moore and Booth, this volume) studies, within national contexts normally seen as fairly inhospitable to the phenomenon.

The simultaneous development of institutional change and academic study in the 1970s created the impression in the public debate that there was something very recent about corporatism, though commentators were usually aware that the term had a longer, rather murky, past. Academic studies have of course traced continuities back in time over a lengthy period. Most of the projects reported in this volume were required to concentrate on the recent past and were therefore unable to capture this. But, clearly, as our earlier example of the medieval corporations suggested, corporatist arrangements have a long history. It is worth looking back at that history before trying to answer questions about a recent growth of such arrangements. The phenomena we study are the product of a mixture of forces: on the one hand structural changes common to all industrial societies; on the other styles of politics, habitual responses, underlying assumptions about the public and the private which are peculiar to individual national political cultures.

NATIONAL TRADITIONS

Most recent comparative studies, based on the central terrain of industrial relations tripartism, rank the UK as either moderately or extremely low on any scale of corporatism, but by other criteria the society is rich in corporatist arrangements. The British have had (1) a fairly well-developed ability to recognize collective goods which cannot be achieved by private action; but (2) a tendency to mistrust the central state which manifests itself in: (*a*) a preference for local control when those public goods can only be achieved by public power (for example, policing or much of education); (*b*) a preference for non-state action as a means of achieving public goods wherever possible (as in the distinctive British concept of the charity); and (*c*) a strong concern with the supremacy of Parliament *within its allotted sphere*—not to let constitutional rules fetter it, judicial authority rival it, or (in the nineteenth century) executives dominate it. It is a delicate and paradoxical mix, but important to grasp if the British approach to public action is to be understood.

In addition, and running parallel to the well-remarked tendency for the British to avoid positive as opposed to negative freedoms, is their sense of public interests as protective, disaggregated, not concerned with strategic goals. Indeed, outside wars, the British have not had strategic goals. The tradition is bound up with the British pattern of industrialization and the well-known 'early developer' characteristic that marked the country out from nations that industrialized later and under Britain's shadow. Industrialism 'happened' to the British; it emerged from the entrepreneurial profit-seeking of individuals in the market. It was not something sought for the nation by its leaders. There was no 'project' of industrialism, *deutscher Art.*

This was political soil in which corporatist arrangements of a certain kind could flourish extensively; but which would not nourish arrangements of another kind. Able to flourish were passive, unambitious means of regulating affairs so that conventionally, often implicitly, recognized public interests would be served and protected from market forces by cosy, often essentially medieval practices, offering sometimes obscure forms of self-discipline. Important to such a procedure was the 'gentlemanly' code of British public affairs, resting on implicit understandings and trust among a social élite linked by networks of family, friendship, and club. Indeed, there may often be room for doubt as to exactly how 'public' the public interests ostensibly served by such practices really were, but the claim was often made. To the extent that all this had an aristocratic and in particular monarchical base, it was a world in which the interests of some families were almost regarded as constituting the public interest, since they were its guardians. So, when the gentlemanly code *was* breached, in a Lloyd's or a Stock Exchange, it could be seriously argued that the best way of serving the *public* interest was to sustain public confidence by hushing up.

For ease of reference we shall call this 'old' corporatism. Falling on stony ground would be any attempt, by government or whoever, to 'use' this rich tissue of associations to achieve some defined national task. We shall call mechanisms of this kind, the kind that was intended by most of the corporatist analyses of the 1970s, 'new' corporatism.

We can place these characteristics in a comparative perspective. If it is only lately, as international competition intensifies, that the British have come to *use* organized interests for purposes of public policy in the way that some of the European late-developers (like Germany or Scandinavia) have long since become accustomed to doing, there has nevertheless been no rejection of the idea that such interests should participate in political activity, as was long the case in France. It has been more like US pluralism, but with an elaborate, informal, and implicit code of self-restraint that has limited lobbying activity, has tended to aggregate interests to form, in contrast with the USA, a relatively small number of non-competing organizations. The USA lacked the 'gentlemanly' social élite that long blunted and channelled unrestrained individualism in the nineteenth century's other major liberal society.

If the British have a large sense of the public sphere but a small sense of the scope of the state within that sphere, then Americans might be said to have a small sense of both; the French to have an extensive sense of the state but a limited idea of any public sphere outside it; and Germans to have an extensive state *which shares its role* with those organized interests that it accepts as co-operating with it, and excludes from participation those that it does not accept.

Maitland's remark that there was in England no such thing as public law has been overtaken by historical change (Maitland, 1901, quoted in Dyson 1980: 115), but it remains difficult for the British to understand the idea of organized interests as *staatstragende Kräfte*—literally, 'state-bearing forces' (see, for example, Böckenförde 1977). Burke's reference to the great oak trees that guard the constitution was a reference to aristocratic families, and it was only by an unofficial extension of that notion that old Tory and Whig traditions accustomed themselves to the ideas of interests that formed a part of the state. It is by a similar anachronistic extension that the British sometimes speak of the unions, the press, or some other institution as extra 'estates of the realm'.

These points can be illustrated in a number of ways. First, the Church of England has been an established national Church, with the monarch at its head, but retained its autonomy, private wealth, and right to make many of its appointments itself. This differs sharply from the state Churches of the Lutheran countries, but is not dependent on an international status as is Catholic autonomy. A second instance has been the manner in which the ancient universities and the major public schools have served as implicit, informal *écoles d'administration* while remaining private in constitution and non-specific in their aims. A third would be that nineteenth-century phenomenon so often re-marked by European observers: a lay, unpaid local magistrature instead of a state prefecture. In the twentieth century something similar has developed in the creation of public institutions that are seen as separate from the state: for example, the British Broadcasting Corporation and the former University Grants Committee.

The greatest instance of a private body taking on a public task is probably the National Trust. That creation of Octavia Hill and her circle came originally from the same ideological stable as the Charity Organisation Society, embodying the ideal of essentially voluntary, though statutorily based, non-state but public activity. When one recalls that this group was part of the same circle as the Bosanquets and T. H. Green, the so-called English Hegelians, one realizes just how far the state-centred philosophy of Hegel changed *en route* from Prussia to England.

Within the business world there has been the central paradox of the City of London. The institutions within the City constitute some of the most perfect markets in the world, but they were long encased in and regulated by a non-market system of familial and other informal links that tied them to the Bank of England (before 1946 itself a private institution) and from there to the Treasury (Cassis 1985; Harris and Thane 1984; Lisle-Williams 1984a, 1984b). Despite its virtual 'official' status, the City long behaved like an offshore island, more concerned with oversea economies than with the British.

At the heart of 'old' corporatist arrangements were the licensed professions. Provided they undertake to discipline their own miscreants and meet certain public needs for the provision of a service, the professions have been free to, or in many cases have been given statutory authority to, organize their recruitment, training, fees, and practices. Contrast the USA, where, though once more state-regulated than in Britain in some of the New England states, they nowadays barely escape subordination to market forces. Contrast France or Japan, where the state has always kept a tight rein on recruitment and training. Professional regulation has always been concerned with the relation between domestic service producers and domestic service consumers. It has had nothing to do with attempts to mobilize the economy for international competition. When, more recently, the professions have been called upon to participate in this latter task, there have been great difficulties, as Laffin's discussion of the engineering professions elsewhere in this volume shows.

The integration of organized labour into old corporatism was of course very tricky, as workers were not gentlemen. However, if admitted gradually and starting with the most highly skilled, their representatives could at least become cadet gentlemen. And this is precisely what they did, as any number of works on the conduct and deportment of late Victorian trade unions have told us. It is still significant, however, that the Act of 1871 that legalized some trade union activity did so by exempting many labour actions from what would otherwise have been the consequences of the common law. There was no desire to tamper with the inability of that law to recognize anything other than individuals (or joint stock companies artificially defined as individuals). Organizations as such remained implicit.

Impact of the world wars

During the twentieth century's two world wars certain major ingredients of the British system changed. War provided a clear mobilizing function for this least mobilized of societies. The state became more centralized, deeply involved in many areas of life that had previously lain outside its scope, and needed to incorporate organized interests, including labour, to help it with these tasks (Lowe 1986). The trends were there before 1914 itself; concern at both the German armament programme and the growing importance at home of organized labour worked towards the same end. It is from this period that Middlemas (1979) dates the 'corporate bias' of British politics: the tendency for governments to work closely with organized producer interests, especially the unions, the producer interest whose organization sharpened class divisions in society. He rightly suggested only a corporate 'bias', for few of the corporatist bargains between government and unions were ever spelt out explicitly until the 1960s, except in wartime. And in both wars mobilization rested more on statutory executive action than on corporatist arrangements.

Although the immediate aftermath of the First War saw an ostensible reinforcement of corporatist trends (Lloyd George's summoning of the National Industrial Conference 1919–21 (Lowe 1978); Speaker Whitley's proposals for a works council system in most sectors of employment), this declined as the threat of worker militancy receded and as economic policy returned to *laissez-faire* normalcy. Further changes came in the 1930s as, in the wake of the Depression, corporatist arrangements were established to limit competition in a number of sectors: e.g. shipbuilding, shipping, milk distribution (Booth 1982). While statutorily based, these arrangements were managed by trade or producer associations, though with no involvement of labour. These policies were initiated with considerable reluctance by ministers, who saw them, accurately, as temporary emergency measures, not a major new path for the British economy.

The early 1930s were the years when coalitions of agricultural and labour interests were initiating corporatist departures in Scandinavia (enduringly) and the USA (temporarily). In Britain, without labour participation, these were the years when the great agricultural marketing boards—for milk, potatoes, hops, etc.—were established. Representative organizations, mainly the National Farmers' Union, were formally and legally integrated into the administration of systems for regulating, limiting, and financing agricultural production (Self and Storing 1962; Grant 1985; Winter 1984). From that point, as Cox, Lowe, and Winter demonstrate in their chapter in this volume, agriculture joined the licensed professions as the purest cases of corporatism in British society. It is notable that even societies that normally rank low on corporatism scales, like France, have highly corporatized arrangements for agriculture.

The Second World War had more extensive corporatist implications than the First, because its more advanced technology required an even greater economic mobilization and because organized labour had become more important. Boards and committees representing employer and employee interests were used to ensure commitment to the war effort and the achievement of its production targets. The pattern lasted into the later 1940s, being used for initial post-war reconstruction. The contrast between this kind of national mobilization and the relaxed 'domestic' corporatism of the liberal professions shows clearly the distinction between old and new corporatist arrangements.

Something of the change survived throughout the 1950s. Many wartime institutions remained, and there was a constant trickle of new bodies that routinely incorporated affected interests. However, immediate reconstruction having been accomplished, the British economy returned to its nonmobilized pattern. Keynesian demand-management techniques were interpreted by the Treasury to mean the manipulation of a few arm's-length regulators, avoiding the need for more substantive entanglements with the actual conduct of the economy.

Many of the newly developing tripartite organizations were consultative rather than administrative. A recent Scandinavian study (Olsen 1983) has contrasted the role of organized interests in that part of the world with the British case. While there has been a similarly extensive incorporation of organized interests into public bodies in Britain, Denmark, Norway, Sweden, and in recent years also Finland (Helander and Anckar, 1983), in the Nordic cases this is more likely to include direct participation in the administration and running of services.

The internal structure of interest organizations themselves was quite varied. Employer and trade associations remained relatively decentralized and loosely structured, relaxing their temporary wartime hold and barely resembling their German counterparts, who were actively engaged in both economic and industrial relations developments. Where regulation of some kind seemed inevitable, however, industry was readily able to provide representatives to contribute to the task (e.g., as well as agriculture, in pharmaceuticals and the denationalized iron and steel industry).

On the union side, skilled workers had already shown their irritation with the constraints of any incomes policy involvement by their leaders in the late 1940s, and their unions were in any case decentralized. Among unions of the less skilled, powerful union 'boss' figures survived, and played a part in restraining conflict and in achieving certain economic goals. The most important case was probably the coal-mining industry. The National Union of Mineworkers and the National Coal Board worked together to close redundant pits, reduce the level of conflict, and centralize the industry's collective bargaining system, with remarkable success in all three respects (Burgi 1983).

With occasional exceptions of this kind, the 1950s saw no real extension along the 'Scandinavian' path towards which Britain seemed to be developing throughout the 1940s. However, neither did they constitute a return to 1920s 'normalcy' in corporatist practice.

The corporatist high tide: the 1960s and 1970s

By 1961 (the year in which plans were laid for the National Economic Development Council and the National Incomes Commission) a heightened awareness of Britain's relative economic decline produced new changes. For the first time since the 1930s the country experienced unemployment of more than a few hundred thousand, and for the first time in normal peacetime there was now a limited acceptance of the idea of organization for the pursuit of national economic goals. Governments wanted interest groups to co-operate in this pursuit. Policies might vary within and between governments, but the basic pattern remained the same until the end of the 1970s.

Income restraint was the rather restricted prime goal, but improving productivity and the quality of labour were also on the agenda. In both cases workers and their organizations were the problematic element, and thus the object of action. But, given the political assumptions of the period, the organizations themselves were also to be the initiators of action. They were invited to participate in solving the problems they were deemed to be creating (Crouch 1977).

Institutional change took place gradually during the 1960s. Such organizations as the NEDC and its attendant sector-level bodies provided fora in which corporatist bargains might well have been worked out; but for the most part they were confined to information-sharing and exhortation on how productivity and industrial relations could be improved (Middlemas 1983). Labour market organizations, especially the TUC and newly formed Confederation of British Industry (1965), were increasingly pressed to take on a disciplinary, corporatist role within incomes policy, though they largely lacked both the internal structure and access to detailed administrative participation that would make such a role feasible. Meanwhile, the spread of radically decentralizing tendencies among organized labour was rendering unions less capable of performing such a task. Ironically, many of them would have been able to respond to such a challenge in the 1950s, when they were rarely asked to do so.

In other fields of policy the increasingly technical nature of government intervention or at least of politically salient problems led to a growing interdependence between government and functional interests. For example, within the construction sector alone the National Building Agency (1964) was formed and the National Housebuilders Registration Council (founded 1936) acquired teeth (1967) (the Council was strengthened again six years later and renamed the National House-Building Council).

Training became an important issue after the Industrial Training Act 1964 led to the establishment of tripartite industrial training boards, eventually in forty-two sectors. Training is one of the areas that raises the question posed above (p. 4), concerning when a collective good for a group is also a general good. Training is often a collective interest for firms within a given sector, because in a free labour market trained workers become a semi-public good for that sector. Training clearly also matters to customers, but they are expected to use the market to express their preferences. Does it matter in any more general sense whether training for a particular occupation is of adequate quality?

The licensed professions have always been distinctive here, since their statute-based self-regulation includes preparation for and admission to occupations that have managed to convince governments, clients, and the public that they have some special importance. The public services are also distinctive in that, by maintaining a particular occupation as a public service, governments have declared it, and presumably therefore the quality of its practitioners, to be of public concern. But where is the line drawn in the perception of a public interest in the quality of normal labour-market occupations—such as maintenance fitters, night-club hostesses, steel erectors, bricklayers, computer programmers, hairdressers, professional darts players? What makes the difference between a Britain where, in a recent House of Lords debate, speakers expressed horror at the idea that the state should ever be involved in deciding what constitutes a good plumber, and a Japan where state skill tests for plumbers have long been regarded as a useful service to the public?

The answer seems to be two things. First, traditional concepts of the state and how far it is legitimate for it to interfere in the market; and second, how far the performance of the economy is seen to be a matter of national concern, how far there is what Katzenstein (1985) calls a sense of international vulnerability.

The greater the concern with international competitiveness, the more extensive the range of occupations likely to be seen as relevant to that task and, in a sense, 'mobilizable' for it. The extent of government interest in occupational training may thus stand as an indicator of how far government perceives a national economic mobilization task—a characteristic likely to lead to corporatist mechanisms of the new kind (Finegold and Soskice 1988).

The shift from various *ad hoc*, specific industry-level training networks to a national training policy may therefore be seen as an indication of the 1960s shift from old to new corporatism. But it was a limited shift. The ITBs were equipped with few powers and, it is usually argued, had few major achievements to their credit.

Early in the 1970s the pace of corporatist change quickened; it is notable that the timing of this and nearly all preceding changes was not related to a change of government. These were the years of the dismemberment of the old Ministry of Labour and the allocation of most of its functions to tripartite organizations: the Advisory, Conciliation, and Arbitration Service (1974), the Health and Safety Commission (1974), the Manpower Services Commission (1973); a virtually self-conscious switch to a Swedish mode of operation. Less widely remarked, the Office of Fair Trading (established under the Fair Trading Act 1973) was given, among its duties, the encouragement of voluntary schemes whereby trade associations would act as guarantors of the quality of the goods and services provided by their members; several such schemes have subsequently developed, covering direct selling, double glazing, electrical goods, footwear, funerals, furniture, insurance, laundries and dry cleaning, mail order purchase, motor vehicles and caravans, photography, and travel.

The problems of the labour market—incomes, inflation, restrictive practices—remained high on the list of issues generating these developments, and attempts at tripartite incomes policies, both statutory and voluntary, were the most striking instances of corporatist policy style. Incomes policy itself was often conducted through informal mechanisms, formal embodiments proving too controversial, though the Price Commission (1973) and, more remote from labour issues, the National Enterprise Board (1975) were elaborately tripartite bodies.

But the most important indicator of growing corporatism was the MSC. Taking over responsibility for the ITBs and developing wider programmes than their coverage, amalgamating public job-search agencies with training in the manner of Scandinavian labour-market policy and developing a co-ordinated tripartite national approach for the whole exercise, the MSC marked a further transition from old to new corporatist arrangements in the area of vocational preparation.

In general, one can discern increasing government involve-ment as problems were articulated and demands for action grew. There was also increasing demand for participation by affected interests, and attempts by government to respond to these by incorporating them; and, in some areas, a problem of unmanageability emerged as British secular economic decline coincided with a global crisis. Government's room for manœuvre was being reduced, and as it became increasingly dependent on organized groups to assist it in the task of maintaining order it became correspondingly difficult to mobilize those groups for constructive action. In a still sharply divided society, no government succeeded for long in winning support for concerted action based on deeply held perceptions of a shared *national* interest. Incomes policies crumbled as much under the strain of inter-union rivalries as because they could not reconcile the divide between wage-earner and profit-taker. Training boards degenerated into arenas in which individual firms could fight for larger grants and smaller levies; and unions could fight to the death to defend the principle that skill qualification should depend on the number of years spent in apprenticeship, not the ability to pass tests.

These corporatist ventures were still being launched through classic British organizations often ill-prepared for such a tight role. They were often internally decentralized—on the rise of labour becoming even more so as the 1970s progressed. Among employers perhaps even more than among workers, members often resented their organizations' participation in corporatist arrangements (Grant and Marsh 1977; Grant with Sargent 1987). The issue had been addressed, though primarily with reference to workers' organizations, by the Donovan Commission, 1965–8, which had analysed the split national–local system of industrial relations that prevailed in the engineering and several other industries, and had proposed various measures for articulating the two parts (Royal Commission 1968). However, this had been almost entirely related to collective bargaining as such, and not to co-operation in an overall national system of income development. The Commission almost coyly avoided a detailed investigation of incomes policy.

The conflict between the decentralizing force of individual organizations' self-interest and the demands placed upon them for concerted action in a common interest finally erupted in the conflicts of the 'winter of discontent', 1979. It was shortly following those events that a Conservative government came to office which overtly set its face against a continuation of the corporatist approach, along the lines of the new right critique that had been developing for some years past.

STOCK-TAKING: THE SITUATION BY 1979

Before assessing the impact of any changes during the 1980s, it will be useful to take stock of the situation reached by the end of the 1970s. It is not always easy to determine whether or not an organization is involved in arrangements which are genuinely corporatist without intensive study of its operation. Most research therefore takes the form of a study of institutions within a particular field, with some means of inquiry to discover their inner workings. But our need here is to give some overview of the extent of corporatist arrangements in Britain as a whole, requiring summary judgements.

Answers to three questions are needed to determine whether an institution is a corporatist arrangement, but they all involve ambiguities. First, an institution must make use of *representatives* of the interests whose behaviour is involved. This is often straightforward and easy to detect. Thus, universities were heavily represented on the University Grants Committee; but the suppliers of telecommunications are not represented on OFTEL, the regulatory body of that sector. The UGC would be a candidate for corporatist research; OFTEL would not. It must be remembered that it is the institution (formal or informal) that *brings together* the organized interests that may be corporatist, not the interest organizations themselves.

However, matters are not always so clear. Frequently a regulatory agency does not include representatives as such, but does contain persons with relevant technical expertise who happen to work with one of the interests being supervised. Various food and drug industry scientists, for example, serve on committees to oversee the health issues that arise from these products. Prima facie this is not corporatism because they are there for their expertise, not in order to co-opt the authority of industry associations to a regulatory scheme. But it is possible that they play a role mediating between organizations in their industries and the official machinery. This is related to the familiar American concept of 'regulatory agency capture'. One can be more confident that the Arts and Crafts Councils should not be listed as corporatist, since there are no significant associations in their field. Some members of these Councils may represent the arts and crafts 'worlds' in a non-specific way, but they have no organizational base. We shall here have to ignore the more complex and limit ourselves to the more explicit cases of representative incorporation.

Second, for an institution to be corporatist it must have power to *constrain and sanction*, either through its own resources or by effectively co-opting those of its constituent representative bodies. A purely consultative body is of interest to us only if there is evidence that constituent organizations will be willing to back its judgements with their own authority.

Again, this is sometimes clear when representative regulatory agencies are equipped with formal disciplinary powers (the Securities and Investment Board and the General Medical Council are examples). But the power to constrain extends beyond discipline. Whenever an agency is responsible for administering its service it allocates resources, even if they are only intangible ones like recognition. It therefore decides who among its constituents should benefit. This automatically embodies constraints. Hence the importance of the distinction between representative bodies that merely consult as opposed to those that administer. This is generally a reasonably straightforward matter to determine, though on occasion the distinction between administration and consultation is not that clear. Much depends on how effectively the authority is constrained by advice. In general, the more technical the matter, the more binding is expertise; but one cannot easily tell.

Cases where constituent organizations are willing to use their own authority to support non-binding judgements within a consultative organ are of course even more difficult to identify. We shall limit attention here to agencies that seem to have clear resources to allocate or sanctions to wield.

Finally, to speak of corporatism we need some notion of *orientation to a public interest*, as explained above (p. 4). This is bedevilled by the fact that the public interest is such an elusive concept. We can start by including all agencies in which government has played some part, whether by placing the agency on a statutory basis, being represented on it itself or merely playing an unofficial midwife role. It may be objected that not everything governments do is for the public interest, but it is at least an external interest.

But, by itself, this leaves out of account those important cases of pre-emptive action by private groups, setting up an agency themselves precisely to avoid what would otherwise be likely government intervention (e.g. the Press Council or the National House-Building Council); or cases where the government informally encourages a voluntary scheme (as in the trade association guarantee scheme, the NFU's straw-burning code, or non-statutory training organizations); or groups who try to establish a structure of external accountability even though government is not interested in them (e.g. the General Council and Register of Osteopaths, representing a form of medicine not recognized by the GMC or the NHS). We must therefore add to the statutory list other instances of explicit self-regulation, though in practice it will be difficult to locate all such cases.

Our aim, then, is to produce a list of all bodies that were: (1) at least in part representative of organizations of those interests whose behaviour they sought to affect; (2) equipped with some resources that would enable them to exercise sanctions over those interests; and (3) equipped with some discernible mandate to bring external interests to bear on them.

Appendix 1.1. (p. 36) presents an extensive, though probably not an exhaustive, list of such agencies as existed at the end of the 1970s. It is based on similar sources to Table 3.1 in the paper by Norman Lewis later in this volume. An attempt has been made to allocate these to different sectors, so that some answer may be given to the question: what areas of British life were governed by corporatist institutions? We start from the historical heartland, the professions. These were largely behaving in the 'old' corporatist way. One must note that, the more recently formed a profession, the more likely it is to comprise employees rather than independent practitioners, and the more likely they are to lie within the public service. The degree of self-regulation is thereby diminished, and corporatist mechanisms decline in importance in deference to employer–employee relations. One notable case among the professions is accountancy, where competing rival bodies were active for well over a century until scandals revealed the inadequacy of their professional codes in the 1970s, leading to formation of an umbrella organization (Willmott 1985).

Administering the professions overlaps heavily with supervising acquisition of qualifications for professional practice, and therefore with the entire area of training. The significance of the shift, first from *ad hoc* arrangements to the ITB system, and then to the MSC, has been discussed above. In general therefore this is a field that has developed strongly as an area of important public interest only since the 1960s. A question mark as to whether we are dealing with general or merely collective interests remains over some of the surviving training instruments outside the MSC's reach.

Particularly through the medical profession, the professional sector also overlaps with a form of organization that is charged with securing the generally accepted desired goals of health, safety, and welfare. Many of the institutions here are very specific—modern examples of old corporatism. But the occupational health and safety network established under the HSC moved this area indirectly towards new corporatism, as it was launched at a time when government was encouraging maximum co-operation among organized producer interests for the sake of national economic goals. We also list here the strange role played by the National Council of Social Service (now the National Council of Voluntary Organisations) since 1928 in co-ordinating voluntary welfare bodies with the allocation of government grants as an important sanction (Wilson and Butler 1985).

Concern for the quality of goods and services on health and safety grounds overlaps with other issues of quality. There is here a somewhat arbitrary collection of organizations that can be defined as being charged with ensuring good standards among producers. There has never been an attempt to secure anything systematic here in the general marketed sector of the economy where public interests become difficult to define. Of particular prominence are the subgroups concerned with the education and communications sectors (some of them very old and in the latter cases reflecting traditional if often controversial censorship concerns), agriculture (primarily the 1930s package, reflecting both the importance of food and the political salience of farmers), and the City of London (the informal networks of which had already come under strain, leading to the institution of a more formal structure in the early 1970s). None of these was part of a mobilizing corporatism, though arguably this is what the MMB has become with the advent of dairy quotas.

The much discussed industrial relations area provided a further separate focus of organization, but at several points it overlaps with the professional, training, and health and safety sectors. They also overlap with the small but politically salient group of organizations concerned with promoting macro-economic performance. This in turn overlaps slightly again with the quality of production sector. It is here, in the industrial relations and macro-economic fields, that we find the distinctive, high-profile creations of 1970s mobilizing corporatism. This was however developing out of an older, mixed pattern. Some of the existing structure of institutions originated in the earlier attempts, discussed above, to create wartime or post-war cross-class unity of a macro-social kind. Others however can be seen as less grandiose, old corporatist instances of setting up arrangements to keep the peace in discrete sectors. Institutions originally established with the latter object in mind may find themselves caught up in something more ambitious at times, like the 1970s, when there is a national 'project'. But again, the component parts of grand schemes may eventually come to play a routine, sector-specific role, as did the Whitley Councils.

The institutions around the NEDC and those concerned with regional development are included because of their prominence, but strictly speaking the NEDC and the English regional bodies have been purely consultative. It has always been difficult to determine what effect the NEDC economic development committees and sector working parties have had within their industries. In some cases they have enabled employer and union representatives to reach understandings on priorities, though their lack of any significant sanctions has always cast doubts on their capacity to reach into individual firms.

The papers by Erridge and Connolly and by Moore and Booth in the present volume discuss some aspects of regional corporatist arrangements in Northern Ireland and Scotland. Organizations here *do* have both executive and policy powers, though their membership is only indirectly representative of organized interests. Their work demonstrates the importance of centres of political decision-making for institutions at this level.

There was much that was arbitrary and random about this set of institutions. It must be remembered that corporatist regulation is one of three options for the governance of a sector. The other two are: (1) direct government regulation without interest representation and (2) reliance on market forces, *caveat emptor*, backed up by various forms of legal redress in the event of flagrant malpractice. There is nothing predetermined about government's choice between direct and intermediary regulation. Industrial safety was, from 1832 to 1974, carried on through the former mechanism; since then it has been run through a corporatist body. The weights and measures inspectorate is a non-corporatist departmental responsibility; but the grading of eggs is supervised by an agency containing producer representatives. Trying to discern a rationale for the particular pattern is as quixotic a task as producing a theory of why some occupations become professions and others do not. Any approach that starts from assumptions about basic or important functions without a strong alloy of ideas about political convenience, historical accident, being in the right place at the right time, and power plays will not take us far.

Similarly, market forces are likely to be supplemented by representative regulation only in the event of some widely accepted need or the occurrence of scandal or outrage. Dissatisfaction with the quality of new houses and fears by the industry of government intervention led to the tightening of the NHBRC scheme in 1967; prominent news stories about holidaymakers stranded by bankrupt tour operators led to the introduction of the ABTA guarantee scheme. Without scandal much depends on the particular circumstances of individual representative organizations. The list of trades that have responded to the Office of Fair Trading's appeals for quality guarantees is hardly comprehensive.

Appendix 1.1 helps our consideration of the central conundrum: why can Britain seem both a country shot through with corporatist arrangements and yet also a country in which corporatism has been weak? The majority of institutions listed here are 'old corporatist', concerned with small corners of activity, mainly dealing with day-to-day 'business as usual'. Organizations of a macro- and proactive kind, concerned with mobilizing for new economic tasks—'new corporatism'—are of recent creation, and often purely consultative or informal. The history of similar such institutions after 1918 and 1945 also suggests that these more active agencies are likely to be temporary. What has been the subsequent fate of the creations of the 1960s and 1970s?

Change in the 1980s

Appendix 1.2 (p. 40) indicates the main developments that have occurred since the change of government and official approach to corporatist institutions in 1979. They can be analysed summarily as follows:

1. There has to date been little attack on the infrastructure of more or less passive corporatist arrangements identified in Appendix 1.1. A few institutions have come and gone; most have largely stayed where they were. In some fields of policy there have even been new corporatist initiatives. Bent as the government was in general principle on restoring to markets the allocative functions which had been 'distorted' by the intervention both of government agencies directly and of the great jungle of intermediate agencies created under one or another variety of corporatist arrangements, it was inevitable that these arrangements should come under scrutiny and attack. The word 'corporatism' was explicitly used to describe what Labour governments and centrist Conservative governments such as that of Mr Heath had allowed to go wrong with Britain's economy and society, and although people primarily had in mind incomes policies and central-level tripartism, the term was also used generally to refer to the expanding pretensions of government and the blurring of its functions through delegation to interest groups. A senior retired civil servant was appointed to survey, and to find suitable candidates for destruction among, the nation's stock of what had come to be called 'quangos and

quagos' ('quasi-autonomous non-governmental' and 'quasi-autonomous governmental' organizations). The distinction between the two was never a clear one and Pliatsky, the retired civil servant in question (Pliatsky 1980), rejected the terms in favour of a general category 'fringe body'. These fringe bodies he divided into three categories: 'executive bodies'—like the Manpower Services Commission, for example, but including also Regional Water Authorities, New Town Development Corporations, etc.—of which he discovered 489; 'advisory councils', of which there were 1,561; and 'tribunal systems', that is to say networks of tribunals, for example for rent regulation, or (a large and important category) for appeals against administrative decisions—on welfare benefits, immigration, etc. These numbered 67 and were Britain's *ad hoc* substitute for the Continental tradition of administrative courts.

Pliatsky's job was to prune, to review the whole range of these bodies with a view to 'eliminating any which had outlived their usefulness or which could not be justified in the context of the Government's objectives of reducing public expenditure and the size of the public sector' (ibid.: para. 19). In another place he refers to concern about these bodies as representing 'not only a spread of patronage, but a concealed growth of government which does not show up in, say, the size of the Civil Service' (ibid.: para. 17).

Pliatsky, after consulting with the various sponsoring departments, recommended the demise of 30 executive and 211 advisory bodies—a not very impressive catch of 6 per cent of the one and 14 per cent of the other which promised a saving of £11.6m. or 0.2 per cent of the total sum (£5,800m.) which had been spent on these bodies in the previous year (though another 6 per cent was expected to be saved by reductions in the scale of operation of the bodies which remained).

It hardly amounted to a 'dismantling of corporatism'. Not all the recommended abolitions were carried out in any case. There has been no recent re-review of the situation, but it is a fairly safe bet that the number of such bodies now stands at a higher level than when the enthusiastic new government of Mrs Thatcher set out to wield its axe. For one thing the concern of the government to demonstrate its commitment to the 'small government' philosophy on occasion led it to create new bodies—or transform old ones—in order to delegate to them executive functions formerly exercised by civil servants. Admittedly, this was done not for the 'corporatist' reasons for which, say, the Manpower Services Commission had earlier been created, by transfer of some of the functions of the Department of Employment (i.e. in order to extend those functions, to make their prominence more efficient by capturing interest groups' co-operation and commitment, to provide bargaining forums, etc.). The aim was rather to reduce the number of civil servants on the books: the transfer of the Department of Education's student fellowship scheme to the administration of the British Academy is an example.

Apart from such instances—stubborn survivals, functions of government which refuse to go away, whether formally within the sphere of government or delegated to other bodies—new corporatist arrangements have continued to be created.

In the industrial field the discretion allowed to ministers whether to refer proposed mergers to the Monopolies Commission, or, having referred, whether to accept its recommendation, has been used by ministers to strike bargains—as in the very recent case of British Aerospace's acquisition of the Rover Group—to extract promises about future business strategy as a condition for not exercising veto power over the merger or acquisition—or, in the case mentioned, for writing off considerable debts to the public purse.

There were also much more systematic developments, however. The enhanced concern with Britain's declining international competitiveness (Britain's imports of manufactured goods began to exceed manufactured exports for the first time in nearly two centuries during the early 1980s), the intensification of international trade competition (see e.g. the rapidity of the swing in the US–Japan trade balance), and the growing importance of R. & D. and innovative capacity as a factor in competitiveness all conspired to promote such arrangements as the Alvey Project for joint pre-commercial research co-operation among leading firms and university research teams. Development support schemes which allow civil servants to negotiate support of individual firms' development projects—schemes which started in the late 1970s—have grown in number, in budget allocation, and in take-up, and in spite of recent announcements that the schemes will be less discretionary in character, it seems unlikely that they will—or can—be greatly changed.

One example, insufficiently institutionalized to appear in Appendix 1.2, is the demand placed on the Football Association to control the law and order problems occasionally surrounding the professional game. Another is the Farming and Wildlife Advisory Group, established by agricultural and conservation interests, which, with encouragement and financial support from government, has assumed a central role in persuading farmers and landowners to adopt conservation practices. A further case is the part-corporatist structure of the Audit Commission, established to oversee the efficiency of local government and other public-service agencies, and including representatives from those sectors on the Commission. Corporatist arrangements for regulating the chemical industry have been strengthened (Grant 1982); and local chambers of commerce (generally pale shadows of the Austrian and German opposite numbers) have acquired delegated powers in the administration of urban aid (Grant 1983; Stewart 1984).

Perhaps because of its relationship to the European Community, corporatist structures in agriculture have been left largely intact, though with the MMB acquiring something of a 'new corporatist' assertive role in marketing British dairy products. Giving a corporatist agency the form and style of a marketing *company* in this way is characteristic of the present government's approach to problems of delegated authority in several fields (water treatment and training are in many respects being dealt with in this way). However, in agriculture this is not entirely novel; meat marketing has been organized in a similar manner since the 1950s (Self and Storing 1962).

There is therefore no overall evidence of a rejection of the corporatist approach, with government seeking to co-opt the powers of associations of interests as supplements to its own authority in difficult areas. The position of the professions is possibly changing, as the government comes increasingly to see them as sources of rigidity in labour utilization, but at the time of writing the practical effect has been limited to some minor arrangements, while a more radical attack on the autonomy, monopoly, and organization of the Bar is being heavily negotiated.

However, if one separates out those particular epitomes of 1960s and 1970s corporatist arrangements, the macro-economic, proactive organizations, there has been more of an onslaught.

The Price Commission, the NEB, and (after a complex career to which we shall return below) the MSC have been abolished. More widely, though more difficult to define, there has been a decline in the importance and reduction in the budgets of organizations that still exist: ACAS, HSC, the sub-corporatist NEDC network—though it will be noted that the HSC has continued to develop its sector-level organizations. The informal arrangements around incomes policy have been abandoned, as has the Labour government's Joint Advisory Committee with the Building Societies Association, an attempt at using the Association to link mortgage interest rates to national economic strategy, described in this volume by Martin Boddy and Christine Lambert.

2. One new corporatist initiative is so important that it demands special attention. This is the establishment of a new, statutorily based system of self-regulation for the financial institutions in the City of London, extensively analysed by Michael Moran in his chapter in this volume. As his account shows, this is a good example of the replacement of 'old corporatist' arrangements by something much more explicit and purposive. And the new structure, though it has been officially dubbed 'deregulation', in fact constitutes a pure case of an elaborate corporatist arrangement, with self-regulatory agencies being granted a legal licence to police their sector according to agreed rules.

Does it however constitute new corporatism in the sense of mobilization for a national task? If that means: does it orientate the behaviour of City institutions towards certain general national economic tasks, the answer is no. The virtual offshore status of the City is unaffected. But in the sense that the financial sector is itself an important component of the economy, it is clear from Moran's account that a major motive of the reform has been to enable the City to regain its former international role.

3. A further initiative that requires separate consideration concerns changes in the organization of the engineering profession, described here in Martin Laffin's chapter. The old structure of a fragmented, highly autonomous set of professional bodies that he describes is another classic example of old corporatism, criticized for not being concerned with national economic tasks. And the response to the situation proposed by

the Finniston Committee (Committee of Inquiry 1980), set up
by a Labour government, was straight new corporatism: bring
the professions under a new council afforced by the usual
corporatist partners—unions and industrial representatives—
and give it the task of reorganizing the profession with national
economic goals in mind.

The response of the Conservative government to which
Finniston in the event reported was to retain the idea of
representation from industry as part of a new, aggregated
authority, but to drop the proposal for trade union representation
and to leave more autonomy to the individual institutes. The
salient characteristics of this outcome are: no rejection of
corporatism; an ambiguous stance on the opposition between
old and new corporatism; and a favouring of industrial but
disapproval of union representation.

4. While the government has rejected 1970s policies for
mobilizing the economy, especially the manufacturing economy,
through representative organizations, it has pursued a mobilization
for this task of education and training institutions. The case of
the engineering profession is again relevant here. Too recent for
our project have been the changes in education: the abolition of
the UGC and its replacement by a Universities Funding
Council including strengthened business and diminished
academic representation; the removal of polytechnics from local
government in favour of a centralized Polytechnic Funding
Council with business domination; a statutory increase in
business representation in the governing bodies of colleges of
further education.

That this is intended to be some form of economic
mobilization of educational and academic research institutions
seems clear; whether it is corporatist is more ambiguous. In
strong contrast to the new arrangements for the City, where
there is almost pure *self*-regulation (under licence), the new
educational arrangements usually see a reduction in regulation
by practitioners in favour of that by external (business) interests.
It is also misleading to speak of business 'representation' if by
that one envisages representation in the corporatist sense of
persons nominated by an organization and having some kind of
responsibility to mediate between it, its members, and the
agency in question. Ministers are more likely to appoint
individual businessmen and women, chosen for personal

qualities, or for their political opinions, not because they speak for a particular organization. With the expulsion from the TUC of the electricians' union (EETPU) and the emergence of a small group of unions outside Congress, the government now has scope to adopt a similar approach where residual surviving areas of labour representation are concerned.

Particularly important and complex in this regard has been the fate of the MSC. During the government's initial years it downgraded the role of the Commission, reducing drastically the number of ITBs, and reducing its budget. This was entirely consistent with the hypothesis that the government was 'anti-coporatist'. However, from around 1983 this changed considerably. The MSC acquired an increasing number of functions and was permitted to play a highly proactive role, achieving a wide range of changes not only in training as such but also within the curriculum of the local authority school system. The budget rose considerably as further aspects of education funding were brought under the Commission's umbrella. The organization remained tripartite, and though the TUC representatives were frequently alienated by such policies as the use of MSC training schemes to reduce the wages of young workers, there were sufficient counter-advantages to persuade them to continue to participate and co-operate. Such a trade-off is of course at the heart of most corporatist arrangements. Not least, they were able to ensure that most schemes for young workers included discussion of the role of trade unions, a theme which might otherwise have disappeared from the agenda in the climate of the 1980s.

There has been much debate over the quality of training dispensed by the MSC; some of its programmes were accused of being more concerned with keeping people off the unemployment register than with equipping them with advanced skills; its achievements continued to be unfavourably compared with those of the French, German, and several other training systems. But there is nothing in the theory of corporatism that says that its outcomes have to be effective. More problematic from this point of view were the doubts expressed whether there was much effective participation in decision-making by the social partners at regional and local levels, as discussed in the chapters by King and Schnack and by Erridge and Connolly in this volume.

As with the other educational initiatives of the government, it was primarily educational, not business, institutions that were mobilized and changed by the MSC. The current needs of firms were taken as the baseline for manpower policy, rather than any strategic aim of changing firms' ambitions, and corporatist mechanisms were used to mobilize educational and training institutions to those needs.

Then, in 1987 the situation changed again abruptly. The Conservative manifesto for the general election of that year, as well as pledging the government to diminish the role of the NEDC, also declared its intention to restrict the role of the MSC to training as such. Indeed, it was to be renamed the Training Commission and have removed from it that oversight of the employment exchange system that had originally been seen as providing opportunities to imitate Scandinavian active labour-market policy. Further, union representation on the new Commission would be reduced and that of business increased, eliminating the 1970s assumptions of corporatist balance. The changes came into force during 1988, but were very short-lived. For some time certain trade unions had been dissatisfied with participation in the Commission and had agitated for a union boycott of its operations. Soon after the Training Commission came into existence it adopted a new programme of job experience for the long-term unemployed which some unions saw as coming close to labour conscription. At the 1988 Trades Union Congress a majority of unions voted to boycott the Commission. The government promptly abolished it and replaced it with a Training Agency controlled directly by government. The MSC's local structure is being replaced by Training and Enterprise Councils comprising individual (not representative) business people. Union and LEA representatives may be co-opted only if the business people choose to do so.

The agency model, now being used for an increasing number of government tasks, involves a certain mix betweeen public authority and private firms; it certainly marks no return to a clear dividing line between state and civil society of the kind demanded earlier by various neo-liberal critics of 1970s corporatist arrangements. In Scotland the plans go further. The SDA and the Scottish wing of the Training Commission are to be merged to form Enterprise Scotland, a publicly funded enterprise development and training body working through a network of local offices run by business executives.

In summary, we can draw the following conclusions about changes in the 1980s to date. The government has, first, sought to reduce the political influence of trade unions. Second, it has reverted *in principle* to the former British approach of treating the state of the manufacturing sector of the economy as an inappropriate area of strategic action—while yet in certain areas (e.g. the promotion of small businesses) intensifying intervention and in others (such as R. & D. and the use of aid to promote exports) initiating new corporatist arrangements. Third, it has sought to advance the influence of businessmen—not necessarily business *representatives* speaking for a corporate business interest— within many areas of life. The fate of corporatist institutions depends on how they are affected by these three preferences, not by any policy towards corporatism as such.

Thus those corporate bodies that included trade unions were more likely to be downgraded than those (like the professional bodies, agricultural boards, and City institutions) that did not. Corporatist arrangements in manufacturing (like the NEDC) were more likely to be diminished than those in other areas of life (the City again, the Milk Marketing Board, or education). And if a corporatist or quasi-corporatist form provided a means for increasing business influence, there would be no qualms about using it. Given that an institution was likely to be acceptable on these three grounds, this administration has, like its various predecessors in the post-war period, made use of corporatist forms when these provide a useful adjunct to its own authority. The rejection of labour as a major corporate partner is an important breach with a fairly lengthy tradition, but the general uneasiness over 'new corporatist' arrangements alongside complete tolerance of 'old corporatist' forms marks a return to the old British pattern.

APPENDIX 1.1. CORPORATIST INSTITUTIONS IN BRITAIN, LATE 1970S

Many of the agencies listed are restricted in their scope to England or England and Wales, with separate arrangements for Northern Ireland, Scotland, and Wales. These have not been mentioned separately unless of particular importance.

(Institutions in square brackets lack a formal government involvement or statutory base.)

Professions

Medical, including: General Medical Council (1858); General Nursing Council (1919); [General Council and Register of Osteopaths (1936)]; Dental Estimates Board (1948); General Dental Council (1956) (previously General Dental Board); General Optical Council (1958); a number of bodies formed under the Professions Supplementary to Medicines Act 1960, covering chiropodists, dieticians, medical laboratory technicians, occupational therapists, orthoptists, physiotherapists, radiographers, remedial gymnasts.

Legal, including: Bar Council (1873) (became Senate of the Inns of Court and the Bar (1974)); Law Society (1825).

Accountancy: Accounting Standards Committee (1976), acting as a central forum for a number of bodies of varying dates of foundation, back to 1858.

Engineering: Council of Engineering Institutions (1962), acting as a central forum for a number of bodies of varying dates of foundation, back to 1860s.

Others, including: Architects Registration Council (1932); Hairdressing Council (1964).

Training

MANPOWER SERVICES COMMISSION (1973), which *inter alia* took over responsibility for the INDUSTRIAL TRAINING BOARDS established following Industrial Training Act 1964 and eventually covering the following trades (most of these supplanted organizations of much earlier foundation): agriculture; air transport and travel; carpet industry; ceramics; glass and mineral products; chemical and allied products; construction; cotton and allied textiles; distribution; engineering; food, drink, and tobacco; footwear, leather, and fur skins; foundry; furniture and timber; hotel and catering; iron and steel; knitting, lace, and net; man-made fibre-producing; paper and paper products; petroleum; printing and publishing; road transport; rubber and plastics; shipbuilding; wool, jute, and flax.

Public services: Environmental Health Officers Education Board (1926); Fire Services Central Examinations Board (1958); Council for the Education and Training of Health Visitors (1962); Local Government Training Board (1967); Joint Board for Clinical Nursing Studies (1970); Council for Post-Graduate Medical Training (1970);

Central Council for Education and Training in Social Work (1971); National Training Council for the National Health Service (1975).

Other, including: [Radio, Television and Electronics Examinations Board (1942); National Council for the Training of Journalists (1952); Distributive Trades Education and Training Council (1956); Pharmacy Assistants Training Board (1963); Licensed Trade Training and Education Committee (1973); National Council for Drama Training (1976); International Freight Forwarding Training Council (1978); Joint Training Council for the Hairdressing Industry (1978).]

Health, safety, and welfare

HEALTH AND SAFETY COMMISSION (1974), and its associated industry advisory committees, some of which took over functions from much older organizations: construction; foundries; oil; paper and board; railways; safety in mines research advisory board.

Other health and safety, including: Poisons Board (1933); various committees on water treatment and disposal (1957–73); Civil Aviation Authority (1971), but replacing the earlier founded Air Transport Licensing Board and Air Registration Board).

Medical, including: various committees under the Medicines Act 1968 governing the safety of medicines, medical equipment, medical use of radiation, etc., incorporating some bodies founded much earlier, e.g. the British Pharmacopoeia Commission (1928); Pharmaceutical Price Regulation Commission (1958, restructured 1978); Hearing Aid Council (1969).

Welfare, including: National Council of Social Service (1919, but not acquiring role until 1928); Housing Corporation (1964); Occupational Pensions Board (1973).

Quality of services and products

Education, including: University Grants Committee (1919); Council for National Academic Awards (1964); Council for the Accreditation of Correspondence Colleges (1969); Schools Council for Curriculum and Examinations (1964) (NB lacked real sanctions to impose its policies on LEAs or teachers but of considerable influence in practice).

Communications, including: [Poster Industry Viewing Committee (1981)]; Defence, Press and Broadcasting ('D Notice') Committee (1912); British Board of Film Censors (1912); [Outdoor Advertising Council (1947); Press Council (1953)]; Independent Broadcasting Authority (1954); [Advertising Standards Authority (1962); Mail Order Publishers Authority (1976)].

Financial institutions, including: [Panel on Takeovers and Mergers (1967)]; various City regulatory authorities, of various and *ad hoc* origin, systematized in 1973 under the auspices of the Bank of England as: City Liaison Committee, City Capital Markets and Company Law Committee, City EEC Committee, City Taxation Committee, City Telecommunications Committee; Council for the Securities Industry (1978).

Agriculture, including: Hops Marketing Board (1923); Milk Marketing Board (1933); Potato Marketing Board (1933); Pig Marketing Board (1933); Herring Industry Board (1935); Wool Marketing Board (1950); Egg Marketing Board (1956) (becoming Eggs Authority, 1977); White Fish Authority (1959); Home Grown Cereals Authority (1965); Fatstock Marketing Corporation (1954) (only indirectly corporatist, being established as a private company but wholly owned by the NFU and being allocated producer subsidies by government. Replaced by Meat and Livestock Commission (1967)); Wine Standards Board of the Vintners Company (1973).

Other, including: [National House-Builders Registration Council (1936, reconstructed 1967 and again as National House-Building Council 1973); National Industry Council for Electrical and Insulation Contractors (1956); Electronic and Technical Appliances Board of Household Equipment (1960)]; Horserace Betting Levy Board (1961); [British Aerial Standards Committee (1961)]; National Building Agency (1964); Sports Council (1971, consultative only from 1965); British Tourist Authority (1969), and its attendant national and regional boards; [National Supervisory Council for Intruder Alarms (1971); National Joint Council of Approved Driving Instructors Organisations (1973)]; various trade association guarantee schemes under auspices of Fair Trading Act 1973; Hallmarking Council (1974); Insurance Brokers Registration Council (1977); [British Air-conditioning Appliances Board (1979)].

Industrial relations

Supporting weak labour groups: Wages Councils, originally Trade Boards, starting in 1909 for a few sweated trades, and expanding in 1913, 1919, 1920, and at various later dates, to cover a wider range of low-paid occupations, consolidated under Wages Council Act 1945; Agricultural Wages Board (1924); National Dock Labour Board (1947).

Resolving conflict: conciliation boards in many industries, dating from early twentieth century, and developing especially in public services as Whitley Committees after 1918; Advisory, Conciliation and Arbitration Service (1974); Central Arbitration Committee (1974); Standing Committee on Pay Comparability (1979).

Restraining incomes: unofficial incomes policy network of Social Contract (1974).

Macro-economic development

National: NATIONAL ECONOMIC DEVELOPMENT COUNCIL, its industry-level economic development committees, and sector working parties (1961, largely consultative); Price Commission (1973); National Enterprise Board (1975).

Regional: Industrial Development Agencies for Scotland, Wales, and Northern Ireland (1964); Highlands and Islands Development Board (1964); English regional planning councils and boards (1964, largely consultative).

Sectoral, including: Export Group for Constructional Industries (1938); Joint Advisory Committee between government and Building Societies Association (1976).

APPENDIX 1.2. CHANGES TO CORPORATIST INSTITUTIONS, 1979–1989

Professions: replacement of Council of Engineering Institutions by Engineering Council (1983); uncertain attempt to downgrade Bar Council (continuing).

Training: abolition of thirty-five ITBs, leaving the seven largest in existence; major extension of role of MSC until its replacement by Training Commission in 1988 and the abolition of that shortly afterwards during same year, to be replaced by *ad hoc* non-representative agencies under non-representative Training Agency; restructuring of NHS training institutions under NHS Training Authority (1983).

Quality of goods and services

Education: Council for the Accreditation of Teacher Education (1984); replacement of UGC by Universities Funding Council (1989); Polytechnic Funding Council (1989).

Health, safety, and welfare: continuing formation of HSC industry committees; suspension of various committees for control of water quality and their replacement by a private company, but with committees supervising much of the former work (1983).

Communications: Direct Mail Standards Board (1983).

Financial institutions: SECURITIES AND INVESTMENTS BOARD, overseeing formation of a range of self-regulating organizations, to replace City regulating system.

Other: establishment of Farming and Wildlife Advisory Group (1981); establishment of British Approvals Board for Telecommunications (1982); estblishment of Audit Commission (1983).

Industrial relations

Abolition of Social Contract mechanisms (1979); abolition of Standing Commission on Pay Comparability (1981); restructuring of Wages Councils, with discussion of their probable abolition.

Macro-economic development

Abolition of BSA consultation scheme (1979); abolition of Price Commission (1979); abolition of NEB (1981); downgrading of NEDC (1987).

REFERENCES

BEER, S. H. (1965), *Modern British Politics* (London: Faber & Faber).
—— (1982), *Britain against Itself* (London: Faber & Faber).
BEYME, K. VON (1984), 'Unregierbarkeit im westlichen Demokratie', *Leviathan*, 39–49.
BÖCKENFÖRDE, E. W. (1977), 'Die politische Funktion wirtschaftssozialer Verbände und Interessenträger in der sozialstaatlichen Demokratie', in Hennis *et al.* 1977, 1979: 233–54.
BOOTH, A. (1982), 'Corporatism, Capitalism and Depression in 20th Century Britain', *British Journal of Sociology*, 33/2: 200–23.
BRITTAN, S. (1975), 'The Economic Consequences of Democracy', *British Journal of Political Science*, 5: 129–60.
BURGI, N. (1983), 'Le Néo-Corporatisme en question: État et relations industrielles dans les charbonnages britanniques' (doctoral thesis, University of Paris I).
CAMERON, D. R. (1985), 'Does Government Cause Inflation? Taxes, Spending and Deficits', in Lindberg and Maier 1985: 224–79.
CASSIS, Y. (1985), 'Bankers in English Society in the Late 19th Century', *Economic History Review*, 38/2: 210–29.
CAWSON, A. (ed.) (1985), *Organised Interests and the State* (London, Beverly Hills: Sage).
—— (1986), *Corporatism and Political Theory* (Oxford: Blackwell).
Committee of Inquiry into the Engineering Profession (1980), *Engineering Our Future*, Cmnd. 7794 (London: HMSO).
CROUCH, C. J. (1977), *Class Conflict and the Industrial Relations Crisis* (London: Heinemann).
—— (1985), 'Conditions for Trade Union Wage Restraint', in Lindberg and Maier 1985: 105–39.
CSSP (Council for Studies in Social Policy) (1976), *The Corporate State: Reality or Myth?* (London: CSSP).
DAHRENDORF, R. (1980), 'Effectiveness and Legitimacy: On the "Governability" of Democracies', *Political Quarterly*, 51/4: 393–410.

Department of Trade and Industry (1988), *DTI: The Department for Enterprise*, Cmnd. 278 (London: HMSO).

DYSON, K. (1980), *The State Tradition in Western Europe* (Oxford: Martin Robertson).

ESSER, J., *et al.* (1983), *Krisenregulierung* (Frankfurt-on-Main: Suhrkamp).

FINEGOLD, D., and SOSKICE, D. (1988), 'The Failure of Training in Britain: Analysis and Prescription', *Oxford Review of Economic Policy*, 4/3: 21–53.

GOLDTHORPE, J. H. (ed.) (1984), *Order and Conflict in Contemporary Capitalism* (Oxford: Clarendon Press).

GRANT, W. (1982), 'Studying Business Associations: Does Neo-corporatism Tell Us Anything We Didn't Know Already?' (Political Studies Association, conference paper).

—— (1983), 'Chambers of Commerce in the UK System of Business Representation' (University of Warwick, working paper No. 32).

—— (1985), 'Private Organizations as Agents of Public Policy: The Case of Milk Marketing in Britain', in Streeck and Schmitter 1985*b*: 1–31.

—— and MARSH, D. C. (1977), *The CBI* (London: Hodder and Stoughton).

—— with SARGENT, J. (1987), *Business and Politics in Britain* (London: Macmillan).

HARRIS, J., and THANE, P. (1984), 'British and European Bankers 1880–1914: An Aristocratic Bourgeoisie?', in P. Thane, G. Crossick, and R. Floud (eds.), *The Power of the Past* (Cambridge: Cambridge University Press), 215–34.

HELANDER, V., and ANCKAR, D. (1983), *Consultation and Political Culture: Essays on the Case of Finland* (Helsinki: Finnish Society of Science and Letters).

HENNIS, W., *et al.* (eds.) (1977 and 1979), *Regierbarkeit: Studien zu ihrer Problematisierung* (Stuttgart).

HILFERDING, R. (1910), *Das Finanzkapital* (Vienna: Wiener Volksbuchhandlung).

KATZENSTEIN, P. J. (1985), *Small States in World Markets: Industrial Policy in Europe* (Ithaca, NY: Cornell University Press).

LANGE, P., and GARRETT, G. (1985), 'The Politics of Growth: Strategic Interaction and Economic Performance in the Advanced Industrial Democracies, 1974–1980', *Journal of Politics*, 47: 792–828.

LINDBERG, L. N., and MAIER, C. S. (eds.) (1985), *The Politics of Inflation and Economic Stagnation* (Washington, DC: Brookings Institution).

LISLE-WILLIAMS, M. (1984*a*), 'Beyond the Market: The Survival of Family Capitalism in the English Merchant Banks', *British Journal of Sociology*, 35/2: 241–71.

—— (1984*b*), 'Merchant Banking Dynasties in the English Class Structure', *British Journal of Sociology*, 35/3: 333–62.

LOWE, R. (1978), 'The Failure of Consensus in Britain: The National Industrial Conference 1919–1921', *Historical Journal*, 21: 649–75.

—— (1986), *Adjusting to Democracy: The Role of the Ministry of Labour in British Politics 1916–1939* (Oxford: Clarendon Press).

MAITLAND, H. (1901), 'The Crown as Corporation', *Law Quarterly Review*, 17: 131–46.

MARIN, B. (1982), *Die Paritätische Kommission* (Vienna: Internationale Publikationen).

MIDDLEMAS, K. (1979), *Politics in Industrial Society* (London: Deutsch).
—— (1983), *Industry, Unions and Government* (London: Macmillan).
OLSEN, J. P. (1983), *Organised Democracy* (Bergen: Universitetsforlaget).
OLSON, M. (1982), *The Rise and Decline of Nations* (New Haven: Yale University Press).
PANITCH, L. (1976), *Social Democracy and Industrial Militancy* (Cambridge: Cambridge University Press).
—— (1980), 'Recent Theorizations of Corporatism: Reflections on a Growth Industry', *British Journal of Sociology*, 31/2: 159–87.
PLIATSKY, L. (1980), *Report on Non-Departmental Public Bodies*, Cmnd. 7797 (London: HMSO).
ROSE, R. (1979), ' "Ungovernability": Is there Fire behind the Smoke?', *Political Studies*, 79: 351–70.
Royal Commission on Trade Unions and Employers Associations (1968), *Report*, Cmnd. 3623 (London: HMSO).
SABEL, C., *et al.* (1987), 'Regional Prosperities Compared: Massachusetts and Baden-Württemberg in the 1980s' (Berlin: WZB).
SARGENT, J. A. (1985), 'The Politics of the Pharmaceutical Price Regulation Scheme', in Streeck and Schmitter, 1985: 105–27.
SCHMITTER, P. (1974), 'Still the Century of Corporatism?', *Review of Politics*, 36/1: 85–131.
—— (1981), 'Interest Intermediation and Regime Governability in Western Europe and North America', in S. Berger (ed.), *Organizing Interests in Western Europe* (New York: Cambridge University Press), 287–330.
SCHOTT, K. (1984), *Policy, Power and Order* (New Haven: Yale University Press).
SCHUMPETER, J. A. (1942), *Capitalism, Socialism and Democracy* (London: Allen & Unwin).
SELF, P., and STORING, H. (1962), *The State and the Farmer* (London: Allen & Unwin).
STEWART, M. (1984), 'Talking to Local Business: The Involvement of Chambers of Commerce in Local Affairs' (School of Advanced Urban Studies, Bristol, working paper No. 38).
STREECK, W., and SCHMITTER, P. (1985a), 'Community, Market, State—and Associations? The Prospective Contribution of Interest Governance to Political Order', in Streeck and Schmitter 1985b: 1–29.
—— (eds.) (1985b), *Private Interest Government: Beyond Market and State* (London, Beverly Hills: Sage).
WEISS, L. (1988), *Creating Capitalism: The State and Small Business since 1945* (Oxford: Blackwell).
WILLMOTT, H. C. (1985), 'Setting Accounting Standards in the UK: The Emergence of Private Accounting Bodies and their Role in the Regulation of Public Accounting Practice', in Streeck and Schmitter 1985b: 44–71.
WILSON, D. C., and BUTLER, R. J. (1985), 'Corporatism in the British Voluntary Sector', in Streeck and Schmitter 1985b: 72–86.
WINTER, M. (1984), 'Corporatism and Agriculture in the United Kingdom: The Case of the Milk Marketing Board', *Sociologia ruralis* 24/2: 106–19.

2. Japan: A Nation Made for Corporatism?

Ronald Dore

JAPANESE political scientists have, not surprisingly, written a good deal about corporatism in recent years. Much of the discussion has revolved around the search for overall characterizations of the Japanese political system—whether it should be seen as conforming to the 'pluralist model', or a 'strong-state pluralist model', or a 'bureaucratic-dominance model', or a 'business–politician–bureaucrat triadic model', or even a 'neo-corporatist model' (see e.g. Yamaguchi 1986; Miyake 1985). Some, however, have been inspired by discussions of corporatism elsewhere to look usefully in detail at the involvement of unions in decision-making and their influence thereon.[1] I shall draw on their findings in a moment.

But if we first take our disaggregated approach and ask: is Japan a society which exhibits a high density of corporatist arrangements? the answer must surely be 'yes'. Fringe bodies and advisory committees proliferate in rank profusion, and a powerful Administrative Reform Commission of extremely high prestige, sitting in a blaze of publicity for two years, did very little to reduce their size and number in spite of its mandate to make 'small government Japan' into 'even smaller government Japan'. Not all of these bodies, by any means, count as genuine corporatist arrangements. They do not all involve the exchange of privileges or concessions and commitments. But many do.

The Textile Subcommittee of the Industrial Structure Council, for example, is not just a body charged with thinking about how the textile industry can best serve the interests of the country. Every five years there is a limited-period law put on the statute book which provides for a variety of funds to help the development of the industry, to compensate those who choose to exit from the industry's less profitable branches, and to give

[1] Tabata 1987, Tsujinaka 1986. I am greatly indebted to Professor Kato Tetsuro for putting me in touch with these sources.

reduced interest loans for certain kinds of development projects. The size of these benefits and the conditions under which they are granted are, of course, matters of great moment to the various sectors of the industry. The Subcommittee, on which there is a wide variety of interests represented, becomes the bargaining forum in which the terms of the Bill are hammered out—sometimes including gentlemen's agreements to put in the next Bill, five year's hence, something which one of the parties has vociferously held out against this time round. (As, in the last round, MITI gave up its insistence on abolishing the loom registration system—in which the various weavers' co-operatives have a strong financial stake—in return for a promise to let it go through next time.) Not much of the bargaining takes place in the formal meetings. Most of it is at informal dinners (or, indeed, office meetings) at which only the interested parties appear—*together*, sometimes, when there are a lot of votes or discretionary subsidies involved, with the relevant *zoku*—the LDP Diet members who sit on the relevant party policy committee. The 'token' members—the two trade unionists, for example, or the lady who does duty as both the sole woman and the sole consumer representative—rarely get to play very much part in these more serious matters; nor, probably, the rather larger number of university economists appointed under the rubric 'persons of learning and experience', though they can sometimes, when they are trusted by the Ministry involved, play important legitimating and persuading roles and sometimes, also, if they are men of exceptional energy and conviction (some do occasionally get appointed, if only by mistake), they can act as an independent force.

In the various industrial sectors, the value of these various *shingikai* (consultative council) forums as arenas for the striking of genuinely effective corporatist bargains is much enhanced by the (in internationally comparative terms) remarkable cohesiveness of the various industry associations. The strength of the inherited Tokugawa guild tradition, the long training protected infant industries have in a developmental state in calculating finely where to draw the dividing-line between cartel-like co-operation and inter-firm competition must be among the reasons, as well as a strong communitarian *mochitsu-motaretsu* ethic (not just 'live and let live', but rather 'help and be helped to live'). In recent years—see Hollerman (1987) on 'the recomposition of Japan Inc.'—the increase in managed trade and the increasing need to share quotas for 'voluntarily restricted' exports have further enhanced the co-ordinating power of industry association in the flourishing export industries, while in the ailing industries the various government schemes for aid have done the same for shipbuilding, plywood, aluminium smelting, and so on.

The representatives of strong industry associations, bargaining in these arenas, can deliver the co-operation of their members, and that is what makes for reasonably functional and efficient corporatist arrangements. The Ministry of Transport, having got agreement in principle to a capacity-cut scheme from the two shipbuilding associations (one for large and one for medium builders), can actually succeed in implementing it—knocking together the heads of nine single-berth small shipbuilders, for instance, and getting them to take their 20 per cent cut collectively by closing two firms, and making it the responsibility of the other seven (with cheap loan assistance) to provide jobs or compensation to the workers and owners of the triage victims.

In local government, again, bargained corporatist arrangements proliferate. In the interests of a gentler and less uneven distribution of the traumas of change, the rationalization of Japan's distribution system has proceeded at a far slower pace than unfettered market forces would have achieved—even given Japan's space-shortage problems. The commerce departments of local towns have seen it as their role partly to look to the interests of the unrepresented consumer, but partly to act, with the local chamber of commerce, as gradualist mediators in the hostile negotiations between the supermarkets and the associations of local retailers. And to find compromises that will stick.

AND THE UNIONS?

So, in terms of behavioural propensities, in terms of the lack of any doctrinaire commitment to the superior virtues either of market allocation or of conventionally political (statutory, administrative, or judicial) allocation, Japan is God's own corporatist country. But what about the *core* corporatist arrangements—taxation and welfare policy, demand management, inflation control, incomes policy? How far, on the European model (or, for that matter, on the Nixon US model in the brief period when the incomes policy approach to inflation control was tried), have these matters been subject to formal or informal corporatist arrangements involving the participation of trade unions?

Only to a derisorily small degree, was the answer of Pempel and Tsunekawa in a well-known article (1979). They have recently been taken to task by Tsujinaka. Even for the time when the article was written, their characterization seriously underrates the involvement of unions in the policy process, he suggests. And subsequent developments have further considerably enhanced the trade unions' role. If you count only representatives of national bodies—industry associations or trade union federations—they have gradually approached parity; there were 51 trade unionists to 85 from business in 1973; 76 and 84 respectively in 1983, though the union representatives are concentrated in a smaller proportion of committees. (They have to be in larger numbers to balance left and right on each, presumably.) If you include members of individual firms or individual unions, the imbalance is greater, though still tending towards parity; 50 *shingikai* had trade unionists in 1973, compared with 154 which had businessmen. Ten years later the numbers were 57 and 142. Still a third of the trade union representation was concentrated on committees of the Ministry of Labour, but the increase in representation over the ten years was concentrated in the central economic committees of MITI, and the Economic Planning Agency (Tsujinaka 1986: 250–2).

Another institutional innovation to which Tsujinaka and others have drawn attention is the so-called Sanrokon or Industrial Labour Round Table—in form a personal consultative organ of the Minister of Labour with a dozen representatives each of business and labour and half a dozen 'men of scholarship and experience'. It was formed under inspiration from a German model in 1970 and meets about nine times a year. Other ministers and officials may also attend in addition to the Minister of Labour and his officials. Since the oil shock the Economic Planning Agency has frequently been represented, nineteen times by its minister. The Prime Minister attends about once a year; the Deputy Prime Minister a little more often. Increased attendance of ministers was noticeable after the Round Table resolved in 1977, at the suggestion of the leading trade union member, first that any consensus reached in the Round Table should be reported to the Cabinet and secondly that the Minister of Labour should formally request in Cabinet the attendance of other ministers (Tsujinaka 1986: 288–9).

But has all this had anything more than ritual significance? Muramatsu thinks it has, but can only cite opinion surveys in which union leaders themselves claim satisfaction with the extent to which they exercise political influence—equally interpretable as evidence that they respond deferentially to flattery (Miyake 1985). Even Tsujinaka, who provides all the positive data reported above, claims only that the Sanrokon has 'increased its presence in the governmental structure', but gives no instance of its positive effect on policy and reminds us in his concluding sentence that the Sanrokon remains, after nearly twenty years, merely a private consultative organ of the Minister of Labour. As for the presence of trade unionists on the *shingikai*, it 'remains on the formal level'; and 'seems not to have contributed much to the invigoration of these bodies'.

Three questions are worth asking.

1. Have there been issues on which the unions have been united against the current LDP–bureaucracy–business–world consensus; have they used their position in these bodies to argue for distinctive policies? Have they been successful?

2. Have there been issues on which the ruling establishment (shorthand, henceforth, for what was called above the LDP–bureaucracy–business–world consensus) has needed the positive co-operation of the unions—or had reason to be fearful of union opposition to measures which it proposed—and has it used consultation in these organs to secure co-operation?

3. Has there been any overt bargaining—the unions getting what they were pressing for, in return for concessions to the ruling establishment?

Perhaps the best route to a direct answer to those questions is via a brief historical sketch of the evolution of national trade union federations in Japan.

THE EVOLUTION OF NATIONAL CENTRES

With the exception of a few industries like shipping, which has a single national seamen's union, the real locus of financial and people-mobilizing power has, for the last forty years, been the enterprise union. Enterprise unions are grouped in industry federations of little authority and varying degrees of influence over their constituents. Some of the most powerful are, or at various points in history have been, the Iron and Steel Federation, the Electrical Workers Union, the Private Railway Workers Union, the Synthetic and Chemical Workers Union, and, in a separate category, the Union of Central and Local Government Workers. These have in turn been grouped in a small number of national centres whose *raison d'être* has been ostensibly political. They have existed to represent the unions' and (not always the same thing) union members' interests on the national political scene, usually by commitment to support of a particular political party.

There was a brief period in 1947 when union leaders directly in touch with the Communist Party (public sector union leaders, be it noted for later reference) succeeded in dominating a loose coalition of the existing centres and bringing it to the edge of a general strike. (General MacArthur stopped it by the simple act of forbidding it.)

Since the Red Purge three years later, the roll-back of union power within the enterprise, and the effective elimination of union leaders who put the prosecution of class interests ahead of the interests of the enterprise to which they belonged—since, in effect, the settled institutionalization of the enterprise union system as a set of accepted rules for the management of conflict and co-operation within the enterprise—trade unions whose leaders have committed them to support of the Communist Party have been rare.

Hence, since the mid-1950s, there have effectively been two major central federations; Sohyo, committed to support of the Socialist Party, and what became successively the Sodomei, the Zenro, and then Domei, committed to the centrist break-away from the Socialists, the Democratic Socialist Party. The DSP, in recent years, has not been easily distinguishable from the ruling LDP in outlook and ideology. The Socialist Party, locked into oppositional postures deriving from the heroic Marxist age of the 1940s, has been steadily losing votes as it ceases to be able to offer either effective destructive criticism of the government or constructive alternatives. The gap grows between the abstract militancy of its rhetoric and the daily behaviour of its Diet members, happy to be allowed to amend legislation at the margins and share in brokerage influence.

And there has been no doubt about the direction of change in the 'labour movement'. Sohyo has been steadily losing members and increasingly confined to public sector unions. The Domei succession has steadily increased its affiliations, almost exclusively in the private sector.

There was one early development which served as a watershed to mark out the difference between the two union centres in interest and policy (as well as in terms of which coteries of politicians benefited from their money and provided a home for superannuated union leaders who had to be kicked upstairs). This was the debate about rationalization and productivity in the mid-1950s. A clear difference emerged between the Sodomei, which showed itself ready for 'co-operation within the system', and Sohyo, which did not. The Sodomei agreed to support the aims of the Japan Productivity Centre, which had been set up—with American help—as a joint initiative of the bureaucracy and business organizations. But it did so only after negotiating an agreed statement that productivity drives should conform to its 'eight principles'—that they should lead to higher wages, expanded employment, *and* greater independence of the national economy (the last, presumably, with left-wing charges of being 'running dogs of American imperialism' in mind—and the American sponsorship of the productivity movement, in Japan as, earlier, in Europe). The expansion of enterprise joint consultation committees in the years that followed has been attributed to the effect of this agreement; 'promotion of industrial democracy' had been one of the eight principles (Garon and Mochizuki 1988).

The functions of supra-enterprise union organization—but not necessarily of the centres—were considerably enhanced by the development of the 'Spring Offensive' wage bargaining system. (This was made possible by the fact that wage bargaining in all major companies is concentrated around a 1 April settlement date, a feature almost unique among industrial countries and an incidental consequence of the lifetime employment system and the timing of the school year.) By the mid-1960s annual wage settlements in individual firms took place in a context in which:

1. Following the formulation, some three months ahead of the opening of enterprise negotiations, of a co-ordinated union demand for a target percentage increase, and the response by employers' organizations (specifying the maximum possible incease which could be conceded), there had been widespread debate, at the national level, of what would be a *just or appropriate or affordable* level of wage increase from the point of view of the national economy—given the need to control inflation, increase or lower the savings ratio, etc.

2. As a result of that debate (in addition to a certain amount of popular education in the structure of value added and the national accounts), real expectations of the bargaining outcome had converged, even though the rhetoric of demand and response may have been little modified.

3. A bargaining schedule had been set by the unions, seeking to get early settlements in industries where a high percentage increase could be expected, and setting schedules of half-day, one-day, two-day strikes in order to make that schedule stick. Equally, a schedule had been set by the major companies, seeking to set the pattern by early settlements in those sectors where unions were relatively weak and could be expected to accept a low figure.

The system had effects which spread beyond the major unionized firms which it directly affected. The publicity surrounding the Spring Offensive and its 'emergent norm'—the weighted average of all settlements—had a coercive effect on wage rises in smaller non-union establishments too. By the 1960s it was delivering wage rises equivalent to the double-figure economic growth rates—10–12 per cent in the first half of the decade, rising steadily to 18 per cent in 1970 and then, after a brief pause, to 20 per cent in 1973. Unions had built up the dual expectation, first that each year's settlement would be followed, in real and not just nominal terms, by a higher one the following year, and secondly that inflation showed a steady secular increase trend and should be fully compensated for.

Such was the momentum that when the oil crisis and the commodity price rises gave a sharp push to inflation, the 1974 wage demands shot up to nearly 40 per cent and, after an unprecedented 10 million man days had been lost in strikes (those lasting at least half a day only), settlements averaged 33 per cent.

Then the jawboning started. An excellent recent account (Hancock and Shimada, forthcoming) chronicles the following events:

March 13. (Before the outcome of the 1974 round is entirely clear) Keidanren (the major business federation dominated by the large corporations, which usually leaves wage and industrial relations matters to its specialist sister organisation, Nikkeiren) sets up task force, including bureaucrats and academics to study economic effects of impending high wage settlement and to draw up a strategy for the 1975 round.

26 April. Cabinet: Minister of Finance said to report on grave consequences of the high wage settlements.

May. Economic Planning Agency economic forecast puts numbers on those grave consequences, but the Minister of Labour says that the economy can absorb the increase without too many ill-effects.

Summer. Discussion in the Sanrokon. Much press discussion of the need for an income policy. Ministry of Labour sets up an expert group on wages and prices.

August. Labour conventions. Influential leaders of moderate unions say: we can't just continue asking for last year's increase plus alpha—and are denounced for defeatism by leaders of Sohyo.

September/October. People start talking figures. Government adopts a consistent theme; inflation can be brought down to 15 per cent by March 1975; unions should be accordingly restrained. Keidanren chairman: companies should steel themselves not to concede more than 20 per cent. Report of business-oriented research organisation, (Nikkeicho), puts target at 17–18 per cent. Nikkeiren's task force sets out a long-term strategy; 15 per cent in 1975, 10 per cent in 1976, single figures thereafter.

December. Economic Planning Agency issues results of simulations using 20 per cent and 15 per cent 1975 wage increases. Higher growth in GNP and real wages results from the lower figure.

December. New Government. New PM meets leaders of four central federations of labour while Minister of Labour meets Nikkeiren officials. Reaffirmation of the March 15 per cent inflation target.

January onwards. The line now firmly set, Ministers, from the Prime Minister downwards appear at the Sanrokon to urge union cooperation in the fight against inflation. Every opportunity for dialogue with union leaders is sought.

March. Major steel and shipbuilding firms meet and agree to concede no more than 15 per cent. Firms in some hard-hit industries with big trading losses announce that their unions have agreed to zero increases and cuts in bonuses as the only way of avoiding redundancies.

The in-built mechanisms for formulating wage demands at the enterprise level were still little altered, and demands still averaged 32 per cent. But in the denouement, settlements averaged only slightly over 13 per cent. And so much had real expectations been lowered that, despite the vast increase in the gap between demand and concession, days lost in strikes amounted to 1½ million fewer than in 1974. Inflation that year was about 14 per cent. The employee share of national income, which had been below 60 per cent until 1973, stabilized around 67–8 per cent for the next six years. Days lost in strikes have fallen unidirectionally to half a million in 1987.

Meanwhile the union movement has moved towards (1) unification; (2) increasingly overt claims to 'take part in the policy process'—no longer by street demonstrations but by participation in all those closed meetings in which the Japanese consensus evolves. The participation of the leaders of both the main national centres in the Ad Hoc Administrative Reform Commission in 1982–3 is seen by many as a definitive turning-point.[2] They saw their concern with lower taxes as justifying co-operation with the Commission's 'small government' drive—the highly publicized application of Reaganomics to Japan.

The process of unification and the process of accommodation of trade union aspirations for formal incorporation in the policy process fed on each other. It seemed apparent that the stronger the unions' organizational unity, the more those aspirations were likely to be fulfilled. Since 'unification' effectively meant the right wing swallowing up the left wing, the government was understandably amenable to the idea of offering bribes.

And there were secular forces pushing in that direction which meant, in effect, that not too much bribery was needed—notably the long-term decline of the Socialist Party and of the public sector unions which supported it. Privatization, particularly of the national railways and of NTT, the telecommunications network, was a particularly telling blow, and partially designed as such. The new private companies into which the railways were divided took a tough line with any signs of union militancy—and, some would say, any signs even of a determination to preserve the union's basic independence.

[2] Shinohara Hajime coined the term *Rincho Corporatism* (Rincho is the abbreviated name of the Commission). See Yamaguchi 1986.

The latest stage: unification of the private sector unions in a new national centre with nearly 5½ million affiliated members, known by its abbreviated title of Rengo, in November 1987. Sohyo agreed to allow its private sector unions to have dual membership, and agreed on 1990 as the target date for working out terms on which public sector unions could join the new combined centre. Unions within Rengo which were committed to the DSP have formed their own separate political support organization (reverting to the name of their ancestral organization, the 1911 Yuaikai) and the supporters of the JSP within Sohyo have done the same in anticipation of the 1990 union.

CORPORATIST ARRANGEMENTS?

We can now briefly answer our original three questions. Have the unions pressed distinctive demands? There seem to have been few incidents of clear opposition between the trade union movement and the ruling establishment in recent years except over the predictable issue of the size of the annual wage settlement—an issue which, because predictable, is confrontational only within managed limits. Most of the expressed demands of the unions seem to have been of the protection-of-motherhood type. The new Rengo has stressed the reduction of the demands which work-life places on home-life and devised slogans like 'a workplace fit for family men'. But it was left to the ordinary bureaucratic EPA's Economic Council to make the concrete suggestion of an 1,800 annual work hours target for 1995. (The present measured work year is around 2,100 hours.)

Has the ruling establishment needed the support—or needed to buy off the hostility—of the unions? It certainly did in 1975. Never in any serious way since.

And (third question), as for striking bargains, not even in 1975 did the unions gain concessions in return for their co-operativeness—unless there were pacts of such secrecy that their leaders have not wished to lay claim to their bargaining successes. What they have gained is recognition, honour, respect—accorded more particularly to trade union leaders than to the unions collectively. And, as Tom Smith pointed out, using newspaper and other writings from 1890s, a demand to be treated with respect—to be incorporated into a community in which basic equality rules—has always been a strong theme in the Japanese labour movement (Smith 1984).

Is this all easily summed up by saying that Japanese unions have been weakened? If weakness is measured by their influence *either* specifically on the management of their individual enterprise *or*, collectively, on the management of the national economy, the answer must be yes. There are three elements in an explanation of this trend, all of which suggest that it is a continuing one.

First, unions, by the nature of their enterprise structure, always did share sufficiently closely the objectives of their companies' managers that it would be not unreasonable to let those managers speak for them in matters of inflation control, welfare policy, and so on. Given the very big difference in income and life chances between the workers in the privileged corporate sector where unions are strongest, and the small-firm sector, there was in reality very little economic basis for a sense of a 'common interest of workers as a whole'. What inhibited their recognizing this hitherto was a lingering attachment to ideologies which told them that they *ought* to have class feeling, that unions *ought* to be 'fighting for the workers'. The attenuation of these ideologies with the steady deterioration of the Socialist Party has brought attitudes closer to underlying reality.

A second element is the managerial offensive—not as strong generally as in the newly privatized former public sector corporations, but slow and relentless none the less. Managements, prepared until recently to accept that they had to live with unions and that they had to expect that the unions would fight their corner, have come increasingly to expect—and to use their control over union officers' future careers to engineer—much greater docility. No wonder that the buzz-word in union circles, according to Inagami (1988), is UI—'union identity' and how to establish it. The quality of the discussion is indicated by the punning games which it generates—UI is also 'you' and 'I' and 'yuai' ('friendship', as well as the name of the very first national union of 1911). The tone of the discussion is set by the new-style magazines which seek new ways to capture union members' hearts and minds. Inagami describes them as trendy ('high sense', 'visual', 'colourful'). They have exotic English titles like *Joinous* and *Welcome our Union*.

The third factor is the decline in the quality of union leaders.

Many of the union leaders of the heady crusading days of the 1940s subsequently became the company directors of the 1970s. The few who stayed with the labour movement as professionals were often men of considerable education and intellectual ability.

The next generation contained a lot of clever people too. In the 1950s and early 1960s many of the former union-leader departmental managers encouraged young university graduates to take a spell working in the union, as something that would do no harm to their career, even if they played their union role with a fair toughness. They often played a stimulating grass-roots role, even if very few of them stayed and moved on to professional union work in the federations. Those who did were for the most part high-school graduates (for whom unions offered better career prospects than the firm). A lot of these were very able. Theirs was still an unequal educational opportunity generation. Many of them had left school at 15, or 18, not because they did not have brilliant prospects of a university career, but because their families were too poor to afford it. They are the generation now coming up to leadership of the national federations; intelligent, often, but without the intellectual self-confidence of university graduates and without a lifetime helped along by the halo effects which graduation from a 'good' university confers.

And the odds are that the next generation behind them, now forming the leadership of the enterprise unions, will be even more disadvantaged. They came through the system at a time of greater affluence, a time when the educational system was effective as never before in 'creaming off' those of high academic ability and recruiting them for jobs in the ruling establishment. Many fewer of those entering their firms from high school in this generation, and becoming union professionals, are the intellectual equals of their age-peers who went on to university. In capacity for massive mental storage of relevant facts, for quick retrieval of those facts, and long-logic-chain thinking, fewer can match the managers whom they confront in negotiations or the fellow-members of the *shingikai* on which — in a decade or so, after their careers have developed—they will sit.

THE SHAPE OF THE CORPORATIST FUTURE

What do we learn from this attempt to trace trends in corporatist arrangements in Japan in the light of the previous chapter's discussion of the other island ex-empire? Three things, I think, two to do with structures and the other with ideas.

1. The first has to do with the operations of meritocracy. The social selection mechanisms just described are at work to weaken the labour movement in Britain too. Who has there been in the TUC of recent years who was the intellectual equal of Ernie Bevan? Does this mean that ruling establishments will have less need to resort to institutionalized forms of tripartism as a means of accommodating vigorous assertion of workers' interests? Or does it mean that the mere recognition, respect, flattery, of formal participation will be an increasingly adequate substitute for a substantive share in governance? Or does it mean that union opposition will grow more impotently resentful; less amenable to anything but the sharp assertion of *force majeure*?

2. Tripartism is not the only form in which 'core' corporatist arrangements might be revived. In Britain we have seen a growing differentiation between the workers in the corporate oligopolistic private sector, able to secure continuing wage rises in a period of slow growth; the tax-dependent public sector, falling steadily behind in wages and increasing in militancy; and a third small-firm market-wage sector. Those differences emerge even more sharply in Japan. Organizationally, it seems doubtful if the tryst of 1990 will in fact be kept. The public sector unions may well never join the new Rengo.

More than in Britain wage mechanisms give the two sectors a common interest. The public sector arbitration award is given in the form of an across-the-board percentage increase soon after the private sector's Spring Offensive, but already this arrangement was put under stress in the early 1980s, when the drive to cut back the accumulated national debt delayed the granting of what were acknowledged to be 'just' increases. The willingness of the private sector unions to join all populist demand for tax cuts means that the occasions for such rifts are more likely to increase than diminish.

There is one other factor specific to Japan. The basic

framework of private sector industrial relations has been settled and accepted as legitimate since the mid-1950s. In the public sector the very framework has been in bitter dispute. Public corporation workers have been allowed to organize and bargain collectively but not to use the strike weapon. Administration workers, central and local, have been allowed to organize but not collectively to bargain. The unions have never accepted the legitimacy of these restrictions. It has been a live issue which has maintained the militancy of those unions' attachment to the Socialist Party. In spite of the gradual demoralization of the teachers' union and the removal of the railway and telephone workers to the private sector, it remains a dominant concern of the public sector unions to which the private sector unions are largely indifferent.

A third element is common to all industrial societies. It was illustrated in Japan in the 1950s when Sodomei signed up in the productivity movement and Sohyo did not. This is usually seen as an ideological difference, but it was not solely that. 'Rationalization' in manufacturing *could* mean a leap in productivity, expanded output, higher profits, more employment, as well as better wages. In the public sector output does not easily expand. On the railways, in the telephone exchanges, in the vehicle licensing department, 'rationalization' meant redundancies.

This is a difference of importance. Office automation may improve productivity in some routine areas of government administration, but by and large measured increase in productivity is far slower than in manufacturing, where rapid technological change occurs. For public sector wages—teachers' and health workers' and civil servants' and policemen's salaries—to keep up with the rest of the economy, their services have to become relatively more expensive, which itself—as is exemplified in current British disputes over costs in the National Health Service—is a source of political tension. If the strength of the private sector unions in the privileged corporate sector allows them largely to keep to themselves the gains of technological advance, those tensions could become more and more overtly tensions between the private and the public sectors.

But, if not tripartism, why not quadripartism? Why do we have to stick to Marxist paradigms which tell us that there are only two class interests and one dubious umpire in a capitalist society? Why not separate representation for the unions dependent on oligopoly markets and for the unions dependent on the level of taxes? And if that principle is accepted, why not quintipartism, with representation also of the secondary labour-market sectors, where wages are much more determined by the forces of supply and demand?

Japan may well be the first industrial society which ends up with one major private sector and one major public sector trade union centre. Perhaps it will be the first to institutionalize quadripartism.

3. The third point is this. We offered, in the first chapter, a definition of corporatist arrangements which emphasized bargaining exchange and contractualist reciprocity. That is the typical instinctive thinking of an individualistic society. Interest groups like unions have to *get* something for doing what the state—the ruling establishment—considers to be in the public interest. However, unions in Japan in 1975 were persuaded into acting in the public interest without more concessions than recognition as talking partners. British unions in the same year were walking out of their social contract negotiations with all kinds of promises about pensions and taxes.

Anyone who knows the tenor of the negotiations in the two countries will know that the difference is not just a difference in deference, in power of self-assertion, though it would be wrong to discount that as *one* element.[3] It is also a difference in the persuasive power of appeals to national interest. Stronger national sentiment in Japan, a stronger sense of being members of an embattled nation to which the world was once again giving a hard time, made Japanese union leaders try harder to understand the 'shared public interest' arguments the government deployed—about the long-run effects of high wage settlements on export capacity, the competitiveness of the economy, investment, and ultimately real wages. It also made those arguments more persuasive when they had understood them.

The difference mirrors the enterprise level difference. The extreme contractualist position—'If *they* want our co-operation in technical change, *they* must guarantee that we will be adequately compensated' (in cruder form: 'they will have to buy out our restrictive practices')—contrasts with Japanese enterprise

---

[3] I have wrestled with this question elsewhere, not by any means to my own satisfaction, see Dore 1987: ch. 5.

union bargaining which assumes that there is a *shared* 'company interest' as well as the separate interests of the bargaining parties. Likewise, the TUC's contractualist 'what will you give us if we exercise wage restraint?' contrasts with a Japanese national debate which never loses sight of the *shared* 'public interest' in competitiveness and inflation control, even when the separate sectional interests are being argued.

So, to our definition of a 'corporatist arrangement' we might be bold enough to make an addition. A corporatist arrangement, it will be recalled, was:

1. the substitution of bargaining for markets or politics
2. in which a privilege, concession, is granted for a promise to act in the public interest.

Let us add one more condition and offer a suggested definition of 'a *successful* corporatist arrangement':

3. and there is some degree of consensus between the bargaining parties as to what the public interest is.

REFERENCES

DORE, RONALD (1987), *Taking Japan Seriously* (London: Athlone).

GARON, S., and MOCHIZUKI, M. (1988), 'Negotiating Social Contracts: State and Society in Postwar Japan' (unpublished conference paper).

HANCOCK, M. D., and SHIMADA, H. (forthcoming), 'Wage Determination in Both Countries', in H. Fukui *et al.* (eds.), *Economic Growth and Public Policy in Japan and Germany.*

HOLLERMAN, L. (1987) *Japan Disincorporated: The Economic Liberalization Process* (Stanford, Calif.: Hoover Institution Press).

INAGAMI TAKESHI (1988), 'Rodo-kumiai-undo no shin-jigen: Yunion-aidenteitei o motomete' ('The New Dimension of the Trade Union Movement: The Search for Union Identity'), *Rodo-kyokai-zasshi,* 342 (Jan.): 46.

MIYAKE ICHIRO (1985), *Nihon-seiji no zahyo (Coordinates of Japanese Politics)* (Tokyo: Yuhikaku).

PEMPEL, T. J., and TSUNEKAWA, K. (1979), 'Corporatism without Unions', in P. C. Schmitter and G. Lehmbruch, *Trends Toward Corporatist Intermediation* (London, Beverly Hills: Sage), 231–70.

SMITH, T. C. (1984), 'The Right to Benevolence: Dignity and Japanese Workers', *Comparative Studies in Society and History,* 26/4 (Oct.): 587–613.

TABATA HIROKUNI (1987), 'Gendai Nihon no roshi-kankei to kokka' ('Industrial Relations and the State in Modern Japan'), in Fujita Isamu (ed.), *Keni-teki chitsujo to kokka (The State and Authoritarian Order)* (Tokyo: Tokyo University Press), 229–62.

TSUJINAKA YUTAKA (1986), 'Gendai Nihon-Seiji no Kooporatizumu-ka' ('The Shift to Corporatism in Modern Japanese Politics'), in Uchida Man (ed.), *Koza Seiji-gaku (Introduction to Politics)* (Tokyo: Sanrei-shobo), 223–62.

YAMAGUCHI SADAMU (1986), ' "Sengoshi" kenkyu no kakuritsu to kakushinha-rekishigaku no kasseika no tame no mondai-teiki' ('Establishing the Identity of Post-war History: Setting the Agenda for the Revitalization of Left-Wing Historiography'), *Rekishigaku Kenkyu* (Oct.), 173–81.

3. Corporatism and Accountability: The Democratic Dilemma

Norman Lewis

WORK on corporatism has varied between that which sees the phenomenon as heralding a new state form, as one among competing theories of the state, as a contribution to the problems inherent in social theorizing, and, more humbly, as one among several possible forms of policy intervention. I have experienced some difficulty in coming to terms with the epistemologies of those who see in corporatism a new state form, and in consequence I have not been seduced to follow their lead. In the end I have adopted the view that corporatism is most usefully seen as a form of policy intervention while recognizing that such an approach assumes a theory of the state; otherwise, policy interventions would simply appear to materialize out of the atmosphere.

As a constitutional lawyer, my main concern is to describe the parameters of legitimate public power and to examine the conduct of public life thereafter. Having a view of 'the constitution' and its problematics allows me to be interested in all manner of policy styles and approaches, and if corporatism can be regarded as a particularly identifiable style which operates, for the most part, outside the constitutional orthodoxies, then it is surely opportune to take a close look at its influence on our affairs. I hope to show that corporatism is one major, perhaps the major, strain of stable non-parliamentary public action and that the time for drawing it into our constitutional analyses is long overdue.

I shall be addressing what has now become widely accepted as 'societal' or 'neo-corporatism', and shall therefore have nothing to say about those strains associated with fascism. Nor, for the most part, will I be dealing with tripartism as a macro-economic strategy. Tripartism is but one form of corporatism and there is now no doubt that corporatism without organized labour is possible at all levels and is of growing importance in Britain at the time of writing. Whether, in the longer term, Britain will become more like the United States in relegating organized labour to the dug-outs, or whether British labour traditions will prove more durable, remains to be seen. None the less, trade unions have been historically significant actors in Keynesian planning experiments and they continue to participate in such remaining tripartite structures as look likely to survive a third term of Thatcherism. However, at the time of writing such structures appear increasingly fragile. That being said, the stable bargained arrangements between the public and private sectors have now to be primarily sought for elsewhere.

The crucial determinant in identifying corporatism is, in my view, how locked into each other the private and public actors are; how interdependent and with what degree of institutionalization? There is no one simple test for identifying this phenomenon but it remains an issue of central constitutional significance; that is, one of public visibility and accountability. Since corporatist relations require by definition a degree of stability then they become, inevitably, 'undignified' aspects of the constitution. We shall see that not only do we have few or no conventions to deal with these outgrowths, but that we possess little in the way of legal control.

It is not only possible but common for both pluralist and corporatist styles of political behaviour to be found within the same functional state activity. Indeed, modern politics at large will operate with both styles of intervention and representation. For corporatist styles of intervention it is the bargaining element that is crucial; gains for both 'state' and interest groups, though not necessarily in the same measure, must be present. Let me now short-circuit a complex debate by providing an ideal-type definitional restatement of the preconditions for corporatist intervention. Given the overarching concern with legitimation or constitutionality, the following characteristics represent the core requirements;

1. Governmental–interest group association or concertation so that the interest groups are in a real sense part of the extended state.
2. Limited numbers of organized interests or interest groups

so that 'competition' is limited and the issue of exclusion is raised.

3. The interest groups will possess sources of information, expertise, finance, or executive–organizational capacities.
4. A degree of brokerage between government and the interest groups.
5. The interest groups will be granted recognition (so that again the limiting of competition and the issue of exclusion are raised), licensed, possess a degree of representational monopoly, etc.
6. The interest groups will use (3) above on behalf of certain government aims. This is the process usually referred to as intermediation and it should be stressed that I see no point in restricting this to the situation where interest groups exercise powers of discipline over their members. I shall develop this point shortly.
7. The linkages between the groups and government must possess a degree of stability.

Intermediation has perhaps caused more dispute amongst scholars working in the field than almost any other concept. I have no wish to weigh and measure these disputes but again to cut through them and substitute a loose and inexact alternative which nevertheless captures the spirit of the corporatist initiative, while leaving the honing down to empirical inquiry. Governments often afford favourable treatment to a particular group or groups, sometimes to the extent of constituting them as the sole legitimate spokesman of the movement concerned. In return, agreements are negotiated which provide for government a 'simplified external environment' (Dunleavy 1982: 189). We must remember that the simplified external environment criterion must operate in harness with at least most of the other variables which have been outlined. This is, at the least, what the private body affords to the governmental body in return for government 'favours' within stable institutional relationships. Normally, what we shall find is that the private body performs or at least assists in performing tasks which have either traditionally been thought of as public or are in the process of becoming matters to which government believes it can no longer turn a blind eye.

Stating the intermediation requirement in this loose and inexact fashion alerts us to the fact that the structures employed within what are, in effect, symbiotic relationships are infinitely variable and that we should not be deflected merely by the verbal characterizations of institutions. To take an example to which I shall return: many advisory bodies are unambiguously corporatist on almost any contemporary definition, in spite of the nomenclature. Their number has certainly not diminished in the Thatcher years and there is growing evidence that strategic examples of such bodies are being emplaced in which like-minded appointees are unarguably sharing the business of governing. A number of examples will unfold in the course of what follows.

Table 3.1 ranks a selection of public and 'hybrid' bodies on a pluralism–corporatism scale. The ranking, which was carried out as part of our research for the ESRC Corporatism and Accountability project, can be only approximate, but is based on the assessments of the position according to the above list (1)–(7). It should also be borne in mind that these categories are fluid and that the location of the bodies within them will be contingent on political and other changes. The sample was culled from the Pliatsky Report (1980) and a number of other publications and directories, most notably *Councils, Committees and Boards, Public Bodies*, and the *Directory of British Associations*. We wrote to each of the bodies concerned asking for copies of their constitutions, Minutes of Incorporation, annual reports, and other official documents. From these we culled our information. On a number of occasions we wrote for supplementary information and constructed a series of structured interviews. We excluded the better-known non-departmental public bodies, such as ACAS or the Civil Aviation Authority, on the grounds that a great deal is already known about them.

THE STATE AND ITS PARTNERS

To speak of the state is to speak of a set of institutions operating legitimately in conjunction with civil society. That said, and having identified at a theoretical level the constitution of any particular country, the actual disposition of power between state organs and private interests is clearly very much an empirical matter. Thus, differing interpretations about where power actually lies as between an activist state and organized private interests are ultimately resolvable empirically too. However (and this is a central feature of corporatist arrangements), in modern society only the bureaucratic state is capable of producing the organized responses from civil society thought necessary for the effecting of public purposes (see e.g. Schmitter 1985: 33–5).

Tracing the contours of the state is made that much easier where a formal constitutional document exists and where yardsticks of legitimation are readily to hand for the purpose of mapping out power configurations and, to some extent, the sites of private and public authority. In general terms, however, there is no doubt that different sites of state power exist, so that the skeins of corporatist conduct need to be traced at different levels. This is not always readily appreciated in corporatist writings with the result that much genuine state–society brokerage has been overlooked. This has been especially true of the 'arm's-length' state institutions such as quangos, advisory committees, nationalized industries, and the like, although recent scholarship has recognized the split-site problem in relation to both the local and the regional state (see King 1985: 202; Cawson 1985: 126).

I have spoken elsewhere about the 'extended' state (Harden and Lewis 1986), but a little more needs to be said for the purposes of unravelling some of the corporatist tangles. For analytical purposes, extended government in general, and quangos in particular, may be classified as government properly so-called or as essentially private interests. A third characterization would see quasi-government as consisting of both public and private actors so that, within its institutional framework, corporatist bargaining can take place. Quasi-government organizations such as the Royal Mint, HMSO, and the former Supplementary Benefits Commission are all so nearly government properly so-called as to make no difference. At the other end of the scale, the 'private' organizations can frequently easily be identified, even if they are, so to speak, 'tainted' with government; bodies here include the National House-Building Council, the Advertising Standards Authority, and so on. In between, we face genuine problems of classification, not least in relation to the 'classic' quangos such as the Housing Corporation and the Independent Broadcasting Authority. Much depends on the membership of such bodies (and their consequent loyalties) and the interests which they represent. This will, to a

Table 3.1. Categorization of the sample bodies on a pluralist–corporatist scale

	Pluralist				Corporatist
	1	2	3	4	5
British Technology Group			✓		
English Industrial Estates Corporation			✓		
Development Commission			✓		
Industrial Development Advisory Boards		✓			
Regional Industrial Development Boards		✓			
English Tourist Board				✓	
Co-operative Development Agency				✓	
London Docklands Development Corporation				✓	
Property Advisory Group		✓			
Export Guarantees Advisory Council	✓				
Energy Efficiency Office	✓				
Advisory Committee on the Safety of Household Electrical Equipment		✓			
Advisory Council on Research and Development for Fuel and Power	✓				
Standing Advisory Committee on Trunk Road Access	✓				
Advisory Committee on Landscape Treatment of Trunk Roads	✓				
Information Technology Advisory Panel	✓				

Advisory Council on Applied Research and Development

Insurance Advisory Panel

Manufacturing Advisory Service Steering Committee

Joint Contracts Tribunal

British Board of Agrement

National House-Building Council

Horse Race Betting Levy Board

Horse Race Totalisator Board

Policy Holders' Protection Board or Insurance Bureau

Wine Standards Board of the Vintners Company

Nationalized industries[a]

Privatized bodies[a]

National Council for Voluntary Organisations

Access Committee for England

Milk Marketing Board

Joint Committee of the Dairy Trade Federation and MMB

General Medical Council

United Kingdom Central Council for Nursing

Law Society[b]

Institute of Chartered Accountants

Bar

Advertising Standards Authority

Press Council

Engineering Council

	Pluralist 1	2	3	4	Corporatist 5
Wages Councils				√ ←→	√
Industrial Training Boards (statutory)				√	
Industrial Training Boards (non-statutory)			√		
Community Industry	√				
Race Relations Employment Advisory Group	√				
School Curriculum Development Council		√ ←→	√		
Industry/Education Advisory Committee		√			
Council for Educational Technology		√			
Business and Technician Education Council			√		
Council for Accreditation of Correspondence Colleges					√
Advisory Board for the Research Council		√			
Advisory Council for Applied Research and Development		√	√		
Arts Council		√	√		
Chemical Industries Association Ltd.				√	
British Agrochemicals Association Ltd.				√	
British Aerosol Manufacturers' Association				√	
Society of British Aerospace Companies				√	
Defence Manufacturers' Association			√		
British Naval Equipment Association				√	
Review Board of Government Contracts				√	

Defence Technology Enterprises			
Committee on the Safety of Medicines		√	
Association of British Pharmaceutical Industries			√
UK MEIG[c]		√	
Medispa[c]			√
Pharmaceutical Price Regulation Scheme			√
Proprietary Association of Great Britain[d]			
Office of Fair Trading[d]			
OFTEL[d]			
Monopolies and Mergers Commission	√[e]		
City Takeover Panel			√

[a] Difficult to categorize in simple terms. On occasion, powerful nationalized industries can be seen as a form of strong state corporatism, while privatization has periodically witnessed bilateral corporatism.

[b] Although we have categorized the Law Society towards the corporatist end of things, considerable changes were being discussed at the time this study was being conducted. A renewed assessment may be called for under contemporary conditions.

[c] Trade associations for medical equipment.

[d] In themselves these cannot be ascribed as pluralist or corporatist—but they may facilitate corporatist tendencies (e.g. self-regulation).

[e] But cf. OFT and OFTEL.

considerable degree, be a matter for empirical investigation. The fieldwork conducted for the ESRC Panel made a preliminary attempt at posing and answering some of the attendant questions.

Another way of addressing the issue is to ask whether such bodies are essentially ciphers for government policies, in which case they may be classified as government properly so-called, or whether they to some extent share interests with those who are to be regulated. The reasons for seeking to draw out this classification should by now be obvious. The analysis should help in identifying the sites of bargaining; where to address the empirical questions—a vital matter for corporatist scholarship in itself, but it should also help in highlighting the issues of constitutionality and accountability. A classification is set out in Fig. 3.1.

A word or two of explanation may be called for. Where quangos are classifiable more as government than not, then it must be asked whether bargaining is taking place with private actors in a corporatist framework or whether essentially pluralistic forces are at work. Many advisory bodies are, in fact, squarely within the 'essentially government' category and in general operate most frequently in a pluralistic rather than a corporatist fashion. There will, however, be the usual axis where one form of policy intervention shades into the other, depending upon such matters as differential access, structured exclusion, and the like.

Where a quango shares both public and private features (e.g. the Housing Corporation, which has members closely associated with government as well as representatives from the building societies, housing associations, and indeed architects), then the sites of any potential bargaining are more complex. Their relations with 'clients', members, the regulated, and so on are likely to be a mixture of bargained relations and those of intermediation, in differential proportions, depending on the issue. That is to say that bargaining may take place at three different levels and at different policy peaks. By the hybrid nature of the beast, bargaining may first of all take place within the institutional framework that is the quango. Secondly, the quango may engage in levels of bargaining with those it has the duty to regulate, while the regulatory function of itself may partake strongly of intermediation. The precise mix can be

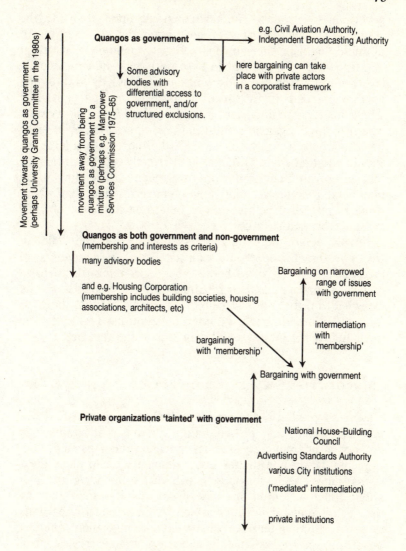

FIG. 3.1. *A classification of public bodies*

expected to vary from case to case. Thirdly, given its hybrid nature, it might well bargain with its sponsoring department over a narrowed range of issues; narrowed, since the majority of issues will have been resolved elsewhere. Again, it is important to stress that such bodies can move from one part of the governing spectrum to another depending upon, *inter alia*, the contingent policy interest of government at the centre. An example might be the University Grants Committee, which at one time might be thought to have been very much a second-layer, non-government body which moved quietly towards the government end of the spectrum towards the end of its life. These matters are important from the point of view of deciding what is really bargainable and what not; where the power really lies and where it may be shared. Furthermore, at this level, we should add that advisory bodies are perfectly capable of being a mix of government and non-government, depending upon membership, interests, and policy concerns, and that where some degree of executive power or strong influence obtains, genuine corporatist forces are at work.

Finally, where the bodies are essentially private but 'tainted' with government, one could expect most of the bargaining to take place between these bodies and their sponsoring departments. In such a case, their relations with the 'regulated' can be expected, in the normal course of events, to be those of intermediation, although the intermediation itself will often be mediated by the interests and concerns of the regulated.

CORPORATISM AS A STYLE OF POLICY INTERVENTION

Having adopted a fairly broad definition of corporatism, it will be unsurprising that I should find a number of strains in a number of different areas of policy formation and implementation. Implementation is a matter upon which I wish to place great stress since it seems obvious that there are few ways in which public functions could be more obviously 'off-loaded' than by their being implemented, at least in part, by private groups. This is perhaps the other face of classic intermediation whereby private groups are expected, in some fashion, to exercise control or discipline over their membership in return for privileges afforded by the state. This seems to me to be only one form which this side of the bargain can take. If the essence of corporatism is an institutionally stable set of arrangements for the mutual advantage of both public and private actors, then securing the implementation of 'public' tasks by private parties would seem to represent corporatism with a vengeance. The empirical work to which I have referred makes it abundantly clear that there is a great deal of such activity currently on offer.

'Off-loading' is by no means restricted to the voluntary and welfare sector and we uncovered numerous examples of government soliciting the private sector to undertake both industrial and general economic functions which have traditionally been within the public domain in return for advantages conferred upon the private parties by government. Even so, the trend is perhaps most in evidence in the field of welfare, and especially through the use made of the voluntary sector. It needs to be added, however, that systemic encouragement of such offloading may be accompanied by a particular philosophy of macro-economic management. To this extent, arrangements in response to fiscal crisis may be characterized as corporatist in no less a sense than the 'classic' concertation policies with the representatives of labour and capital.

Winkler, in particular, has argued that recent governments, not least British governments, have been developing institutions for involving the community in the provision of welfare services. These developments are commonly presented as being better for the recipient, more cost effective, and perhaps ideologically valuable too (Winkler 1981). Stripped of its essentials, this movement amounts to the state off-loading traditional welfare functions back on to groups of citizens. The institutions chosen for this shift are many and various; voluntary associations, community groups, user co-operatives, non-profit corporations, mutual aid societies, and the like. A government committed to a reduction in the burden of direct taxation was bound to find such alternative styles of welfare delivery particularly attractive, and so it has proved.

This off-loading combines three related strains. It transfers existing services to the community, it helps to pre-empt demand, and it mobilizes new community provision. This trend is an international one and is as clearly visible, for example, in the United States as in Britain, a fact which helps to expose the canard that corporatism is alien to the politics of the US (see e.g. Kramer 1979). There is clear evidence of corporatism as I define it in these relationships. Not only is there a two-way process whereby both the ends of the state and the voluntary organizations and those they represent are to various degrees satisfied, but in many of the instances we uncovered during the course of the research, the relationships were relatively stable, institutionally speaking. Whether or not one can identify 'classic' intermediation, there is clearly a great deal of policy *implementation* by the voluntary organizations. Moreover, although *exclusion* as such is not normally apparent, there is, in most instances, either an umbrella or 'lead' organization which receives favourable governmental treatment and support.

Let me attempt a brief summary. The short-term economic policies of government both constrain and are constrained by social programmes, while, in the longer term, the inseparability of economic performance from education, housing, and income-maintenance provision in particular is crucial, whether the nexus be analysed in terms of the reproduction of labour or in more complex ways. In this sense I agree with the view that significant corporatist tendencies should be regarded primarily as a response to problems of economic management and the need to find institutional and ultimately political substitutes for the declining efficiency of market mechanisms (Goldthorpe 1984: 325).

One upshot of defining corporatism in this broader fashion, including the identification of differential, devolved sites of government at one end of the relationship, is that it becomes possible to regard not only sectoral-level concertation with government as potentially corporatist in nature, but also single-firm–government relations as of the same order. This must naturally depend upon the strategic nature of the firm in question but the point is worth making that not only is one-firm corporatism theoretically coherent, it is perhaps a greater likelihood in Britain than elsewhere. It has frequently been observed, for instance, that the domestic and international importance of large British firms creates a climate in which direct relationships between government and industry are likely to be of more importance than, say, in West Germany, where trade associations will be much more active (see e.g. Grant 1984). Multinational corporatism in West Central Scotland has also been identified as a potentially rich study for corporatist intervention (Reed 1981). This, incidentally, raises the issue of differential government sites, since it has been stressed that where there is a degree of devolved government, as in Scotland, the articulation between the Scottish Office and a large company might well exhibit features which are quite as corporatist as those exhibited by business interest associations elsewhere (see Moore and Booth, this volume).

Having said that, it is perfectly feasible for such corporatist practices to flourish at the national level. Particular kinds of markets, especially those of a multinational variety, might furnish patterns of corporatist interaction, not least in the form of regulated autonomy. This is currently in the process of being researched by others, but I would expect that the 'big bang' of late 1986 in the City of London would ultimately produce a handful of giant global securities dealers whose activities would, at the very least, be of considerable interest to government, howsoever the sites of government are identified in this context. Oil might provide another example, particularly in the 'hybrid' case of British Petroleum (see e.g. Arnold 1978: 79–81). The final illustration I want to make in this section is that of self-regulation, which, for present purposes, can be allowed to absorb the recent phenomenon of privatization of state assets.

Cases of self-regulation are often seen as rearguard actions against government legislation/regulation, threatened or imagined. This is a trite view. Self-regulation is frequently the result of bargains struck between government and the group or industry concerned where the issues at stake are clearly of exceptional national interest. Depending on the degree of give and take, we are often once more talking corporatism, given the definition which I have adopted. Arguably public tasks are being performed by private actors exercising 'classic' intermediation which can, in appropriate circumstances, be highly advantageous for government in that it avoids committing resources to day-to-day policing.

AN ENDEMIC PHENOMENON

Contrary to the beliefs embedded in 'crude' corporatism, it should now be plainly asserted that corporatism is endemic to modern liberal democracies. Fashions and styles of government may change but partnerships of various sorts are an inevitable accompaniment of the pursuance of social and economic goals (see e.g. Berger 1981: 10; Maraffi 1983). Corporatism in its modern forms is combined with liberal parliamentarism under the dominance of the latter (e.g. Sweden with its social

democratic corporatism, Holland with its consociational democracy, Austria with its *Proporz-demokratie*, and so on). But this
pattern does not obviate, and indeed may provoke, contradiction
and conflict between corporatist representation and parliamentary
representation. Indeed, there is every reason to suppose that the
constitution of Britain, as I have recently argued (Lewis 1988),
is becoming increasingly a marriage of prime ministerial
centralism and neo-corporatism. Furthermore, corporatist patterns
of policy-making and delivery, though requiring a degree of
stability for effective performance, may represent transitional
phases from one form of representation to another. Perhaps
'third-force' housing in Britain in the post Second World War
period is a good example. More generally, the more the modern
state underwrites the capitalist state (*a fortiori* the mixed or
welfare state) by expanding its regulative and integrative tasks,
the more it finds that it needs the professional expertise,
specialized information, prior aggregation of opinion, contractual
capability, and deferred parliamentary democracy which only
corporatist structures can provide (see Schmitter 1979: 26–7).

This general point can be reinforced by returning briefly to
the matter of welfare corporatism. Winkler shows how, after the
Wolfenden Report, the voluntary sector was seen as an
extension of the state, yet in circumstances where they were
'essential partners in the provision of services' (Winkler 1981:
130). There must then, to whatever extent, exist a sense of
shared purpose, unlike versions of state corporatism where social
peace is enforced in circumstances where the interest groups are
too weak to respond. Degrees of mutuality are just that and no
more, for it is rare to institutionalize a setting for total
'concordance' as appears for a long time to have been the case in
Austria (Marin 1985: 114–15).

Self-regulation (or 'regulated autonomy') necessitates that a
broad range of groups, voluntary, professional, and otherwise,
may be chosen instruments for corporatist practices. The
professions, for example, may be seen, for the purposes of
accountability at least, through the eyes of corporatist scholarship.
Thus it might be asked how far the exercise of professional
power, or privilege, is partly exchanged for and expressed in the
profession's regulation of its own members, whether by seeking
to underwrite competence or through discipline. Some of these
issues have been addressed by other researchers operating

under the ESRC initiative, though we have found examples in our own fieldwork (see e.g. Moran, this volume).

It might be supposed that, just as Keynes is seen as the forerunner of modern attempts to use corporatism as a policy instrument to stabilize and make markets more manageable, so anti-Keynesian economic policies would be anti-corporatist. This, however, is clearly not the case. Supply-side policy generally requires corporatism, and arguably so does monetarism. Ensuring that goods, services, and labour are available in sufficient quantities at the right time and without bottle-necks will require planning and co-operation in modern economies. The market unaided is seen to be insufficiently sensitive to produce results which are conterminous with any government's economic objectives. Furthermore, governments will have to depend upon the action of salient industrial agents, albeit that the latter will often receive considerable injections of governmental assistance. This has clearly been the case with supplies to the offshore oil industry, training, and finance and credit. It might be added that, as a policy instrument, or an instrument for increasing the capacity of the state to make and implement policy, arrangements at the *micro-* or *meso*-level may have considerable impact at the macro-level. Indeed, it can be argued that the most important role of the NEDC, a macro-level body, has been to provide a framework for the operation of the meso-level sector working parties (Middlemas 1983), though, at the time of writing, they look to be becoming increasingly unpopular in governmental circles. On the other hand, the links between City institutions and the state, which operate at meso-level in relation to the workings of financial markets, may have greatest significance in terms of the operation of macro-economic policy.

CORPORATISM: EFFICIENCY AND ACCOUNTABILITY

There exists within governing circles a habit of mind which regards accountability mechanisms as an impediment to efficiency. This is a view which I am unable to share. As is argued elsewhere, not only is efficiency a highly problematic concept but, within the policy communities involved in corporatist relations, bargaining postures make a clean measurement of optimum outcomes extremely difficult (Birkinshaw, Harden, and Lewis 1987: ch. 3; *ibid* 1990).

My belief is that, in modern conditions, effective action by organizations, public or private, economic or political, requires *learning capacity*. Learning capacity includes institutional arrangements for setting and revising objectives, goals, and policies, and for monitoring performance (see Pizzorno 1978). Such institutions and procedures constitute accountability mechanisms, although accountability exists in a number of different forms: hierarchical, democratic, internal/external, and so on. These correspond to different types and forms of learning, and thus to different conceptions of the effectiveness of organizations, networks, or public policy initiatives. My central claim is that evaluation of the effectiveness as well as the legitimacy of an institution or of a strategy (for example, corporatism as a strategy of political intervention) requires an examination of arrangements for accountability.

For public policy, I would argue, the concept of efficiency is logically subordinate to that of *effectiveness*. This latter concept presupposes a set of objectives and priorities. Furthermore, given the limits to central control and co-ordination imposed by (1) the scarcity and costs of information and (2) the absence of hierarchical control over the behaviour of relevant actors, the process of institutional design cannot be effective if it is guided by purely instrumental considerations.

Given the need for learning capacity, substantive criteria of evaluation which can guide a purely instrumental process of institutional design are not available for public policy as a whole. In order to achieve the co-operation needed to generate information and use it effectively, the process of institutional design must involve both decentralization of decision-making and taking sufficient account of affected interests. This, in turn, requires sufficient trust to make the rules of decentralized 'games', involving strategic and instrumental behaviour by the actors, revisable in a learning process, which itself necessitates machinery for monitoring and evaluation. In sum, the relevant issues are ones of accountability.

Another, simpler, way of stating the issue is perhaps to say that government has at its disposal a number of instrumentalities for governing. The extent to which government is effective in the way in which these instrumentalities operate depends upon making the right assumptions about the particular mode of rationality concerning organizations in a specific sector (see

Butler 1985). Absent techniques for performance review, quality control, and systems assessment, the search for optimum effectiveness is likely to be impeded.

The thin gruel of corporatist accountability

The public tasks of social co-ordination, conflict resolution, and policy-making have, for some time, been shifted further away from the dignified parts of our constitution to the private or hybrid sectors. There has been an extremely significant bypassing of territorial or political loyalties with little in the way of public law control to put in its place. In so far as private or voluntary groupings assume tasks which are matters of pressing public concern, then it seems to me to follow that they owe constitutional allegiance to our collective belief-system. They become, with government, subject to canons of public account-ability. These agencies will frequently exercise a degree of control over their constituencies as part of the corporatist bargain, as well as being to some extent the source of power and influence over other actors and state institutions. In the ESRC Report, we argued that since public functions are in effect being delegated, then canons of 'internal' accountability ought logically to be required of such bodies.

Because corporatism has frequently been associated with total systems—the formal and hierarchical representation of estates—instead of being characterized in something like the fashion adopted here, its insidious growth has not always been recognized, with alarming repercussions for the rule of law. Corporatist arrangements, often of the 'weak' variety, have been grafted on to parliamentary structures as and when the need has arisen. Given that this process has been incremental and pragmatic, it has rarely been exposed to the constitutional limelight.

Within the clear dissolution of the boundaries between civil society and the state, I shall want to concentrate not upon shifting alliances between the public and the private sectors, but upon the more stable institutional relations. This is an attempt to redress a major constitutional omission, for an examination of the accountability of corporatist arrangements is an examination of a vital part of the governmental system; a patterned way of conducting public business. It involves asking for a constitutional reassessment of a development which is likely to continue in the heart of modern governments for the foreseeable future.

Although corporatist styles of intervention are not alone in escaping adequate 'supervision', one specific problem has to be faced at the outset. Corporatist arrangements, by their nature, tend to foreclose or exclude all individuals or groups save the favoured ones. This is to raise the spectre of insiders and outsiders in the political game, a central feature of British politics in any event, but one almost certainly heightened in this particular context.

There is no debate between serious scholars about the fact that the simple constitutional understandings of a world divided between parliamentary institutions and markets can no longer hold, if indeed they ever could. If, therefore, a mixed economy necessitates bargaining, co-operation, and co-optation, as it surely does, how far is it the case that such styles of policy formation and implementation constitute a progressive deterioration of the democratic form of governance? To answer this question it is necessary to concentrate on the role of the state *vis-à-vis* the 'partner' or regulatee, for it by no means follows that whatever control is retained by the state will be exercised publicly or will be reasoned.

Our researches indicate that, with honourable exceptions, the picture is constitutionally bleak, though this unsatisfactory state is part of a larger problem. Whether we are talking of pluralist politics, corporatists structures, market dominance, or whatever, the constitutional arrangements of most of the European states have been those designed or developed between the late 18th and early 20th centuries (see e.g. Maraffi 1983: 21). As such they have been slow to respond to the emergent patterns of new policy communities. This is exacerbated in Britain since: (1) we do not possess Continental-style systems of public law; and (2) we have not adapted through the espousal of open-policy processes, as has occurred to a considerable extent in the United States. Table 3.2 indicates the main accountability mechanisms in use, though it cannot be taken as exhaustive.

THE MODERN FACE OF CORPORATISM

Since I wish to concentrate upon accountability mechanisms from now on, I shall resist the temptation to litter this essay with

Table 3.2. Forms of accountability of corporatist bodies

Institution	Heads of Accountability[a]																
	1	2	3	4	5	6	7	8	9	10	11	12	13	14	15	16	17
1. Industry/Education Advisory Committee		✓							✓			✓					
2. School Curriculum Development Council			✓✓						✓	✓	✓	✓					
3. Advisory Board for Research Councils	✓	✓		✓					✓	✓	✓	✓					
4. Advisory Council for Applied Research and Development		✓							✓	✓	✓	✓					
5. University Grants Committee	✓	✓							✓	✓	✓	✓					
6. Council for Educational Technology	✓	✓		✓					✓	✓	✓	✓			✓		
7. Business and Technician Education Council	✓	✓	✓						✓	✓	✓	✓					
8. Council for Accreditation of Correspondence Colleges			✓				✓[c]			✓	✓	✓[e]					
9. Engineering Council	✓[b]	✓	✓			✓			✓	✓			✓	✓			
10. English Industrial Estates Corporation	✓	✓	✓	✓		✓			✓	✓		✓[d]	✓	✓		✓	

Institution	Heads of Accountability[a]																
	1	2	3	4	5	6	7	8	9	10	11	12	13	14	15	16	17
11. Co-operative Development Agency	✓									✓		✓	✓				
12. British Technology Group		✓	✓	✓	✓	✓				✓		✓	✓				
13. English Tourist Board		✓	✓	✓	✓	✓				✓		✓	✓				
14. British Tourist Board		✓	✓	✓	✓	✓				✓		✓	✓				
15. Joint Committee of Dairy Trade Federation		✓	✓		✓	✓						✓	✓e				
16. Milk Marketing Board	✓	✓				✓	✓e					✓	✓				
17. Industrial Development Advisory Boards		✓	✓	✓	✓					✓f		✓					
18. Regional Industrial Development Advisory Boards		✓	✓	✓						✓f							
19. London Docklands Development Corporation	✓(?)	✓	✓	✓	✓					✓		✓	✓				
20. Property Advisory Group		✓	✓	✓					✓	✓		✓					
21. Export Guarantees Advisory Council		✓	✓	✓								✓					
22. Policy Holders' Protection Board	✓	✓	✓	✓	✓	✓						✓	✓				
23. General Practice Finance Corporation	✓	✓	✓	✓	✓	✓						✓	✓				

24.	Offshore Oil Advisory Committee		√					
25.	Chemical Industries Association		√	√g	√	√	√	
26.	British Agrochemicals Association Ltd.		√	√eg	√	√	√	
27.	British Aerosol Manufacturers' Association		√	√eg	√	√	√	
28.	Review Board for Government Contracts	√	√e	√h	√		√e	
29.	Society of British Aerospace Companies			√e	√eg	√e	√	
30.	Defence Manufacturers' Association			√	√eg	√e	√	
31.	Medicines Commission (and its committees)	√	√	√e	√		√	
32.	Proprietary Association of Great Britain			√e	√e	√e	√	
33.	Association of Consulting Engineers			√e	√e	√e	√	
34.	General Medical Council	√	√	√e	√e	√	√	√√
35.	United Kingdom Council for Nursing	√	√	√e	√e	√	√	√√
36.	Law Society		e		√f √e	√e		√√
37.	Senate of the Inns of Court; Bar Council and Inns of Court						√√	√√

Institution	Heads of Accountability[a]																
	1	2	3	4	5	6	7	8	9	10	11	12	13	14	15	16	17
38. Institute of Chartered Accountants	✓						✓		✓	✓	✓			✓			
39. British Board of Agrément	✓	✓	✓						✓		✓	✓					
40. Horse Race Totalisator Board	✓	✓		✓					✓		✓	✓	✓				
41. Horse Race Betting Levy Board	✓	✓		✓					✓		✓	✓	✓				
42. Arts Council	✓	✓	✓e						✓	✓	✓	✓					
43. Advertising Standards Authority	✓	✓					✓e		✓	✓	✓	✓		✓		✓	
44. Press Council[i]																	
45. Wages Council	✓	✓			✓				✓		✓	✓	✓				
46. Advisory Committee on Houseworking[j]					✓	✓											
47. Industrial Training Boards (statutory)	✓	✓		✓	✓				✓	✓	✓	✓	✓	✓			
48. Industrial Training Boards (non-statutory)									✓ek	✓	✓l						
49. Community Industry	✓	✓e	✓m								✓						
50. Race Relations Employment Advisory Group												✓					
51. National Council for Voluntary Organisations		✓							✓	✓	✓						

52. Access Committee for England[n]
53. National Federation of Self-Employed & Small Business
54. Energy Efficiency Office
55. Advisory Committee on Safety of Household Electrical Equipment
56. Advisory Council on Research and Development for Fuel and Power
57. Legal Aid Advisory Committee
58. Legal Services Conference[q]
59. Standing Advisory Committee on Trunk Road Access
60. Advisory Committee on Landscape Treatment of Trunk Roads
61. Information Technology Advisory Panel
62. Insurance Advisory Panel
63. Manufacturing Advisory Service Steering Committee
64. Association of British Pharmaceutical Industries

Institution	Heads of Accountability[a]																
	1	2	3	4	5	6	7	8	9	10	11	12	13	14	15	16	17
65. Advisory Council on Race Relations		√[e]										√					
66. Health authorities	√	√	√	√	√	√		√	√			√[s]	√				
67. Health Service Supply Council (disbanded 31 Dec. 1985)		√	√	√	√				√			√	√[e]				
68. Office of Fair Trading	√	√	√[e]		√	√			√	√		√[t]	√				
69. Monopolies and Mergers Commission		√	√[e]						√[u]	√		√	√				
70. Office of Telecommunications	√	√	√[e]		√	√			√	√		√	√				√
71. Nationalized industries		√		√	√			√	√	√		√	√				
72. Development Commission		√		√	√			√	√	√		√	√				
73. Council for Small Industries in Rural Areas[v]					√												
74. British Naval Equipment Association							√[f]		√	√	√						

[a] Column headings as follows. 1: Comptroller and Auditor-General oversight; 2: Parliamentary Select Committee scrutiny; 3: controlled (by provision of appeals, statutory standards imposed by civil servants, or guidance likewise imposed; Secretary of State directions/approval, etc.); 4: reports or accounts to the Secretary of State; 5: report to Parliament; 6: annual accounts to Parliament; 7: elections; 8: public meetings; 9: public reports, annual or otherwise; 10:

consultation with other bodies; 11: Companies Acts requirements; 12: members appointed by the Secretary of State; 13: created by statute; 14: created by royal charter; 15: created by trust deed; 16: established disciplinary hearing or complaints procedures; 17: ombudsman supervision.

^b For first three years.
^c To an extent.
^d Board members.
^e Statutory instrument.
^f Limited.
^g Not internal committees.
^h General.
ⁱ None of the devices exists. A newspaper only publishes a judgement if found to be in the wrong.
^j Has not met since 1979.
^k Variable.
^l Not all.
^m MSC.
ⁿ Registered charity.
^o Not for internal meetings.
^p Lord Chancellor.
^q Informal offshoot of (57).
^r PM.
^s Some nominated.
^t DGFT.
^u Published by 1968.
^v Agency of 1972.

consultation with other bodies; 11: Companies Acts requirements; 12: members appointed by the Secretary of State; 13: created by statute; 14: created by royal charter; 15: created by trust deed; 16: established disciplinary hearing or complaints procedures; 17: ombudsman supervision.

[b] For first three years.
[c] To an extent.
[d] Board members.
[e] Statutory instrument.
[f] Limited.
[g] Not internal committees.
[h] General.
[i] None of the devices exists. A newspaper only publishes a judgement if found to be in the wrong.
[j] Has not met since 1979.
[k] Variable.
[l] Not all.
[m] MSC.
[n] Registered charity.
[o] Not for internal meetings.
[p] Lord Chancellor.
[q] Informal offshoot of (57).
[r] PM.
[s] Some nominated.
[t] DGFT.
[u] Published by 1968.
[v] Agency of 1972.

empirical examples of corporatism in modern Britain, but if I did not say a little then the accountability arguments might carry less weight. With that in mind, I shall refer to just a few illustrations from both the welfare and the industrial fields and then top them up with some examples which emerged from our empirical work.

First, the field of social welfare. Even here, a disclaimer needs to be lodged. There is some evidence, both convincing and less so, that patterns of welfare policy are emerging which are highly ideological and discriminatory, in what might be crudely characterized as class terms. (For the more convincing, see e.g. Harrison 1984: 17, 35–6; and for the less so, see Gould 1981.) Further research is needed to give us the necessary information about these claims, but if true they are enormously important. However, the point to make here is that some of my examples are merely tip-of-iceberg corporatism.

The Volunteer Centre and the National Council for Voluntary Organisations are centrally important in the development of 'off-loading' functions, though for the sake of brevity I shall concentrate on the former. Founded in 1973, its purpose is to encourage volunteering in as many settings as possible: hospitals, social services, schools, independent voluntary associations such as MENCAP, neighbourhood care schemes, even supporters of the local museum. It offers to voluntary organizations an information and advice service, organizes training courses, development work, and promotes the work of self-help groups in the countryside, inner cities, *et al.* The Centre is a registered charity, and receives grants from the Home Office Voluntary Services Unit, other government departments, charitable trusts, and elsewhere. The degree of its societal penetration not only supports Winkler's thesis but comes very close to sustaining some of the larger claims about 'consumption' corporatism made by Harrison and others. Although there is no classic intermediation, the Centre does a great deal more than help to create a simplified or sympathetic external environment. It is clearly instrumental in assisting in the co-ordination of the implementation of large areas of social policy.

The voluntary or 'third-force' housing movement is another good example. The relations between the D.O.E., the Housing Corporation, the housing associations, and the National Federation of Housing Associations are extremely complex, even if we leave out of account the extra involvement of both local authorities and the building societies, which logically one cannot. Most recently, governmental encouragement of linkages between the associations and private finance capital has further complicated the patterns of development. Deep-layered corporatist forces are, however, very clearly at work.

The National Association for the Care and Rehabilitation of Offenders is a body which rarely figures in the corporatist literature but very clearly should, although its relations with government are of a very mixed sort on the pluralist–corporatist spectrum. Its principal activity is the provision of local services through local projects, the day-to-day work being concerned with helping offenders meet their practical needs for housing, education, employment training, neighbourhood improvement, and so on. It is a major sponsor of the Youth Training and Community Project schemes, which aim to give some of the most disadvantaged school-leavers and long-term unemployed adults training and work experience (see e.g. NACRO 1985). In spite of considerable ideological differences with recent governments, the Association has become a major plank in the official training programme, thereby underlining an important corporatist strain: namely that differences may be sunk between public and private actors providing that there remains something of interest to be defended by both sides of the relationship.

There is also the example of the Independent Television Companies Association. The IBA seems incapable of dealing with a range of matters thrown up, in part, by the fragmented nature of British broadcasting. The machinery for programme planning has to come through the ITCA to the Programme Controllers Group, which plans network schedules. Regular meetings take place on programming and related matters, formally, institutionally, and stably, between the ITCA and the IBA. There is, in reality, a sharing of the governing functions between a distinctly private body and a quango which is near to the government properly so-called end of the spectrum.

Finally, to turn to economic and industrial affairs, there exists an Industrial Development Advisory Board to advise the Secretary of State on regional and national assistance under the Industrial Development Act 1982, as well as Scottish and Welsh IDABs and an Industrial Development Board for each of the English regions. Support for local enterprise agencies is provided through tax reliefs with the promotional body being Business in the Community. A bargained, quasi-legislative framework exists in relation to the supply of goods to the offshore oil industry, while the financial services industry is riddled with corporatist arrangements. In short, there is abundant evidence that neither a 'pure market' nor a 'social market' industrial policy (Grant 1982) operates in Britain and that, on the contrary, a range of quasi-government and quasi-non-government bodies, as well as central departments, are engaged in various forms of selective support for industry and business (see Birkinshaw, Harden, and Lewis 1987: ch. 4).

Our wider project uncovered a huge range of articulations between the public and private sectors, some clearly corporatist, some less obviously so, and some seeming to be on the point of shifting from one sector to another. A much abbreviated list of institutions will be mentioned, simply to show how pervasive such linkages are and how unremarked in terms of constitutional scholarship. The following then are merely some of the most interesting: the British Technology Group (springing out of the National Enterprise Board), the English Industrial Estates Corporation (England's largest industrial and commercial landlord), the Development Commission (which advises on all matters relating to the economic and social development of rural areas), the London Docklands Development Corporation, the Property Advisory Group, the British Board of Agrément, the Joint Committee of the Dairy Trade and Milk Marketing Board, the Advertising Standards Authority, the Council for Educational Technology, the Review Board for Government Contracts, Defence Technology Enterprises, the Defence Manufacturers Association, the Committee on the Safety of Medicines, the Pharmaceutical Price Regulation Scheme. I have deliberately omitted the professions, the privatized industries, and most self-regulatory bodies.

This is not the place to elaborate on our empirical work to any very great extent, but let me refer briefly to the Development Commission in order to lend some substance to the rather perfunctory list which I have just cited. The Commission acts as adviser to the D.o.E. on all matters relating to the economic and social development of rural areas in England and may carry out or assist others to carry out measures likely to further such development. In fact it possesses considerable executive powers including the ability to make grants and loans, give guarantees, acquire land, provide premises for partnership with others, and so on. The Commission operates only in Rural Development Areas. The English Estates Corporation operates as agent for the latter's factory and workshop programmes. The Council for Small Industries in Rural England administers the Commission grant, which amounts to up to 25 per cent of the cost of renovation and modernization of redundant buildings. The Commission also has partnership arrangements with some housing associations and enjoys grant-giving relationships with local authorities. In fact the multi-layered arrangements need to be carefully unpicked in order to see the dense relations between the public and private sectors, a matter which our research reinforced in context after context.

My object here has only been to indicate the enormous spread of corporatist arrangements which has received so little attention from lawyers and from constitutionalists generally. Massive accountability, or rule-of-law, implications are thereby raised. I shall here be able to touch upon only a few

THE DEMOCRATIC DILEMMA

I have argued elsewhere that the extended state operates outside canons of democratic acccountability to a very considerable degree (Harden and Lewis 1986). This situation is perhaps more exacerbated within corporatist arrangements than elsewhere, as I shall indicate shortly. Let me, however, summarize the position very briefly: parliamentary (and associated) forms of accountability are subject to well-documented limitations. In corporatist relations, where much bargaining is conducted *sub rosa*, such forms are of even less value than elsewhere. As we argued in *The Noble Lie*, judicial restraints are unpatterned and constrain policy communities in only very minor degrees. Some intermediate bodies, however, such as the Office of Fair Trading and the Monopolies Commission, require accountability arrangements in a limited number of circumstances where corporatist bargaining takes place (Birkinshaw, Harden, and Lewis 1987).

What is clearly required (and what obtains in only a very unsatisfactory degree) is a reconsideration of the range of legal techniques adoptable within the framework of modern policy-making, leaving the courts a minor role but one which is very different from that which they ordinarily play. The primary role of the courts within the modern political system should be to act as the guarantor of 'rational discourse', although without any attempt at second-guessing substantive outcomes. The institutions for rational discourse must be flexible but could be expected to conform to a narrow range of ideal types (Llewellyn 1940; Lewis 1981). These concern, primarily, the provision of information, machinery for resolving disputes, and machinery for policy and corporate planning. Whether or not such institutions need to be constrained, and in what degree, by substantive regulation will depend upon the context and the degree of certainty and/or knowledge which the official state apparatus possesses. A new, more purposive, formal rationality, certainly within corporatist arrangements, should lie at the heart of modern accountability mechanisms.

What I am urging here for corporatist arrangements is a melding of Llewellyn's older insights with those of modern sociology of law. Accountability demands on the hidden agendas of government are growing in an atmosphere where it is becoming increasingly recognized that accountability through the law or formal public structures does not have to be of the traditional court-room, over-lawyerized, variety. The task of the legal order when faced with networks of policy communities is somewhat different from that assumed formerly. As Streeck and Schmitter have said in the context of corporatist arrangements:

> It is true that an associative social order implies a devolution of state functions to interest intermediaries. But this has to be accompanied by a simultaneous acquisition by the state of a capacity to design, monitor and keep in check the new self-regulating system's 'procedural control'. (1985: 26)

This is, in fact, an insight into the work recently conducted by a number of lawyers who have detected shifts in the social universe which, they argue, leave the task of a legal order as primarily one of designing institutions for the achievement of 'purposive' goals (Nonet and Selznick 1978; Teubner 1983; Harden and Lewis 1986: ch. 10).

The legal techniques required for these doings are variously described as being of the 'soft' or 'reflexive' or 'responsive' variety; they are summarized in terms of the arm's-length regulatory techniques overseeing self-regulation in the public interest as 'regulated autonomy'.

Soft law and regulated autonomy

The first requirement of any form of regulation and any form of accountability is, of course, freely available information. Its absence in Britain is too well known to catalogue here and is quite as severe in relation to corporatist arrangements as elsewhere. Indeed, it could be argued that it is, in vital respects, worse in that bodies characterized as 'private' but which perform some public functions will usually be subject to normal private law requirements. These will rarely demand publicly accessible information, save perhaps where the National Audit Office or Parliamentary Select Committees exercise jurisdiction. As we catalogue elsewhere, the designation of public and private in governmental circles is quirkish to say the least (Birkinshaw, Harden, and Lewis 1987: chs. 4, 6). A crude catalogue of when information is available within a typical set of corporatist arrangements can be found in Table 3.2. Suffice it to say here that the availability of information is patchy and incomplete.

The existence of grievance mechanisms is just as sporadic. The absence of an administrative procedure act and constitutional foundation document is a significant impediment to describing how grievances are resolved in British public life (see Birkinshaw 1985). We now possess a fairly compendious treatment of complaints mechanisms adopted in British local government (Cracknell, Lewis, and Seneviratne 1986), and an overview of complaints mechanisms within self-regulatory organizations (NCC 1986). The 'fairness' doctrine is a common law body of jurisprudence which determines, *inter alia*, when and how a case may be stated against a 'public' body, broadly described. This has operated in an expanded fashion in recent years but against no obvious body of theoretical doctrine or understanding of the growth of public/private policy communities.

Policy-making is the great accountability desert of British public law. Both statutory and voluntary consultation occur in a wide range of areas but in circumstances where our constitutional jurisprudence has little to offer, with the possible exception of the land use planning area. Two vital deficiencies occur in the law and practice of British policy-making consultation; the first is the practice of inviting insiders and excluding outsiders, heightened, by definition, within corporatist arrangements. The second is that the terms of the consultation debate are usually called by government or governing institutions without the courts demanding that a 'hard look' at policy objections occurs. The great rule-making procedures of American Federal Law are largely absent and in consequence what debate occurs at the level of the general public is largely determined by what governing institutions feel they can get away with (Harden and Lewis 1986: chs. 8, 9). This is particularly acute in relation to the many quangos and 'advisory' bodies which play such a central role in corporatist relations.

Corporate planning and performance review are perhaps the other two great managerial features which have not been adequately constitutionalized within the process of the extended state at large, and corporatist arrangements in particular. Where, for example, corporate planning occurs, it is normally seen as exclusively a managerial–financial affair. What is manifestly lacking is public input into this process and the failure of our system of public law to force planners to 'hard look' objections from those who are invited to express their views on these matters. The courts have been less unwilling to open up this process than to obstruct it (see generally Prosser 1986: ch. 6). The self-same points can be made in relation to the monitoring or performance review processes so central to judgements about the efficiency of corporatist arrangements, and indeed the general set of judgements required to be made about public policies.

As a device for advancing a number of these 'constitutional goods', a word should be said about codes of practice. They may operate voluntarily or they may be the result of statutory requirements. In either event, they may or may not be bargained between public and private actors. Codes are not, of course, restricted to self-regulatory regimes, though they are especially important for them. The NCC document is particularly valuable in this respect and identifies five categories of code which can be reconstructed by corporatist scholars to advance ideal-type corporatist accountability measures. It also provides some kind of rough catalogue of the current contribution of such codes within corporatist frameworks (NCC 1986). Two of the codes which we identified as being of considerable interest within frameworks of corporatist accountability are the *Code for Voluntary Organisations*, and the one bargained between the Department of Energy and UK Offshore Operators Association Limited (Birkinshaw, Harden, and Lewis 1987).

Sunshine and beyond

Democratic politics requires open conduct. In fact, with the movement of decision-making away from parliamentary institutions, many modern governments, and certainly the British, have also moved away from the open address of public issues. Corporatist arrangements are once again largely more open to such criticism than other forms of managing politics. The bargains are not only made between public and 'private' actors, but it is frequently argued that they must be struck confidentially. The catalogue of closeted government within these arrangements is in fact stark. None of the advisory bodies (many of them effective decision-takers) of which I am aware sits openly; almost all health authorities operate in closed session; and government committees and meetings are invariably closed, save at the local level where the writ of the Local Government (Access to Information) Act 1985 now runs. This need not be so, as American experience shows.

In the United States, the Government in the Sunshine Act 1977 applies to all agencies of the executive branch of the Federal government headed by at least two members, and also their subcommittees and advisory committees. The Act circumscribes what can be dealt with collectively without any opportunity for the public to be present, and provides that every portion of every meeting of an agency shall be open to the public unless the subject-matter is statutorily exempted. There are also procedures for closed meetings, which are judicially enforceable, and for public access to relevant records and documentation. Legal restraints upon *ex parte* discussions (i.e. the agency meeting with interested parties in private) and the conduct of advisory committees are also imposed (see Harden and Lewis 1986: ch. 8).

If considerable power is exercised outside Parliament, then the only constitutional redress left to those who wish to reassert democratic values is through the courts. Unfortunately, judicial review in Britain is next to valueless in this context since closeted conduct will rarely disclose manifest error. The lessons for lawyers are not difficult to learn, but much ground needs to be made up if our constitutional life is to be made accountable again in any real sense.

The issue of *ex parte* relations is particularly acute within corporatist arrangements when it comes to the 'self-regulation' of public tasks. This is because some self-regulation is undoubtedly the result of government threatening the private body with legislation as an alternative to a voluntary reordering of its affairs. This is a loaded revolver which cannot be as effectively held by many other governments in the Western world as in Britain, given the control of the parliamentary machine exercised by the dominant political party. The need for the public to be apprised of these discussions is, by definition, particularly acute. It is a matter of major constitutional concern both whether self-regulation is acceptable, and *on what terms.* The degree of autonomy retained and the degree of oversight demanded are matters over which any government ought to be held to effective account.

The other issue concerning self-regulation and accountability is this: there will often be a regulatory oversight body for the general supervision of the regulatee who will, to all intents and purposes, be exercising semi-public functions, whether it is, for example, the IBA or, for telecommunications, OFTEL. In most cases, this supervision will be exercised by what are now called non-departmental public bodies (NDPBs). The categorization by government of which bodies are public and which private is often baffling, but more to the point is that no general administrative procedure act regulates their conduct or their accountability (see Harden 1987). No regular pattern can be discerned, but in general it can be stated that the law has little to say; influence is mainly 'political' and the political influence is largely shielded. Even the government's own *Guide* is a damning indictment of the state of constitutional accountability in Britain today (Cabinet Office, 1985). The theoretical aridity of official thinking on the public/private divide is of major importance for present purposes. The most recent manifestation occurs in the Parliamentary and Health Service Commissioners Act 1987. This extends the number of agencies subject to the oversight of the ombudsman system and as such is to be welcomed. However, only two of the bodies in our detailed empirical survey have thereby been brought into the net. Furthermore, even the 'classic' quangos are differentially treated. Thus, the Housing Corporation is included, the Independent Broadcasting Authority is not. No rational explanation seems to be forthcoming.

CONCLUSIONS

This treatment of a complex subject has necessarily been unelaborate. There are, however, several points by way of summary which will bear reiteration. They are as follows. First, stable institutional arrangements, which we may call corporatist, are an entrenched feature of our system of government whereby private and public actors share the business of government between them. This is a matter of *singular* constitutional importance which has been largely unaddressed by constitutional lawyers in particular, but by students of our constitution more generally. Secondly, these arrangements are deeply embedded and will almost certainly constitute a major feature of our organized public life for the foreseeable future. Thirdly, these corporatist processes occur largely outside the framework of effective supervision and accountability with the legal system, in particular, having little to say. Table 3.2, though by no means exhausting the range of corporatist relations in Britain, illustrates the total inadequacy of accountability arrangements. Fourthly, there is no evidence that increased accountability would impede efficiency on any sensible interpretation of that term. In conclusion, we now need to bend our minds to creating or borrowing techniques of a flexible legal nature to recapture the essence of the rule of law so that we may harness the many advantages of corporatist relations to the constitutional claims upon which our system of government is based.

REFERENCES

ARNOLD, GUY (1978), *Britain's Oil* (London: Hamish Hamilton).
BERGER, S. (1981), *Organizing Interests in Western Europe* (New York: Cambridge University Press).

BIRKINSHAW, P. (1985), *Grievances, Remedies and the State* (London: Sweet and Maxwell).

—— HARDEN, I., and LEWIS, NORMAN (1987), *Patterns of Accountability within Corporatist Arrangements* (London: Report to the ESRC).

——, ——, —— (1990), *Government by Moonlight: the Hybrid Parts of the State* (London: Hyman Unwin).

BUTLER, R. J. (1985), 'Public Choice, Ambiguity and Regulation', unpublished paper for EGOS symposium, Sweden.

Cabinet Office, MPO/Treasury (1985), *Non-Departmental Public Bodies: A Guide for Departments* (London: HMSO).

CAWSON, A. (1982), *Corporatism and Welfare: Social Policy and State Intervention in Britain* (London: Heinemann).

—— (1985), 'Corporatism and Local Politics', in Grant 1985: 126–47.

CRACKNELL, S., LEWIS, NORMAN, and SENEVIRATNE, MARY (1986), *Complaints Procedures in Local Government* (Sheffield: Centre for Criminological and Socio-Legal Studies, University of Sheffield).

DUNLEAVY P. (1982), 'Quasi-Governmental Sector Professionalism: Some Implications for Public Policy-Making in Britain', in A. Barker (ed.), *Quangos in Britain* (London: Macmillan).

GOLDTHORPE, J. H. (ed.) (1984), *Order and Conflict in Contemporary Capitalism: Studies in the Political Economy of Western European Nations* (Oxford: Clarendon Press).

GOULD, ARTHUR (1981), 'The Salaried Middle Class in the Corporatist Welfare State', *Policy and Politics*, 9/4.

GRANT, WYN (1982), *The Political Economy of Industrial Policy* (London: Butterworths).

—— (1984), 'Large Firms and Public Policy in Britain', *Journal of Public Policy*, 4.

—— (ed.) (1985), *The Political Economy of Corporatism* (London: Macmillan).

HARDEN, I. (1987), 'A Constitution for Quangos', *Public Law*, 27–50.

—— and LEWIS, NORMAN (1986), *The Noble Lie* (London: Century Hutchinson).

HARRISON, M. L. (1984), *Corporatism and the Welfare State* (Gower).

JESSOP, BOB (1979), 'Corporatism, Parliamentarism and Social Democracy', in P. C. Schmitter and G. Lehmbruch (eds.), *Trends Towards Corporatist Intermediation* (London: Sage).

KING, ROGER (1985), 'Corporatism and the Local Economy', in Grant 1985.

KRAMER, RALPH M. (1979), 'Public Fiscal Policy and Voluntary Agencies in Welfare States', *Social Services Review*, Mar.

LEHMBRUCH, G. (1977), 'Liberal Corporatism and Party Government', *Comparative Political Studies*, 10.

LEWIS, NORMAN (1981), 'Towards a Sociology of Lawyering in Public Administration', *Northern Ireland Legal Quarterly*, 32.

—— (1988), 'Undemocratic Centralism and Neo-Corporatism: The New British Constitution' (public lecture to the Centre for Constitutional Studies, University of Alberta).

LLEWELLYN, K. (1940), 'The Normative, the Legal and the Law-Jobs', *Yale Law Journal*, 49.

MARAFFI, MARCO (1983), 'The Neo-Corporatist Model and the Theory of the

State' (paper to Summer School on Comparative European Politics, EUI, Florence).

MARIN, BERND (1985), 'Austria: The Paradigm Case of Liberal Corporatism?', in Grant 1985.

METACALFE, L. (1978), 'Policy-Making in Turbulent Environments', in K. Hanf and F. W. Sharpf (eds.), *Interorganisational Policy-Making: Limits to Co-ordination and Central Control* (London, Beverly Hills: Sage).

MIDDLEMAS, K. (1983), *Industry, Unions and Government* (London: Macmillan).

MORAN, M. (1986), 'Theories of Regulation and Changes in Regulation: The Case of Financial Markets', *Political Studies*, 24: 185–201.

NACRO (1985), *Annual Report 1984–5*.

National Consumer Council (1986), 'Self-Regulation' (NCC, unpublished).

NONET, P., and SELZNICK, P. (1978), *Law and Society in Transition: Toward Responsive Law* (Harper and Row).

PIZZORNO, A. (1978), 'Political Exchange and Collective Identity', in C. Crouch and A. Pizzorno (eds.), *The Resurgence of Class Conflict in Western Europe since 1968*, 2 vols. (London: Macmillan).

PROSSER, TONY (1986), *Nationalised Industries and Public Control* (Blackwell).

REED, M. (1981), 'Theories of Corporatism and the Business Enterprise' (paper to SSRC Conference, Canterbury).

SCHMITTER, P. (1979), 'Still the Century of Corporatism?', in P. C. Schmitter and G. Lehmbruch (eds.), *Trends Toward Corporatist Intermediation* (London, Beverly Hills: Sage).

—— (1985), 'Neo-Corporatism and the State', in Grant 1985.

Social Science Research Council (1981), *Final Report of the Corporatism and Accountability Research Panel*.

STREECK, W., and SCHMITTER, P. (1985), 'Community, Market, State—and Associations? The Prospective Contribution of Interest Governance to Political Order', in W. Streeck and P. Schmitter (eds.), *Private Interest Government: Beyond Market and State* (London, Beverly Hills: Sage).

TEUBNER, G. (1983), 'Substantive and Reflexive Elements in Modern Law', *Law and Society Review*, 17.

WINKLER, J. T. (1976), 'Corporatism', *European Journal of Sociology*, 17.

—— (1981), 'The Political Economy of Administrative Discretion', in M. Adler and S. Asquith (eds.), *Discretion and Welfare* (London: Heinemann).

4. Regulating Britain, Regulating America: Corporatism and the Securities Industry

Michael Moran

'SECURITIES' is a 'generic term for any financial instrument traded on a stock exchange' (Valentine 1985: 176). Behind this innocent definition lies a world of turmoil. The heart of the global securities industry is located in Britain and the United States. The industries of these two countries have in recent decades been revolutionized—in their ownership structures, trading practices, and regulatory arrangements. At the heart of the revolution lies a crisis of corporatist control. This chapter is about that crisis: about its origins and attempted resolution; and about what light the crisis throws on patterns of regulation in Britain and the United States.

Our best starting-point is puzzlement. For over a decade the securities industry in the United Kingdom and the United States has been dominated by calls for deregulation—in particular, for an end to public controls. Since the beginning of the 1980s there have also existed in London and Washington neo-liberal administrations ideologically sympathetic to this deregulation movement. Yet at the end of the decade, on both

This chapter reports work done as part of a project on Anglo-American securities regulation. The research was supported by the ESRC as part of its 'Corporatism and Accountability' initiative (grant no. E04250010). The material subjected to comparative analysis here has been reported separately for each country in Moran (1987 and 1988), where more detailed documentation is also given. Some of the observations also rely on interviews with interested parties conducted in London in 1985 and in Washington and New York in 1986.

I received valuable comments on earlier versions of this paper from participants in seminars in the Department of Politics at the University of York and the Faculty of Law at the University of Warwick. I also benefited greatly from the friendly criticism of members of the ECPR Workshop on 'Deregulation in Western Europe', held at the Joint Sessions in Amsterdam, 1987. I owe a particular debt to the comments of Phil Cerny, Leigh Hancher, and Sir Arthur Knight.

sides of the Atlantic, public intervention in the industry is in significant ways greater than was the case a decade ago. How did Mrs Thatcher, in the name of deregulation, impose on the British securities industry a system of controls more comprehensive than any socialist administration dared contemplate? Why did the Reagan administration, perhaps the most pro-business since the days of Coolidge, launch a ferocious campaign against insider trading, a stock market practice which a generation ago was perfectly respectable? And why did an administration with particularly close ties to Wall Street create, in the Boesky affair, the greatest scandal on Wall Street since the Whitney scandal of the 1930s?

The attitude of neo-liberal administrations towards insider trading is especially puzzling. Economists like Stigler and Manne have advanced the intellectually powerful argument that insider dealing makes markets work efficiently—a view which ought to appeal to supporters of deregulation (Stigler 1975; Manne 1966). Mr Boesky's admission that he indulged in insider trading turned him into a pariah; but if the logic of deregulation were applied consistently it should have made him the toast of Wall Street.

One possible solution to this puzzle lies in the argument that deregulation has perverse consequences. Many participants in the markets, for instance, believe that in recent years traditional controls and standards have been weakened, that this has caused scandalous abuse, and that this abuse has in turn compelled public intervention. But this account is unconvincing. Doubtless in some cases abuses do encourage intervention, but this only begs a more important question: why do particular practices become stigmatized as abuses, and thus the focus of regulatory attention? The striking feature of the campaign against insider trading is the way in which the stain of criminality has been applied to what was once an acceptable business practice. The present campaign is not a sign of the emergence of some novel problem; it is a mark of how changing regulatory standards have converted a common practice into an abuse. A similar sequence marks the evolution of London's elaborate new regulatory structure. The new arrangements were not produced by the excesses of deregulation. How could they be, since they developed alongside, not after, the deregulation of the domestic securities industry? But the experiences of building a new regulatory system, and the rule-making activities of the new institutions, have undoubtedly contributed to a heightened sensitivity to standards of business conduct. In short, the puzzling state of regulation at the end of the 1980s cannot be ascribed to the 'abuses' caused by deregulation, for the changing notion of what is an abuse is itself part of the wider changes in the industry.

An alternative solution to the puzzle is offered by a glance at the changing historical setting of regulation in Britain and the United States. Until recently, Anglo-American securities regulation looked like a study in contrasts.

These contrasts were suggested both by arrangements in financial markets and by the wider culture of regulation in the United States and the United Kingdom. In financial markets it was a truism that Britain and America were very different. 'The City' was hidden from politics. Neither law, nor Parliament, nor Whitehall played a significant part in its control. A network of associations, social groups, and independent institutions like Lloyd's controlled who entered markets and the terms under which, once in, they could do business. The stability of the system was guaranteed by a socially cohesive City élite and by the guiding hand of the Bank of England. The Bank, especially after it was nationalized in 1946, could in a crisis command something like sovereign authority in the City. Yet it also kept its distance (both administratively and geographically) from Parliament and from the central departments of state.

These regulatory arrangements fulfilled two functions: they provided a stable business environment in which 'excessive' competition could be curtailed; and, particularly through the agency of the Bank of England, they protected the markets from the characteristic inconveniences of control by a democratic state.

Observation across the Atlantic suggested a starkly contrasting picture. The control of financial institutions has been a deeply divisive issue in American politics. The existence and purpose of a central bank; the ownership of financial institutions; the power exercised by financiers in the wider economy: all have historically been the object of fierce partisan controversy. Banks and securities markets have been subject to legal regulation, intervention by administrative agencies, and scrutiny by legislators. The starkest contrast of all was presented by the securities industry itself. In Britain the Stock Exchange traditionally worked largely independently of state control, and with only the lightest surveillance by the Bank of England. In the United States the financial crisis associated with the Great Depression produced a political and administrative revolution. The 1933 Securities Act and the 1934 Securities Exchange Act established a comprehensive legal framework for stock exchange trading (supplemented in 1938 by the Maloney Act, which did the same thing for the over-the-counter market). The creation in 1934 of the Securities and Exchange Commission produced one of the most prestigious and successful of the New Deal agencies.

The notion that British and American financial regulation was a study in contrasts was reinforced by consideration of the wider character of regulation in the two countries. American regulation seemed to be influenced by distinctive cultural traits: a manic litigiousness, an adversarial style of personal conduct, and an obsession with public disclosure. These casual observations have recently been systematized, notably by Kelman and by Vogel, in comparative studies of national regulatory styles (Kelman 1981; Vogel 1986). Vogel's is the most pertinent, since it rests on a series of Anglo-American comparisons, principally in the field of environmental regulation. The essence of his subtle and complex argument is as follows. Regulation is shaped less by the particular object of control than by the national historical and cultural setting in which it takes place. The American setting dictates extensive and detailed public controls; adversarial confrontation between regulators and regulated, especially when the regulated are from the business community; hostility on the part of business to regulation and to regulators; and a climate of public opinion suspicious of the activities of business. In Britain, by contrast, the national setting dictates co-operative regulation. British capitalists, unlike their American counterparts, lost their aggressive instincts late in the nineteenth century, when a 'gentlemanly' ethic began to dominate business life. This made businessmen ready to co-operate in public regulation. In turn, the state trusted business to practise self-regulation in a responsible way. An élitist political system ensured that, by contrast with America, the whole arrangement was conducted in a private and informal manner.

The 'national setting' account of regulatory style offers a most attractive solution to both the American and the British parts of our puzzle. The aggressive attack on practices like insider trading can be explained as the result of the American adversarial tradition—perhaps the dying echo of that tradition in an age of deregulation. The rise of regulatory controls in London can likewise be explained in terms of the decline of a distinctively British style of financial regulation. The most striking feature of the securities industry in recent decades is the growing convergence of markets: a global industry has begun to emerge, in which the same small number of multinational giants dominate trading in the major world centres. These structural changes were led until recently by American institutions. It is entirely to be expected, therefore, that a convergence of regulatory systems would occur, and that this convergence would be towards the dominant, American, model.

There is no doubt that in market practices and in regulation a process of convergence is indeed taking place, but as I shall show in these pages the character of this convergence is not at all what one would expect from the initial stereotypes of American 'adversarial' and British 'co-operative' regulation. Securities regulation has, it transpires, long been strikingly similar on the two sides of the Atlantic. Both systems have been corporatist, and remain corporatist. In both countries the prevailing corporatist arrangements have been under intense stress. The particular forms taken by corporatism, and the intensity of stress, have indeed been shaped by individual national peculiarities. But in the two countries, deregulation *and* episodes like the campaign against insider trading are the product of the decay of old corporatist arrangements, and the attempt to recreate new ones. The solution to our puzzle is, therefore, that the contradictory development of securities regulation in recent years is the product of a declining corporatist order.

The notion of corporatism employed here has been expressed in eight words by Claus Offe: 'the attribution of public status to interest groups' (Offe 1985). In both Britain and the United States securities regulation has worked by endowing private institutions with regulatory authority. Wolfe's notion of a 'franchise' exactly describes the arrangement (Wolfe 1977). The franchise to regulate securities was won by (or in Britain granted by default to) particular private interests. The stresses on corporatism arose from the development of new interests, who

challenged those entrenched by the franchise. Deregulation—
an adjustment of market practices to reflect the demands of the
new interests—was one result of this challenge. The reconstruction of the regulatory system and the evolution of new
regulatory standards was another.

In the remainder of this chapter, I elaborate these arguments
by examining in turn the American and British experiences. In
the final section I try to describe the wider implications of the
discussion.

AMERICA: A CORPORATIST FRANCHISE IN DECAY

The campaign against insider trading in the 1980s is in the
distinct American regulatory tradition identified by Vogel—
highly moralistic, adversarial, and legalistic. In these respects,
however, it is entirely uncharacteristic of American securities
regulation. The ferocity of the regulatory attack on Wall Street
actually results from the decay of the traditional system, and the
decline of the interests and the ideologies which made it viable.

To foreign—especially British—eyes the American system
established in the 1930s seemed adversarial and bureaucratic.
The reality was the very opposite: the regulation administered
by the Securities and Exchange Commission was co-operative,
not adversarial, and corporatist, not bureaucratic. It is the decay
of the historical forces and ideologies sustaining that system
which explains the present assaults.

The common misperception of American securities regulation
as adversarial in character is not difficult to explain, for the
present system was undoubtedly created in fractious circumstances. The Wall Street crash, the crisis of American
capitalism, and the rise of Roosevelt as capitalism's saviour
produced an atmosphere ripe for the revelation of scandal
(Parrish 1970). From April 1932 the Senate Banking Committee,
in a series of highly publicized hearings, documented the
malpractices of Wall Street in the years before and after the
Great Crash (US Senate 1934). The Securities Act of 1933 and
the Securities Exchange Act of 1934 were passed in the
atmosphere created by these revelations. Their passage was
fiercely and unscrupulously opposed by the traditional leadership
of Wall Street. This opposition continued during the first four

years of the life of the SEC, ending only with the disgrace of Richard Whitney, the leader of the 'old guard' on the New York Stock Exchange, who was sent to Sing Sing for embezzlement in 1938 (Seligman 1982: 72 ff.).

It is these events which have coloured perceptions of the American system as adversarial. But against this early history must be set a number of important considerations. Even in confrontation with the SEC, the financial community was not united. In its early battles with the New York Stock Exchange the Commission was always able to command allies on Wall Street among reformers who wanted a co-operative system of regulation. After 1934 the Commission also developed close and co-operative relations with the accounting profession and the securities bar, the two key professions in the system of corporate capitalism which was beginning to dominate financial life (Gadsby 1959; Jennings 1964).

The emergence of this system of co-operative regulation was encouraged by another consideration: the influential figures in the creation and implementation of the 1934 reforms themselves believed in co-operation. The system was legitimized by an ideology of self-regulation—by the belief that business affairs were so delicate and complex that they demanded control through practitioners rather than by a bureaucratic agency. Even a comparatively radical figure like William Douglas—the SEC's greatest chairman—argued that the stock exchanges 'should be so organised as to be able to take on the job of policing their members so that it would be unnecessary for Government to interfere . . . that is something more than partnership. That is letting the exchanges take the leadership role with Government playing a residual role' (Allen 1940). The legislation passed in 1934 did not give the Securities and Exchange Commission power to govern the industry; it gave it the power to issue regulatory licences to existing stock exchanges to do that job. By this 'attribution of public status' the exchanges ceased to be private institutions; they became self-regulatory organizations (SROs) supervised by the SEC. The system of control via SROs endures today.

The regulatory arrangements established in the United States under the New Deal thus had a corporatist structure supported by an ideology of self-regulation. The practice of regulation for almost a generation after 1934 reflected these beginnings. Far from confronting the exchanges, the Commission went out of its way not to impose its existing powers. In the first thirty years of its history, for instance, it revoked a licence only once and imposed a rule only twice. It also ensured that in its own independent rule-making operations, 'public comment' was reduced to a ritual: it was standard practice for the Commission to consult privately with the most important institutions in the industry before 'going public' with proposals (US House of Representatives 1963; US Senate 1972; Jennings 1964). This was possible because the top of the securities industry was a small world. An élite circulated between jobs in the Commission, the big law and accounting firms, the leading investment banks and securities houses, and the SROs. They swapped jobs, and communicated naturally and easily in a round of formal and informal meetings.

The corporatist structure and co-operative ideology of securities regulation was evolved to solve the crisis caused by the Great Crash, and the scandals following in its wake. The crisis impelled the state to intervene—an impulsion supported by many in the industry. Yet state intervention—especially the intervention of a democratic state—endangered the autonomy of powerful interests. The corporatist structure equipped the regulatory system with public power—but lodged those powers in institutions in the private sphere or, in the case of the SEC, at one remove from democratic arenas. This system was viable because of the particular historical evolution of securities regulation. By the 1930s the exchanges had a long tradition of, and considerable expertise in, regulation; the Federal government, by contrast, was creating a system almost from nothing. To bypass the exchanges would have involved an administrative and economic revolution inconceivable to all but the most radical of the New Dealers.

Although couched in the past tense, much of the description given above applies to the 1980s. The corporatist institutional structure, the ideology of self-regulation and co-operative regulation, the small élite circulating through the best jobs and mixing in a variety of formal and informal arenas: all these endure. But they endure less certainly: the community is less closed; is more open to penetration by Congress and interest groups; arguments are more abrasive; and, as the insider trading scandal shows, the SEC is more aggressive in enforcement.

These changes reflect the decay of the system established in the 1930s. Corporatism in the securities industry faces the same difficulties as those encountered by any corporatist arrangements established in societies combining capitalism and democracy. Corporatism fixes particular hierarchies of interests. The growth and innovation characteristic of a market economy constantly disturbs those hierarchies: new interests are created, old interests decline, conflicts spring up between those established and those newly flourishing. This is precisely what happened in the securities industry. By the late 1960s newly powerful groups—such as institutional shareholders and financial conglomerates with global ambitions—were demanding reforms in trading practices, and were being resisted by the interests at the top of powerful bodies like the New York Stock Exchange (Sobel 1975). The structure of power within the industry meant that the conservatives could successfully resist pressure for reform. But in a democratic political system suppressed interests do not have to acquiesce; they can take their case into a variety of competitive political arenas. The case for reforming trading practices was taken into the Federal bureaucracy (the Justice Department proving a notable ally), into Congress, and into the media. Competing pressure groups began publicly to argue with each other on behalf of their conflicting constituents. Congress, having largely ignored the industry since the 1930s, conducted a series of public hearings, during which all the competing interests tumbled into the public arena (US Senate 1972; US House of Representatives 1972). In short, the regulation of the industry became what is conventionally called 'politicized'. To put it more accurately, what had been a private world of politics became prey to the public forces of democracy.

Politicization was of course linked to the demand for deregulation, for it was part of the process through which the interests suppressed by the established corporatist structure made themselves heard. But once the industry had been dragged into democratic arenas, it was impossible to confine debate to narrow issues of business organization, such as the rates of commission charged on bargains. Politicians and journalists have a legitimate interest (and a career interest) in 'scandals'—as regulatory failures are commonly characterized. The politicization of the securities industry from the late 1960s inaugurated an age of 'scandalous' revelations which were examined exhaustively in Congress and the press. They encompassed the 'back office' scandal of 1969–70 (abuse of trading practices by New York Stock Exchange member firms, leading to Federal reform of investor protection); the 'corporate bribes' scandal of the mid-1970s (partly a side-effect of Watergate, leading to close Congressional scrutiny of esoteric accounting rules hitherto entirely controlled by accountants and the securities industry); and of course the insider trading scandals of the 1980s (leading to legislation in 1984, compacts between the SEC and foreign regulators, and the still unwinding Boesky affair).

American securities regulation has not hitherto fitted the model of bureaucratic and adversarial regulation identified as characterically American by observers like Vogel. The system established in the 1930s was corporatist and co-operative. It took this form because of the particular regulatory history of the industry. By the 1930s, when the demand for state intervention became insistent, the Federal government possessed neither a tradition of regulation, nor significant administrative resources to do the job; the industry, notably the exchanges, had both. Corporatism gave the regulatory system the stability of public authority without any dangerous exposure to democratic accountability. The institutions controlling this system could not, however, accommodate the new interests created by competition and innovation. These rejected and disaffected interests took their case into democratic arenas. This sparked the public debate about deregulation. Once 'politicized', however, the industry could not prevent scrutiny of operations beyond the areas covered by the deregulation debate. Hence the spate of 'scandals'. To return to the puzzle with which I began: deregulation and the campaign against insider trading are the product of the same process—the decay of corporatist regulation. President Reagan's administration was the scourge of Wall Street because it happened to be in office when that decay was taking place.

The argument outlined here obviously rests to some degree on evidence unique to the United States; but it also involves factors general to societies combining capitalism with democracy. Is the American experience being replicated in Britain?

BRITAIN: THE DESTRUCTION AND RECONSTRUCTION OF CORPORATISM

Britain is a capitalist democracy but it is neither as capitalist nor as democratic as is the United States. Firms are smaller, less efficient, less competitive, less meritocratic in their selection of personnel, and less capable of coping with, or causing, economic change. British government is, by comparison with the United States, more secretive, offers fewer points of access, has a weaker legislature, and a less inquisitive press. These differences obvious though they are, need to be borne in mind in considering the history of British securities regulation.

The most striking manifestation of national differences can be seen in the varying degrees to which the two industries have been politically salient. In America the securities markets secured a corporatist franchise in the 1930s, but they had to fight for that franchise. In Britain the franchise was won by default. An ideology of 'self-regulation' dominated thinking about securities regulation (Wilson 1980). The central department with most obvious responsibility (variously, the Board of Trade, the Department of Trade, now the Department of Trade and Industry) accepted regulatory responsibility for only the fringes of the industry, and even then restricted its role to one of passive licensee (Gower 1982, 1984, 1985). The most important reason for this state of affairs was the domination of the securities market by the London Stock Exchange. The Exchange was, of course, one of that network of City institutions which had established the right to control a regulatory sphere, exercising quasi-public authority but operating free of public accountability. (The importance of the City connection is well illustrated by a comparison with insurance regulation: the Board (Department) of Trade, faced with an insurance industry with strong non-metropolitan roots, developed a comparatively significant regulatory role and built up a comparatively substantial amount of regulatory expertise.)

The most important beneficiaries of the corporatist franchise exercised by the London Stock Exchange were the Exchange's own members. From before the First World War until the 1980s a number of anti-competitive practices (notably minimum commissions on bargains, and a separation of roles between principals and agents) shielded members from many of the disturbances of a market economy. Broking and jobbing, which for much of the nineteenth century were occupations for the socially dubious, became in the twentieth century lucrative and respectable professions.

The Exchange's grip over regulation proved astonishingly resilient. It survived the long debate over the inadequacies of the securities market as a source of funds to British industry, a debate stretching the half-century between the Macmillan and Wilson Committees. It also survived the administrative and economic dislocation of two world wars, Britain's economic eclipse, the development of mass democracy, a succession of Labour governments, and the post-war structural transformations in the British securities industry. In other words, it proved remarkably resistant to the ravages of democracy and capitalism.

But this resistance did not amount to total immunity. In the 1950s a series of take-over battles—themselves tremors from the earthquakes which were beginning to destroy the old financial order—pushed securities regulation into partisan politics and on to the front pages of newspapers. Take-over battles, which are a natural part of a market economy, were a recurrent source of 'scandal' in the intervening decades. The publicity surrounding take-overs has highlighted a range of practices—'asset stripping', sophisticated tax avoidance bordering on evasion, the use of privileged inside information for personal gain—whose exposure to democratic scrutiny proved immensely delicate for the business community. Many of the conventional practices of business life became, in these conditions, the unacceptable face of capitalism (Clarke 1981). The regulation of take-overs has proved a critical weakness in the corporatist structure. It has forced the creation of a separate Takeover Panel, which is responsible for a contentious, increasingly elaborate, quasi-legal set of rules (Business Law Review 1987).

Take-overs and the associated 'scandals' show how the established corporatist structure was damaged by the interaction of market change and democratic politics. But even more serious damage was inflicted by the wider world financial services revolution. We have seen from the American experience that the key factor in the survival of a corporatist order is its capacity to adjust to the changing balance of interests produced by growth and innovation in markets. The London Stock

Exchange miserably failed that test. It could not respond to the demands of institutional investors for competitively negotiated commissions on bargains. The ownership structure which it imposed on members deprived them of the capital base they needed to become significant players in the developing world securities market. The scale of business transacted within the Exchange was dwarfed in London by the transactions of the Eurobond market, the most innovative part of the world financial services industry.

By the late 1970s the failure to respond to market change had created a crisis in the domestic securities industry. The corporatist structure, by hampering innovation, had reduced domestic firms to insignificance in world terms. This crisis was resolved by state intervention, and by the creation of an alliance between supporters of reform in the industry and in state institutions. The first attack came from a public regulatory agency, the Office of Fair Trading (OFT), which in 1979 referred the Stock Exchange's rule book to the Restrictive Practices Court (Office of Fair Trading 1980). There followed a period during which the Exchange simultaneously prepared to defend its own rule book in court, while lobbying central government to have itself removed from the clutches of the court and the OFT. This lobbying was supported by the Bank of England, which nevertheless, with characteristic ambiguity, also used the Exchange's predicament as a way ·of exercising pressure for reform (Plender and Wallace 1985).

These manœuvrings culminated in the 'Goodison–Parkinson' Agreement of July 1983, a compact between the Exchange and the Department of Trade and Industry, whose effect was to remove the Exchange from the jurisdiction of the Office of Fair Trading in return for the abolition of the most important restrictive practices. The structural consequences of this agreement have been momentous: there has occurred in the intervening years a transformation of ownership and market practices designed to reverse London's decline as a world centre of the securities industry.

So momentous are these structural changes that they have compelled equally fundamental changes in the character of the regulatory order. With the passage of the Financial Services Act in 1986 the new structure is now in place. At its heart lies a Securities and Investments Board (SIB), a half private, half public institution. The members of the Board are chosen by a process of consultation between the Department of Trade and Industry and the Bank of England. The Board independently appoints its own staff (and pays them private sector, not Civil Service, salaries). The SIB is funded by a levy on the private sector, its Board is dominated by leading figures from the securities industry, and its headquarters are in the heart of the City. But it is also a statutory body, which is equipped with extensive legal powers and which is required to give a public account of the exercise of those powers. The most significant powers allow the SIB to license self-regulatory organizations (SROs) covering different parts of the industry, and to prescribe a range of substantive practices which SROs must enforce as a condition of their licence.

This system marks an obvious process of convergence with American arrangements—indeed, when the proposals were being developed there was a constant traffic of ministers, civil servants, and leaders of the industry across the Atlantic to observe arrangements there. The crucial change involves a shift to the kind of corporatism practised in America, with a negotiated corporatist franchise, and a conscious 'attribution of public status' to private bodies.

London's recent experiences have, because they produced results resembling the institutional structures created in the United States under the New Deal, been sometimes compared with that episode. A better parallel is with the crisis experienced in the American securities industry in the late 1960s and early 1970s, when the inability of the corporatist structures to adapt to economic change forced alterations in the regulatory franchise. The new arrangements in London are designed to achieve several, not always consistent, objectives: to keep the system corporatist, thus retaining power in the hands of private interests at the expense of public institutions; to combat the sclerotic effect of corporatism, by giving the SIB the job of ensuring that the holders of corporatist franchises do not suppress the structural changes which are a normal part of market competition; to regulate the amount of that competition so as to curb whatever competitive practices happen at any particular moment to be defined as unacceptable; and to equip the corporatist institutions, via the statute book, with the necessary authority to accomplish these objectives.

The crisis of the corporatist franchise in the United States after the late 1960s was resolved in characteristically American fashion—by ferocious public arguments between the main interests. Because financial politics in Britain are more insulated from democratic forces, the process here was more hierarchical and closed. The 'Goodison–Parkinson' Agreement which destroyed the Stock Exchange's traditional franchise was the result of private negotiations between a few practitioners in the world of high politics in Whitehall and the City. It was sprung without warning on an incredulous and hostile public (incredulity and hostility existing, not least, among many members of the Stock Exchange). The new regulatory structure was also shaped by a tiny élite. The most important discussions took place within a special Advisory Group set up in May 1984 by the Governor of the Bank of England. The discussions within this Group (whose members were drawn from the City élite) crystallized the outline of the new structure. This structure in turn protects the regulatory system more fully from public control than does that existing in the United States. The most obvious contrast is in the difference between the SEC, a Federal agency, and the SIB, an institution with a much less marked public status. This outcome is not surprising, because the terms of reference of the Group were to advise on reforms which would 'attract sufficient support from potential participants to be capable of early implementation' (Leigh-Pemberton 1984). It has been common ground between all the parties that practical responsibility for regulation must rest with institutions created by the markets.

The different ways in which the crises of corporatist regulation were resolved in the United States and the United Kingdom reflected differences in the strength of economic competition and political competition in the two countries. Nevertheless, the striking feature of the UK experience is precisely the extent to which the disturbing forces of markets and democracy made themselves felt in the 1980s. The decision to design a stronger and more elaborate corporatist structure was the product of a wide-ranging consensus, but of course the initial agreement left unresolved a list of issues concerning institutional arrangements and business rules. The transformation of that original consensus into the detail embodied in the Financial Services Act of 1986 was dominated by two features: by the struggle to achieve some kind of balance between the established interests, and the new interests created out of structural change; and by the growing intrusion of democratic politics into securities regulation.

Perhaps the most important new set of interests created in London in the last three decades is the houses dominant in the Euromarkets. The struggle between these houses and their proposed SRO (the International Securities Regulatory Organisation) on the one side, and the Stock Exchange on the other, was one of the most significant in the passage of the Financial Services Act. The ISRO lobbied intensively over the details of the legislation, challenged the Stock Exchange's role in the regulation of the industry, and finally forced the Exchange into a merger. The activities of the Euromarket houses are only an illustration of a general difficulty experienced in London since 1983: that of devising a settled corporatist order in markets where growth and innovation have created a complex range of fiercely competitive interests.

This is an obvious echo of the American experience, but there exists an even more striking similarity with developments across the Atlantic. In the USA in the 1970s the struggles between new and old interests pushed the politics of the securities industry into democratic arenas such as Congress. A similar process is taking place in Britain. Only legislation could confer the authority necessary to reconstruct the system of corporatist control. Even in the comparatively hierarchical and closed atmosphere of British politics, the process of legislation released some of the forces of democratic politics. The passage of the Bill was accompanied by intense lobbying in Westminster, in Whitehall, and in the press. As a result, the securities industry in Britain is now more 'politicized' than ever. It is the object of parliamentary and press scrutiny; of bargaining in Whitehall; and of 'adversary' politics, its problems being routinely used by politicians to attack each other. The signs of these incursions can be seen partly in the substantive amendments to the legislation conceded during the passage of the Financial Services Act, notably those strengthening the public status of the Securities and Investments Board. The most important effect, however, lies in the more diffuse 'politicization' of issues once treated as the preserve of practitioners.

The campaign against insider trading is a perfect example of this process. Although insider trading was finally made illegal in

1980, enforcement of the law was notoriously ineffective. The reconstruction of the regulatory system after 1983 was accompanied by three developments: the acquisition by the DTI of new powers of investigation when insider trading was suspected; increased readiness to pursue suspects, even when they belonged to the City élite; and a sustained public campaign by ministers against the practice. The reason is directly connected to the industry's exposure to democratic politics. The government and the City élite now feel immensely vulnerable to public criticism of a practice which a generation ago was perfectly common, and a decade ago not much more than ungentlemanly.

At the root of the recent puzzling evolution of securities regulation in Britain lie tensions between corporatism, capitalism, and democracy. The closed and hierarchical character of financial politics, and the retarded character of capitalism in Britain, meant that corporatist structures suffered less stress than in the United States. The franchise to regulate the securities industry hardly had to be fought for; the hegemony of the ideology of self-regulation meant that it was won, so to speak, by default. The comparative weakness of capitalism and of democracy in Britain thus delayed the crisis which (after the late 1960s) affected the United States. But in the end it proved impossible to protect even the British securities industry from the great changes wrought by the extraordinary dynamism of the markets of advanced capitalism. The very strength of corporatist institutions in the City then proved almost fatal, for the independence of the City's system of regulation meant that adaptation to the new markets could be blocked by those whose interests were served by traditional arrangements. With the Stock Exchange almost frozen into immobility, the pace of structural change by the late 1970s created a crisis whose resolution required an alliance between state institutions and the efficient, progressive sections of the industry. The old corporatism was swept away, and a new, more formally organized and hierarchical order, modelled in some degree on American arrangements, put in its place.

This new order was created for two reasons. First, some central authority was needed to ensure that the system responded to change generated by markets—in other words, that it did not lapse into the sclerotic state of the old corporatism. That is the significance of the new SIB, especially its role as the promoter of competition. Second, growth and innovation had created a set of markets too diverse and complex for the old, informal, and amateurish regulatory system. These two requirements explain the apparently puzzling construction of a complex and hierarchical system of corporatist regulation in an era dominated by ideologies of deregulation. The power and authority necessary to operate the new system had to be appropriated from the state. The price of appropriation was legislation, and the price of legislation was the 'politicization' of the industry. Its practices became the subject of parliamentary abuse, newspaper headlines, and competitive lobbying.

CORPORATISM, REGULATION, AND DEMOCRACY

Corporatist regulation—the exercise of regulatory functions by private institutions endowed with public authority—developed in the securities industries of Britain and the United States out of particular historical experiences. Stock exchanges grew up as significant centres of private regulation before the age of state intervention in economic life. The exchanges acquired a tradition of regulation and—more important—a virtual monopoly of regulatory expertise. Historical crises like the Wall Street crash propelled the state forward as a rival to this system, but the state's capacity to build an independent structure of regulation was obstructed by a number of features: by a hegemonic ideology of self-regulation, which elevated 'flexible' practitioner-based control over 'rigid' bureaucratic control; by the simple fact that most people with expert knowledge were in the securities industry, and were sympathetic to its desire to control its own affairs; and by the sheer administrative and fiscal burden of building a new system of control. These considerations explain why the American reconstruction of the 1930s and the English reforms of the 1980s both took a corporatist form.

The endurance of corporatist creations is determined by how well they cope with the consequences of capitalism and with the challenges of democracy. After 1945 the most distinctive feature of the economies of advanced capitalist nations was their extraordinary dynamism; the financial markets proved the most dynamic of all. Even Britain, a comparatively stunted capitalist economy, was not insulated from innovation and structural change. The interests entrenched by corporatist regulation proved incapable of absorbing the new forces thus created. Regulation in the industry was entwined with a range of restrictive practices which served the interests of the most traditional, and least innovative, parts of the securities markets. The new interests responded with further innovation, designed to bypass controlled markets and to create unregulated arenas. In Hirschman's terms, they responded with 'exit' (Hirschman 1970). But the fact that the tension between capitalism and corporatism was taking place in democratic societies gave disaffected interests the added option of 'voice'—of taking their case into (democratic) political arenas. 'Deregulation' of the securities industry in recent years is shorthand for state-enforced dismantling of restrictive practices, and the re-construction of corporatist hierarchies so as to ensure that the old sclerotic tendencies will not be reasserted. Both British and American securities regulation has become more statist as a result of the reforms of the 1970s and 1980s; and one of the chief purposes of increased state control is to ensure that the industry's corporatist institutions do not once again use their power to preserve established interests in the face of market change. The considerable power and authority of the democratic state is thus harnessed to the task of ensuring that outmoded élites do not obstruct the process of innovation and growth in market economies.

Corporatism is a device for appropriating public authority without the inconvenience of democratic responsibility. This demands considerable feats of constitutional mystification—feats which assume heroic proportions as the state's role in overseeing and licensing securities regulation increases. The act of mystification has been easier in Britain than in the United States, because here democratic ideologies are weaker, and mechanisms of public scrutiny and accountability less well developed. But the securities industries in the two countries have in recent years shared a common experience of demystifi-cation. It has proved increasingly difficult to carry off the prize of public authority without paying some price in public scrutiny and accountability. The reasons are twofold: the need to provide an increasingly elaborate statutory framework for the regulatory system has made more obvious the 'public' character of authority; and the initial debate in democratic arenas about narrow issues of market organization has broadened into a wider scrutiny of business practices.

Securities regulation is not under democratic control in either Britain or the United States. Corporatist structures still dominate, and are still supported by a vigorous ideology of self-regulation. In the United States 'deregulation' has indeed recently resulted in some transfer of responsibilities from a public agency—the SEC—to the SROs. In Britain the physical location, staffing policies, and Board composition of the SIB are all designed to provide even more effective protection from public control than exists in the United States. Even in the USA, with its system of powerful Congressional Committees, democratic intervention in the industry is spasmodic and haphazard. In Britain the possibilities of effective democratic control are, for cultural and institutional reasons, even slighter.

Yet the combination of competitive economics and competitive politics is imposing change. The autonomy of corporatist institutions from public scrutiny and control has declined, is declining, and will continue to decline. The institutions of regulation are becoming more bureaucratic in their operations and more public in their character. Electoral politics and the competitive pressure group system are becoming more salient. The industry's business practices and ethical standards are being challenged in public arenas. In all these respects, the United States is more advanced than Britain; but even the backward British are having to reconcile corporatism with capitalism and democracy.

REFERENCES

ALLEN, J. (ed.) (1940), *Democracy and Finance: The Addresses and Public Statements of William Douglas* (New Haven: Yale University Press).

Business Law Review (1987), 'Judicial Review of Panel on Takeovers and Mergers', Feb.: 29–57.

CLARKE, M. (1981), *Fallen Idols: Élites and the Search for the Acceptable Face of Capitalism* (London: Junction Books).

GADSBY, E. (1959), 'A Private Practitioner's View of the Development of the Securities and Exchange Commission', *George Washington Law Review*, 28/1: 18–28.

GOWER, L. (1982), *Review of Investor Protection: a Discussion Document* (London: HMSO).

—— (1984), *Review of Investor Protection: Report, Part I* (London: HMSO).

—— (1985), *Review of Investor Protection: Report, Part II* (London: HMSO).

HIRSCHMAN, A. (1970), *Exit, Voice and Loyalty* (Cambridge, Mass.: Harvard University Press).

JENNINGS, R. (1964), 'Self-regulation in the Securities Industry: The Role of the Securities and Exchange Commission', *Law and Contemporary Problems*, 29/3: 63–90.

KELMAN, S. (1981), *Regulating America, Regulating Sweden: A Comparative Study of Occupational Safety* (Cambridge: MIT Press).

LEIGH-PEMBERTON, R. (1984), 'The Future of the Securities Market', *Bank of England Quarterly Bulletin*, 24/2: 189–94.

MANNE, H. (1966), *Insider Trading and the Stock Market* (New York: Free Press).

MORAN, M. (1987), 'An Outpost of Corporatism: The Franchise State on Wall Street', *Government and Opposition*, 22/2: 206–23.

—— (1988), 'Thatcherism and the Constitution: The Case of Financial Regulation in the 1980s', in C. Graham and T. Prosser (eds.), *Waiving the Rules: Thatcherism and the Constitution* (Bletchley: Open University Press), 56–72.

OFFE, C. (1985), 'The Attribution of Public Status to Interest Groups', in his collection *Disorganised Capitalism*, ed. J. Keane (Cambridge: Polity Press), 221–58.

Office of Fair Trading (1980), *Annual Report* (London: HMSO).

PARRISH, M. (1970), *Securities Regulation and the New Deal* (New Haven: Yale University Press).

PLENDER, J., and WALLACE, P. (1985), *The Square Mile: A Guide to the City Revolution* (London: Hutchinson).

SELIGMAN, J. (1982), *The Transformation of Wall Street: A History of the Securities and Exchange Commission and Modern Corporate Finance* (Boston: Houghton Mifflin).

SOBEL, R. (1975), *N.Y.S.E.: A History of the New York Stock Exchange 1935–75* (New York: Weybright and Talbey).

STIGLER, G. (1975), *The Citizen and the State: Essays in Regulation* (Chicago: University of Chicago Press).

US House of Representatives (1963), *Report of the Special Study of Securities Markets of the Securities and Exchange Commission*, House Document No. 95, 88th Congress, 1st Session.

—— (1972), *Securities Industry Study*, House Document 92–1519, 92nd Congress, 1st Session.

US Senate (1934), *Stock Exchange Practices: Report of the Committee on Banking and Currency*, Senate Report No. 1455, 73rd Congress, 2nd Session.

—— (1972), Securities Industry Study, *Report*, Senate Document 85–033, 93rd Congress, 1st Session.

VALENTINE, S. (1985), *International Dictionary of the Securities Industry* (London: Macmillan).

VOGEL, D. (1986), *National Styles of Regulation: Environmental Policy in Great Britain and the United States* (Ithaca: Cornell University Press).

WILSON, SIR H. (1980), *Committee to Review the Functioning of Financial Institutions: Report*, Cmnd. 7937 (London: HMSO).

WOLFE, A. (1977), *The Limits of Legitimacy: Political Contradictions of Contemporary Capitalism* (New York: Free Press).

5. The Engineering Profession: From Self-Regulation to State-Sponsored Collaboration

Martin Laffin

IN Britain there is a long history of official and industrial concern over the supply of highly skilled and trained labour. The limited supply and doubtful quality of skilled labour has been seen as a major contributor to the declining international competitiveness of the UK economy (McCormick 1981). This skill gap has been regarded as especially serious in the case of professional engineering skills. This chapter is concerned with how the skills gap in engineering has been defined and acted upon by the various stakeholders—government, the professional bodies, industrialists–employers, and trade unions.

Historically the institutional arrangements relating to the regulation and production of professional engineers took the form of self-regulation, with the professional institutions enjoying considerable formal autonomy. By the late 1970s the system of self-regulation in engineering fell into disrepute and the government intervened to restructure the profession, but this proved to be short-lived. In 1982 the Conservative government reorganized the institutional structure of the profession through the introduction of the new Engineering Council but then resumed a non-interventionist stance. The reorganization took the form of 'state-sponsored collaboration' between the professional institutions and the employers–

This chapter is a revised version of a paper originally presented at an ESRC Workshop on the State and the Professions in British Industry and Commerce at the Policy Studies Institute, Jan. 1988. I would like to thank the Workshop participants for their comments on the paper and especially Kevin McCormick for his detailed comments. I would also like to thank the ESRC 'Corporatism and Accountability' Committee for funding the research on which the paper is based.

industrialists. This chapter will outline the events leading up to the formation of the Engineering Council and then discuss the problems of this form of collaboration between private interests with reference to the work of the Council.

FROM SELF-REGULATION TO SPONSORED COLLABORATION

Phase 1: self-regulation

The professions in Britain developed largely independently of direct state control. Through their associations they acquired rights from the state to bestow a qualification and to manage their own affairs. Engineering was no exception. However, unlike professions such as medicine, professional membership has not become a licence to practise, and the great majority of engineers have been employees rather than independent practitioners. Meanwhile for employers professional self-regulation has meant low employer training cost. Self-regulation has enabled them to externalize a large part of their training and qualification costs on to the professional institutions and the individual aspiring professional as well as on to state-run higher education. In addition professionalism has enabled British employers, traditionally distrustful of the educational system, to combine the advantages of formal educational training with a company-specific 'training' period (Whalley 1986: 60).

Notably engineering did not emerge as a single united profession, comparable to architecture or medicine, but as a loose and fragmented group of specialisms. During the late nineteenth and early twentieth centuries technological change created new engineering specialisms and each new specialism acquired its own institution. By the mid-twentieth century there were sixteen chartered professional institutions, all of which had accreditation functions including the right to award the professional chartered engineer (C.Eng.) qualification.

This high degree of professional fragmentation in engineering has come to threaten one basic reason for the existence of any profession—that is to standardize the type of services offered by practitioners. The proliferation of sub-specialisms has meant that the buyers of engineering skills, mainly employers, experience difficulties in distinguishing precisely what sub-branch of engineering they require.[1] Moreover by the 1970s there were growing suspicions of divergent standards, with a professional qualification from some institutions being worth more than that from others; such suspicions were highlighted by the three larger institutions. Rapid technological change was also deepening these problems as new technological developments were beginning to undermine the traditional division of industrial labour.

The formation of the Council of Engineering Institutions (CEI) in 1965 represented an early move towards resolving these problems. The CEI was a step towards the unification of the profession, though it remained little more than a loose, co-ordinating umbrella organization. It did not represent a break with the traditional model of professional self-regulation, being incorporated under a royal charter in a similar way to the institutions themselves. Even so, during its first years of existence the CEI was able to make considerable progress in ironing out the differences among the institutions; in raising the entry standards of the profession to ordinary degree level; establishing a single C.Eng. professional qualification; and defining an auxiliary occupational grouping in the engineering technicians.[2]

By the early 1970s there were new demands for change as the limits of this still self-regulatory body were becoming obvious. The CEI constitution had created serious internal political difficulties. The smaller institutions had achieved a majority representation on the CEI so that they were able to resist changes promoted by the 'Big Three' institutions (the Institutions of Civil, Mechanical, and Electrical Engineers) despite the fact that the latter contained a clear majority of engineers. The smaller institutions had demanded equal representation with the larger institutions as the price of their participation in the CEI, as they had feared that the CEI was the first step towards their absorption by the big institutions.

[1] Increased specialization is a typical defensive strategy adopted by professional bodies when they see their position being eroded. The engineering profession in Britain has sought improvements in its market position through increased specialization.

[2] In large measure the creation of the technician engineer grade represented a safety net for those who could no longer aspire to professional membership after the raising of entry standards.

The small institutions' built-in majority allowed them to frustrate further moves by the big institutions to raise entry standards, which they saw as a direct threat to their existence. Their concern was, and still is, that high entry standards would restrict the numbers in the profession as a whole and that any fall in membership would have a disproportionate effect on them, new entrants preferring to join a major rather than a minor institution if the entry requirements were the same. Thus the big institutions would be recruiting those engineers who would otherwise have joined the smaller institutions. In other words the small institutions as a group had a strong interest in resisting any standardization that involved a levelling up of entry requirements.

This resistance to raised entry standards and other changes created internal pressures for change within the profession. In particular the Big Three were increasingly concerned by what they saw as the devaluation of the professional qualification by the smaller institutions and a widening divergence in entry standards between the small and the large institutions.

Phase 2: interventionist–transitional

By the mid-1970s there was increased trade union interest in the profession as technical and scientific staff, including engineers, were proving a major growth area for the unions. However, they met some resistance from both the institutions and the CEI. In the union view the latter tacitly discouraged unionization through codes of conduct that rejected the use of industrial action. In addition the unions, anxious to represent professional and technician engineers, had a strong interest in seeing strengthened qualifications which could be used as a basis for 'bargaining units' in collective bargaining with the employer.[3] Consequently there were considerable union pressures against professional self-regulation. These pressures culminated in a TUC conference resolution calling for the formation of an inquiry into the profession.

The internal institutional obstacles to change within the profession had also led some within the major institutions to conclude that the existing system of self-regulation had failed.

[3] For a useful discussion of the relationship between unionism and professionalism in engineering see McLoughlin (1985).

The Institution of Electrical Engineers, in particular, favoured the idea of an inquiry. However the consensus within the world of the institutions was against an outside inquiry, and the CEI and the majority of institutions continued to argue the merits of self-regulation with the government.

There was little support for an inquiry within government circles. Department of Industry (D.o.I.) officials took the view that it would be superfluous and that the profession could and should sort out its own problems. It took considerable union pressure and the involvement of one of the Prime Minister's top advisers before an inquiry was appointed.

The Finniston Inquiry into the engineering profession was announced by the Labour government in 1977. However, the Inquiry reported in 1980 to the new Conservative government. The central Finniston recommendation was the establishment of a new statutory Engineering Authority, reflecting the Committee's view that the traditional model of professional self-regulation had failed (Committee of Inquiry 1980). They preferred the model of a statutory body with control over the registration of engineers and entry standards, bringing British engineering training and qualification closer to the Continental model. The Committee argued that such a body was essential if standards were to be unified across the profession, given the institutional fragmentation of the latter. But such a change would have meant the relegation of the institutions to their original functions as learned societies. Even so the proposed Authority would not necessarily have meant direct state control over the profession as the Authority, although appointed by the government, would have comprised members of the professional institutions, employers, and trade unionists. Essentially the Engineering Authority would have meant weakening the hold of the professional institutions and giving industry–employer and trade union interests representation.

Initially the new Conservative Secretary of State for Industry, Sir Keith Joseph, appears to have been sympathetic to the idea of an Engineering Authority. The early reactions of the industrialist–employer lobbies in the form of the Confederation of British Industry (CBI) and the Engineering Employers' Federation (EEF) were also sympathetic. In addition the trade unions involved responded favourably though by this time the government had effectively marginalized them in relation to industrial policy (for a detailed account of the reception of the Finniston proposals see Jordan and Richardson 1984).

However, the professional institutions strongly opposed the proposed Authority (except the Institution of Electrical Engineers, which later fell into line).[4] The institutions' loss of their accreditation and registration functions to the Authority would have threatened their membership base: much of the incentive for engineers to join an institution would be lost as registration with the EA would have been sufficient to retain use of the professional title. Publicly the institutions claimed that their demise or shrinkage would be a serious blow to the advancement of engineering as a discipline, but they stressed that removing self-regulation opened up the possibility of direct government intervention.

Leading members of the institutions and the Fellowship of Engineering were active in lobbying industry. They targeted some key industrialists and under pressure from certain of these the initially favourable, if weak, reaction of the industry–employer lobbies evaporated. These industrialists were concerned about the statutory nature of the proposed Authority and the spectre of the 'Benn factor'. The 'Benn factor' was shorthand for fears that a statutory authority would provide too easy an opportunity for future ministers to interfere in its running, and that a left-wing minister (such as Tony Benn) would have made full use of such opportunities. In this vein one industrialist, interviewed in this study, stressed that he opposed a statutory body because it represented a move towards a 'corporatist state'.

Meanwhile there was little enthusiasm within government circles for Finniston's Authority. Other departments were at best indifferent and within the Department of Industry only those civil servants most closely involved with the Finniston Committee supported the Authority. At ministerial level, too, there was little inclination to be seen imposing a solution on the profession and creating a 'quango'.

Would Finniston's proposals have been implemented if Labour had still been in power? The answer is in the affirmative. The critical factor was the lack of ministerial commitment rather than the veto power of the profession or of business or the

[4] The IEE would have been the least affected of the institutions by a loss of membership as it had developed a major business as an electronics information agency and as a major international publisher in the electronics area.

supposedly incremental style of British government (Richardson and Jordan's (1984) view). Certainly Sir Monty Finniston himself believed that, if he had reported to a Labour government, his Engineering Authority would have been realized.[5] Industry opposition was not widespread but limited to several influential industrialists with close contacts with the Conservative government. Moreover, a minister less inclined to prevarication than Joseph would probably have acted before opposition had coalesced (McCormick 1985). A Labour minister, too, would have faced considerable union pressure to set up the Engineering Authority and been less ideologically inhibited.

Phase 3: state-promoted collaboration—the Engineering Council

The government rejected Finniston's statutory Engineering Authority in favour of the Engineering Council, which was appointed in early 1982 (under the Industry Act 1981). The new Council represents a government-promoted attempt to institutionalize a collaborative relationship between the professional institutions and industrialists–employers. It emerged as a compromise between the institutions' concern with preserving self-regulation and the D.o.I.'s concern with strengthening the employer interest. Thus the EC combines elements of both the old CEI and Finniston's Engineering Authority. Instead of being a statutory body, like the EA would have been, it is a body established under royal charter like the CEI. The professional interest remains well represented on the Council of the EC as at least two-thirds of the EC membership have to be chartered engineers (that is, members of an institution). In addition the EC has taken over the registration functions of the CEI but, as institutional membership remains a requirement for registration, the institutions were not faced with a loss of membership. Although the Engineering Council has the authority to accredit courses, its limited resources mean that it is dependent on the institutions to act as its agents. Thus much of the substance of professional self-regulation has been retained as the institutions themselves effectively control accreditation.

[5] View expressed in interview with the author.

In line with the D.o.I.'s concerns industrialist–employer interests are heavily represented on the EC, its constitution specifying that at least half of all EC members have to be employers. The initial appointments to the Council were made by the government and an impressive array of industrial members was gathered. Great care was taken to ensure that 'heavyweight' industrialists were included on the Council and that very few of those appointed had a background of activism in the institutions. Over half (fourteen out of twenty-five) of the first appointments to the Council were industrialists, for the rest there were five academic engineers, two trade unionists,[6] one technician engineer, one local authority chief education officer, an assistant director of the Bank of England, and Baroness Platt.

Despite his initial reluctance Sir Frederick Corfield, the then Chairman of Standard Telephones and Cables (STC), was persuaded by Sir Keith Joseph to become the first EC Chairman. Subsequently, another top industrialist, Francis Tombs, Chairman of Rolls-Royce, has succeeded Corfield. Similarly great care was taken to find a Director-General from industry rather than appoint from within the Civil Service or the staff of the institutions.

THE WORK OF THE ENGINEERING COUNCIL AS STATE-PROMOTED COLLABORATION

The major feature of state-promoted collaboration is the very limited role of government. An institutional arrangement is created by government policy-makers who then withdraw from the arena, leaving the remaining organized interests to work out policy. In the case of the EC those private interests are the producers of engineers (the professional institutions) and employers (the industrialists). There is a minimum of formal contact between it and the government. That contact has been limited to twice-yearly meetings between senior EC staff and civil servants from the Department of Trade and Industry, Manpower Services Commission, and Department of Education and Science. However, contacts at the political level have been

[6] One of whom was John Lyons of the Engineering and Managers' Association, who had proposed the original TUC resolution leading to the Finniston Inquiry.

very important. For example Corfield was able to use his ministerial level contacts to increase the initial funding of the EC from £1m. to £3m. over three years and, later, to extend the period over which the funding ran.

Under state-promoted collaboration the 'public interest' is not defined by government policy-makers; the latter allow the participants themselves to produce proposals that are in the 'public interest'. The implicit assumption is that the problems are those of co-ordination that can be remedied through improved dialogue among the organized interest groupings. In other words the state is entrusting the definition of the public interest to the joint deliberations of the representatives of these private interests.[7]

How has the Engineering Council defined the problems facing it? Its appointed officers and leading members see themselves as primarily involved in overcoming the skills gap in order to improve the international competitiveness of the UK economy. EC reports and press releases continually stress the declining competitiveness of British industry and are laced with statistics such as the UK's failure each year since 1983 to export as many manufactures as have been imported. The EC warns of the dire consequences unless Britain raises its industrial performance; to quote the Director-General in January 1987: '. . . unless we get our industrial wealth-creating act together then we will go the way of Venice and Spain as major trading nations and eventually turn into a commercial backwater relying on a tourist trade to eke out a living' (Miller 1987). He has also attacked the view that the service rather than the manufacturing sector can lead the country to economic recovery.

The EC members and officers see the UK engineering skill problem as fundamentally cultural in nature. The continuing failure of the country to produce the necessary numbers and quality of engineers is seen as arising from the anti-industrial culture of Britain. Inevitably the educational system has been a major focus of concern for the Council, reflecting the long tradition of employer criticism of the educational system and its supposed failure to produce the type of skilled workers demanded by employers. Thus a major focus of their activity has

---

[7] Importantly the government appointed those who were to 'represent' these interests to the EC; the CBI, the EEF, and the institutions were not formally asked for nominations.

been trying to promote the 'engineering dimension' in schools and other educational institutions. Nevertheless an important theme of their reports, as will be seen later, is the failure of British industry itself to ensure that its work-force receives sufficient training and education. Even so they have continued to stress the need for changes in attitude rather than in the structural arrangements for industrial training.

The Engineering Council and the institutions

In relation to the professional institutions the EC members and officers see themselves as having a pressing and significant role in rationalizing the profession. The limited funding of the EC is a major constraint on its relations with the big institutions, which have up to ten times as many full-time staff. For financial reasons the EC has to run its accreditation functions through the chartered institutions which are represented on its Board for Engineers' Registration. The Board is divided into five 'executive groups', which are intended as a basis for future institutional amalgamations. The groups encourage the institutions to recognize their shared interests and overlapping professional claims, while each executive group is dominated by a major institution, which is increasingly expected to play a lead role in changes to accreditation.

The promotion of institutional amalgamations is seen as a major part of the EC's rationalizing role. The executive groups are expected to encourage amalgamations, but few have taken place. The obstacles to mergers illustrate some of the difficulties in the way of change and the rigidities that have developed in the profession. Institutional mergers at the very least require the active support of the appointed and elected members of the merging institutions, not all of whom may welcome their personal submergence in a larger body. In addition the institutions' charters require the approval of two-thirds of the institution's membership. Thus the honorary and appointed officers have to take very seriously the need to win over the requisite number of members. Amalgamations become long processes lasting about three years, through the initial joint working parties, votes in the two councils, a campaign amongst the membership, a postal poll, and, finally, Privy Council approval. Although many of the issues thrown up during merger debates seem trivial to an outsider, such as the name of the new body, issues of serious concern to the membership do underlie the debates. Typically the members of the larger institution are concerned that their own standards will be diluted by admitting members of a smaller institution—not only that the supply of 'qualified' engineers will increase but that employers will be even less likely to rely on institutional membership as a guarantee of expertise.

Despite these problems significant mergers of chartered institutions have taken place since the advent of the Engineering Council. Most of these have resulted from the need to adjust to changes affecting the employment of the membership. The Municipals have merged with the Civils as the shrinkage in the public sector has meant that the Municipals have lost members, younger local and central government engineers having opted for a more marketable qualification than a purely public sector one; in any case the two institutions had maintained similar entry standards for some years. The Metals Society and the Institute of Metallurgy have merged as the British Steel Corporation had come to fulfil many of the functions of the Metals Society, formerly dominated by the ironmasters. Finally the Institution of Electrical Engineers has absorbed the Institution of Electrical and Radio Engineers. The latter was a small specialist institution which was experiencing financial difficulties and which already had a considerable overlapping membership with the former.

There has been a significant failed merger between the Institutions of Mechanical Engineering and of Production Engineering. The impact of technological change on the division of labour in manufacturing industry forms the background to this abortive merger. Change at the workplace has flattened what was previously a hierarchy of skills—the work of design engineers (predominantly mechanicals) and process engineers (predominantly production engineers) becoming increasingly blurred. Merger proposals were negotiated between the appointed and the elected officers of the two institutions with the assistance of Engineering Council staff. However the proposals failed to win the necessary two-thirds support of the membership of the Mechanicals. The members of the larger institution were apparently not convinced that the amalgamation was in their interest.

The Engineering Council and industry

The EC has developed close relationships with industry, not only through industrial Council members but also through an Industrial Affiliates Scheme. The government, quite deliberately, gave the Engineering Council a grant which ran for just three years, after which the Council was expected to make up the shortfall itself. One way of doing so has been to increase the other main source of income, engineers' subscriptions, and the Council doubled these in 1985. However, the staff and members of the EC have been very aware of the limits on the extent to which the Council can raise subscriptions without provoking a membership revolt or resistance from the institutions who collect the subscriptions for the Council. Consequently they have looked to industry to make up their revenue shortfall.

Under the Industrial Affiliates Scheme companies can affiliate to the Council for an annual subscription and by 1986 almost 130 companies had joined the scheme. The attraction of this to companies lies in the chance they are offered to express their views on engineering issues and so contribute towards the formation of EC policy. For the EC the industrial affiliates have been important not just as a source of revenue but also as a means of support in backing up its own arguments particularly with government. The EC has also been trying to co-opt the affiliates on to its campaign to overcome industry's tendency to ignore the Chartered Engineering qualification—the great weakness of engineering compared with other professions being the absence of a licence to practise. In a 1987 circular to affiliates the Council suggested that companies should specify the qualification in their job advertising. The circular argued that there were potential advantages to companies in demonstrating a concern to employ well-qualified staff, for example they could attract able staff by showing that the company took training and qualifications seriously and also draw potential customers' attention to a company's stress on employing only highly qualified staff.

The Engineering Council and engineers

So far little has been said about the views or the involvement of rank-and-file engineers. The professional institutions are representative in the sense that their governing councils are elected by member engineers, though in practice only a small minority of members participate in elections. However, member participation does become crucial when major changes in the profession are at stake, as instanced by member votes against mergers. Member attitudes were important, too, early in the life of the EC when, as part of the process of the EC acquiring the registration functions from CEI, two-thirds of voting chartered engineers had to vote for the abolition of CEI. Members and staff of the EC had to tour the country campaigning for support for the EC take-over. Notably this meant that rank-and-file engineers themselves had a veto over change. However, they voted overwhelmingly in favour of the EC, indicating considerable rank-and-file support for change.

During the campaign to take over from the CEI, Corfield was sensitive to the criticism that the EC constitution, unlike that of the CEI or the institutions, meant that it was a 'self-perpetuating oligarchy'. To counter this Corfield committed the EC to the creation of an Engineering Assembly. The Assembly is directly elected by all chartered engineers and has met anually since 1985. The Council members and staff view the Assembly more as a means of communicating with engineers than as involving them in self-government, and they have the resources and organization to enforce this view. As yet there is little indication that it is going to become a significant power centre in its own right.

MAJOR ENGINEERING COUNCIL INITIATIVES

The last part of this chapter will examine in more detail the Engineering Council's role as a collaborative channel between private interests. The discussion will focus on three major initiatives in the areas of professional entry, technician education, and continuing education and training.[8] In addition the reasons why the EC was largely excluded from another major initiative, the Butcher Information Technology (IT) Initiative, will be considered.

[8] There are other important initiatives that have been undertaken by the EC such as Women in Engineering, the Young Engineer for Britain competition, and an Engineering in Schools Initiative.

Professional entry requirements

The first major task undertaken by the EC was the definition of entry standards in its report on Standards and Routes to Registration (SARTR) (Engineering Council 1984). The Report set the EC seal on the lead of the major institutions in raising professional entry requirements to honours degree level across the profession and revising the professional syllabus to include a small quota of management and business studies within engineering degrees. In the Report the EC also indicated its intention to raise entry standards for technician engineers to pass degree level. These proposals were not new and reflected what had become the established view of the larger institutions. Indeed there was some criticism, from these institutions, over whether the Council really needed to engage on a long consultation process before the publication of the final report.

The employers' response to the Report was mixed. Many were disappointed at what was simply a restatement of the professional institutions' approach to entry and training. They were not convinced that they required the type of academically trained specialist engineers that the institutions were intent on producing. Many employers took the view that they required engineers who were not highly specialist but had a wide range of practical skills. Thus the EEF dismissed the Report as:

. . . an accurate and off-putting description of the present, over-complicated qualifying system, with the present inappropriate concentration on education and the neglect of training and experience qualifications. If registration is no more relevant to employers than the consultative document implies, they will not encourage their employees to seek or promote it through their recruitment practices. The EC would then prove no more effective than the CEI.

Officers and members of the EC saw this type of criticism as premature. They believed that they could not risk breaking with the major institutions' approach, as to antagonize them so early on would have threatened the survival of the EC itself. The EC is dependent on the institutions to accredit courses and well aware of the political pressures that the latter can bring to bear. None the less several members and officers have indicated their concern to establish broadly based and less specialized engineering degrees in higher education.[9] However, by 1987 (as far as I am

[9] In interviews with the author.

aware) no such broadly based degree had been accredited by the EC, as the institutions continued to disagree over accreditation procedures and course requirements.

Technician qualifications and training

The skill problem in engineering is not restricted just to professional engineers but is also widely seen as extending to technician engineers. In fact many industrialists argue that the 'shortage' of skills at technician level is a more severe problem than at professional engineer level. Nevertheless the technician-level qualifications have received very little recognition in industry, very few people working in these grades have acquired the qualification, and the technicians' institutions remain small. The EC Report on Standards and Routes to Registration dealt with technician as well as chartered engineers, proposing the raising of entry standards for technician engineers to pass degree level or equivalent.

The EEF and many industrialists interpreted this proposal as the EC and the institutions promoting the grade of technician engineer as a second best for 'failed' chartered engineers (those who failed to gain an honours degree). The EEF has argued, in its response to SARTR, that this level was too high and that to funnel failed professional engineers into that grade was likely to generate discontent; that is make the management of technicians in the workplace more difficult.

At the same time employers were and are unwilling to support effectively the formalization of technician grades, so few technicians actually acquire the T.Eng. qualification. At technician level there is little obvious economic return for employers in providing the more general training and education required by technician qualifications beyond what is required for the specific tasks required for technicians in their immediate work situation. Employers see the provision of too much training as enabling employees either to bid up their remuneration or to increase their mobility, moving on to other jobs and taking with them the company's investment in their training. To prevent such a loss of investment employers try to optimize by providing just enough training for the employee to do his or her job but not enough to encourage regrading claims or mobility. Thus a major reason why the T.Eng. qualification has not caught on is that employers are willing to pay only for company-specific and not occupation-specific training. In addition many employers believe that recognizing technician grades is likely to introduce yet another barrier to the flexibility of their work-forces. Such considerations underlie the problems that the Engineering Industry Training Board has faced over recent years in reorganizing its training programme.

The engineering trade unions are very aware of this employer unwillingness to invest in technician training. Some unions have pressed for improved training provision for their members as a means of improving their marketability and remuneration. The Electrical, Electronic, Telecommunications and Plumbing Trades Union, for example, in its evidence to a House of Lords Select Committee criticized industry for training only in specific skills and not 'providing training in principles'.[10]

Continuing education and training

While the initial training of engineers is vital, rapid technological change also means that engineers have to keep up to date with new developments to be professionally effective. The Finniston Report stressed the need for training to be a life-long process for engineers and the Engineering Council has followed this lead. In its report on Continuing Education and Training (CET) the EC stressed that Britain was falling behind its competitors in providing continuing education and training for its engineers (Engineering Council 1986*a*; see also Coopers and Lybrand 1985, which reached similar conclusions for British industry as a whole). British employers needed engineers who were up to date and able to improve their organization's 'cutting-edge'. The Report urged companies to give greater attention to the continuing training of their engineers and individual engineers themselves to keep up to date.

The evidence gathered by the Council confirmed suspicions that British employers give a low priority to CET for their engineers and technicians. Most companies surveyed were described as having a 'haphazard approach' to CET and giving insufficient attention to the importance of such training in improving their competitiveness. Nevertheless the EC survey

[10] EETPU oral evidence to the House of Lords Select Committee on Science and Technology (1984).

strongly suggested that those companies which were committed to continuing training were commercially more successful than those which were uncommitted. In the survey report the reasons for lack of employer investment in employee training were given as the high cost, expressed mainly as the cost of covering for employees absent on training schemes, and the widespread fears about other companies 'poaching' trained staff. Indeed most companies provided such training solely in response to current problems rather than in the long term and almost half the companies surveyed saw it as more economic to recruit experienced people than to train up raw graduates (Engineering Council 1986*b*).

The recommendations in the Report were mainly exhortatory. Companies were told that their future success depends on improvements in their training provision, while professional and academic institutions were told to improve their course offerings for industry. However, there was a recognition that employers may require a cost incentive to provide enhanced training and the Report suggested that the government consider the possibility of providing tax incentives for companies to provide in-service training. Finally the Report stressed that continuing education is a responsibility of the individual engineer and floated the idea that such updating should become a requirement for continued professional registration.

The Butcher Information Technology Initiative

In April 1984 Kenneth Baker, then Minister for Information Technology, convened a meeting of industry, education, and government representatives to discuss the skills problem in the area of information technology (IT). The meeting arose in response to pressures from the directors of several major high-tech. companies, particularly Plessey and GEC, which enjoy close contact with ministers. There was concern also from other sources, in particular the Alvey Directorate, which estimated that about 5,000 further graduates with IT skills would be required by 1987/8 (IT Skills Shortages Committee 1984: para. 23). At the meeting Baker and the industrialists present agreed to form an IT Skills Shortages Committee which was to be chaired by John Butcher, the then Parliamentary Under-Secretary of State in the Department of Trade and Industry.

The Committee was comprised primarily of senior industrialists, including a director of Plessey, the Director of the Alvey Programme, the Chairman of the University Grants Committee, and a member of the Engineering Council. Notably the Engineering Council was not consulted before the formation of the Committee. Its remit defined the IT skills problem in terms of a simple shortage of IT staff and accordingly its function was to establish more precisely the size of the shortfall and the necessary response to meet it. This shortfall was seen as placing a major limitation on the growth of the IT sector in Britain, which was becoming increasingly urgent in the light of an IT balance of payments deficit of £2bn. (IT Skills Shortages Committee 1984: para. 24).

The main formal recommendation of the Report was that a new Information Technology Skills Agency should be formed. The members of the Committee believed that there was a strong case for a continuing organization to monitor the situation and recommend remedial action to the government. The two ministers involved were concerned that such a body, if connected to government, would look too much like a quango and instead suggested that the private sector should establish and fund the body. The Engineering Council made a strong pitch for the body to be attached to the Council but several industrialists on the IT Skills Committee argued that the EC was too narrow, as IT extended beyond just the engineering sector. Certain key members, too, believed that they would lose influence over the priorities of the new Engineering and Technology Programme were the Agency to be placed with the Engineering Council.

In the event the new Agency was set up under the umbrella of the CBI Educational Foundation and funded by subscribing companies. The Foundation was thought to be more appropriate than the main CBI organization as it would allow non-CBI members, like GEC, to subscribe. The role of the Agency was to monitor developments in the labour market for IT skills and to make recommendations to government, and its first action was to commission a study of future IT manpower requirements (Connor and Pearson 1986). The new Agency consisted of a small staff of two and a Policy Committee, which consisted exclusively of industrialists, though invited 'observers' usually met with the Committee and included the Director-General of the EC and the Chairman of the University Grants Committee. Baker asked that government representatives should not be included to avoid any embarrassment should ITSA decide to question government policy.

The Committee's deliberations also led to a new Engineering and Technology Programme announced in March 1985. The Programme involved an allocation of £45m. to fund an additional 400 higher education places in engineering and technology over three years (IT Skills Shortages Committee 1985: para. 1). University departments wishing to apply for this money had to show that they had a substantial amount of industrial support in forms such as student sponsorship and gifts of equipment. Although the Department of Education and Science actually distributed the extra funding, the ITSA Policy Committee was closely consulted over which courses should be supported. There was considerable debate over the selection of courses. The Engineering Council was largely excluded from the process of selection despite its claims to have persuaded the government to establish the Engineering and Technology Programme. The Chairman and the Director-General of the Council did meet with ministers to argue the case that the EC was the most appropriate body with which to consult over IT courses, but with little success. Moreover many industrialists outside as well as inside the EC were concerned that too small a proportion of the new funds was being spent on courses directly related to manufacturing industry.

An important feature of the Programme and the ITSA initiative has been the strengthening of industrial influence in higher education through direct company influence over specific courses. Not all industrialists agreed with this strategy. A number were critical of the Programme and ITSA. One industrialist interviewed argued that it had been a mistake to have an investigation into skills shortages chaired by a politician and driven by 'narrow sectional interests from the IT industry'. In his view the outcome had been a 'parochial skills agency' which was orientated towards the particular manpower shortages of companies like Plessey, GEC, and Lucas, with large research departments.[11] Thus there is a danger, according to him and other industrialists, of creating an educational system driven by

[11] And incidentally major defence industry contractors whose manpower needs reflect defence rather than domestic manufacturing needs.

the short-term needs of specific employers rather than by the longer-term requirements of industry as a whole, and of producing over-specialized people liable to be rendered obsolescent by further technological advances.[12]

The ITSA initiative, in summary, was driven by the concern of certain large high-tech. companies to externalize a higher proportion of their training costs on to state-funded higher education. Moreover they had a strong economic interest in holding down their labour costs as major employers through raising the output of graduate engineers.

CONCLUSION

> I would like to say that politicians and civil servants are not likely to have skills greater than employers for piercing the cloud of unknowing ahead. (Sir Keith Joseph, former Secretary of State for Education and Science (House of Lords Select Committee on Science and Technology 1984: para. 1003).)

This paper has focused on four groups of participants—the professional institutions, the employers–industrialists, the trade unions, and the government. The trade unions played a major part in persuading the then Labour government to appoint the Finniston Committee of Inquiry. However, Finniston reported to a Conservative government which was more responsive to pressures from the profession and from industry and indifferent to the unions. Consequently the professional institutions, especially the major ones, were able to preserve their interests in the face of pressures for change. As the only organized interests that mobilized on the issue, they succeeded in deflecting the Conservative government away from Finniston's Engineering Authority.

The new Engineering Council adopted an agenda for

---

[12] This view is now quite widespread in industry, cf.: 'Increasingly, the traditional boundaries between types of engineering are no longer relevant. There are few jobs these days that involve pure mechanical engineering without the application of some other discipline. That applies across the whole field of engineering and it is breadth that we need rather than increased specialisation.' John Fairclough, then a director of IBM and subsequently Chief Scientific Adviser to the Cabinet, in oral evidence to the House of Lords Select Committee on Science and Technology (1984: vol. ii).

professional change which was predominantly that of the larger institutions. The latter have preserved their interests despite the apparently widespread reservations within industry and government about the type of professional engineer which they, in conjunction with the universities, are producing.[13] In part this must reflect the 'stiletto' principle—the better organized interests tend to achieve their aims even when the opposing interests are *potentially* the more powerful.

Would Finniston's Engineering Authority have produced more effective change than the Engineering Council? An EA with direct control over registration and accreditation could have moved faster in rationalizing the profession and in accrediting new innovative engineering courses. Indeed some industrialist members of the EC were impatient with the slow rate of change, yet they indicated their dislike of a statutory or 'corporatist' solution. An EA might well have faced considerable resistance in imposing change on the institutions and would have had limited if any support from the Conservative government or industry.

In any case the central problems of employer uncertainty and conservatism over future skill needs would have remained. There was (and is)—in the words of a former President of the CBI, Sir Austin Bide—a 'lack of comprehensive awareness' across British industry of its own needs and future requirements in terms of trained labour (House of Lords Select Committee on Science and Technology 1984). Moreover the Chairman of the House of Lords Committee, in response to Sir Austin's observations, noted that many witnesses before the Committee had indicated their disappointment with the absence of a lead from industry on its skilled labour requirements. Several industrialists interviewed claimed that the majority of British industrialists could not assess even their own skill requirements. There were also wide variations among employers over the type of engineer they required—the traditional employers wanted a strengthened practical component and less academic training, high-tech. employers wanted 'off the peg' specialized engineers, and yet other employers wanted broadly trained engineers able to cross the traditional specialist boundaries.

---

[13] For reasons of time this study has not looked at the responsiveness of the higher education system to changing skill needs. Clearly there is considerable need for research on this area.

The failure of employer–industrial interests to mobilize effectively and push for sustained change in engineering training raises important questions about their pressure group role. One explanation for their limited effectiveness may be British business reluctance to become involved in the political arena and ideological resistance to state intervention. The lack of business support for the Finniston Engineering Authority lends some support to this explanation. Moreover almost all the industrialists interviewed (admittedly most of them were EC members) expressed their strong support for the non-statutory and collaborative approach of the EC over the statutory and 'compulsory' Engineering Authority. Indeed several industrialists elaborated at some length on their objections to state intervention.

Despite these ideological inhibitions industrial interests have shown themselves willing and able successfully to use political channels. Notably these channels have increased in importance under the Conservative government, which enjoys more informal contacts with business than the previous Labour government. In some ways these informal channels can be seen to be substitutes for the more formal ones that formerly existed between the D.o.I. and industry under Labour. The Engineering and Technology Programme is a prime example. Significantly the Programme arose directly out of the immediate skill problems faced by one section of industry. This suggests that industrialists are quite prepared to act when they see their immediate interests at stake, yet there must be doubts about the appropriateness of government policy being formed in response to the skill requirements of just one sector of the IT industry. Those doubts were expressed both by the Engineering Council informally and by other industrialists, who saw the Programme as insufficiently directed towards the interests of manufacturing industry.

The case of engineering labour suggests that employer–industrialist interests tend only to mobilize themselves effectively in respect of their immediate skill requirements. Indeed a few industrialists interviewed criticized British employers' continued tendency to expect the educational system to provide them with, in the words of one, 'off the peg employees'. In addition there is the now widely accepted and documented failure of British industry to train its staff adequately, a failure stressed by Engineering Council and National Economic Development

Office reports (Engineering Council 1986*a*, 1986*b*; Coopers and Lybrand 1985). Thus collectively British industrialists have signally failed to formulate a long-term view of and approach to the skill gap.

The failure of industry interests to mobilize on a collective rather than company-specific view of their future engineering skills should not be surprising. The interests of many companies lie in obtaining highly skilled employees matched to their needs at minimum cost to themselves. Consequently they press for training and education arrangements that externalize training costs on to the state (as was seen earlier this was why historically they assented to training by the academic and professional institutions). Moreover employers' concern not to over-invest in training also means that they are unwilling to prepare very far ahead for new technological change; a picture further complicated by significant differences in skill requirements across industry.

Despite these serious problems the Thatcher government has largely abdicated responsibility for labour-market planning in favour of industrial and professional interests. The government view, summed up in the above quotation from Sir Keith Joseph, has been that industrialists are the right people to take the lead and will come up with the 'right' policies. In other words, the definition of the 'public interest' in industrial training has been entrusted to industry. In so far as ministers have a role it is simply that of non-directive facilitators who bring together 'private' interests, such as the institutions and industry, or who bring government policy in line with the expressed wishes of industrial interests, as in the case of the Engineering and Technology Programme and higher education.

What the government has in effect done is to allow the sectional interests of certain groups of industrialists to make piecemeal 'industrial training policy'. In particular this approach has created the potential of 'trained-in obsolesence', in the view even of many industrialists, and would seem to conflict with the government's stress on labour-market flexibility. In the absence of an 'industry policy' or industrial training policy (or a sector-specific definition of the 'public interest'), the government's approach to labour-market policy in engineering has been fragmented and reactive.[14]

[14] Though the new National Council for Vocational Qualifications represents a move towards a national training policy (Working Group on Vocational Qualifications (1986)).

REFERENCES

Committee of Inquiry into the Engineering Profession (1980), *Engineering Our Future*, Cmnd. 7794 (London: HMSO).

CONNOR, HELEN, and PEARSON, RICHARD (1986), *Information Technology Manpower into the 1990s* (Brighton: Institute of Manpower Studies, Apr.).

COOPERS and LYBRAND (1985), *A Challenge to Complacency* (London: NEDO/MSC).

Engineering Council (1984), *Standards and Routes to Registration* (London: EC).

—— (1986*a*), *A Call to Action: Continuing Education and Training for Engineers and Technicians* (London: EC).

—— (1986*b*) *Annex to A Call to Action*, Industrial Consultants' Survey (London: EC, June).

House of Lords Select Committee on Science and Technology (1984), *Education and Training for New Technologies*, Session 1984–5, 2nd Report (London: HMSO).

HUTTON, STANLEY, and LAWRENCE, PETER (1981), *German Engineers: The Anatomy of a Profession* (Oxford: Clarendon Press).

IT Skills Shortages Committee (1984), *First Report: The Human Factor—The Supply Side Problem* (London: DTI).

—— (1985), *Final Report—Signposts for the Future* (London: DTI).

JORDAN, A. G., and RICHARDSON, J. J. (1984), 'Engineering a Consensus: From the Finniston Report to the Engineering Council', *Public Administration*, 62/4 (Winter): 383–400.

McCORMICK, KEVIN (1981), 'Engineers, British Culture and Engineering Manpower Reports: The Historical Legacy Revisited', *Manpower Studies*, 2 (Spring): 27–31.

—— (1985), 'Engineering a Consensus: Unanswered Questions and Questionable Answers after the Finniston Report', *Public Administration*, 63/3 (Autumn): 360–3.

McLOUGHLIN, IAN (1985), 'Engineering their Future: Developments in the Organisation of British Professional Engineers', *Industrial Relations Journal*, 15/4: 64–73.

MILLER, KENNETH (1987), speech to the Parliamentary and Scientific Committee at the House of Commons, quoted in EC Press Release, 20 Jan.

WHALLEY, PETER (1986), *The Social Production of Technical Work: The Case of British Engineers* (London: Macmillan).

Working Group on Vocational Qualifications (1986), *Review of Vocational Qualifications in England and Wales* (London: MSC/DES, Apr.).

ZUSSMAN, ROBERT (1985), *Mechanics of the Middle Class: Work and Politics among American Engineers* (Berkeley: University of California Press).

6. Corporatist Interest Intermediation: Government–Building Society Relations in the UK

Martin Boddy and Christine Lambert

BUILDING societies are the major source of loans for house purchase in Britain and major financial institutions in their own right.[1] They have accounted for around three-quarters of all lending for house purchase over the last decade, and deposits with the societies represent over half of personal sector liquid assets. Banks and other financial institutions increased lending for house purchase considerably from the mid-1980s, but the building societies still retain the major share of the home loans market.[2] Housing and finance markets have, however, been dramatically transformed over recent years, changes which have had major repercussions for relations between the societies and government. These culminated in the 1986 Building Societies Act, the first comprehensive review of the societies' legislative framework for over a century. In the context of more general financial deregulation and the 'big bang', the Act gave the

This chapter is based on research funded by the Economic and Social Research Council, grant no. EO4250005. We are particularly grateful to those building society personnel and others in the BSA, Treasury, Department of the Environment, and other organizations who very willingly contributed to and commented on the research—we would not, of course, wish to implicate them in the conclusions we have drawn.

[1] On the structure and function of building societies in general in the 1970s and 1980s see Boddy (1979) and Boleat (1986).

[2] Building societies accounted for 76% by value of loans for house purchase in the decade to 1986. This dropped sharply to 50% in 1987, reflecting mainly the upsurge in lending by banks and other financial institutions but also a drop in building society lending for house purchase. Building society lending was however increasing relative to the monetary sector in 1988. Their share of personal sector liquid assets was 53% at the end of 1987—the banks accounted for 33% and national savings 14%.

societies considerable scope to diversify their activities and provided a new regulatory framework.

This chapter looks in detail at government–building society relations over this period, from the perspective of corporatist interest intermediation. Particular attention is paid to the Building Societies Association (BSA), a strong and effective trade association which plays the key role on behalf of around 130 member societies, mediating between them and government. The societies' formal, regulatory framework is largely administered by the Registry of Friendly Societies. The analysis focuses in particular on two case-studies, the one 'historical' and the other more contemporary.[3]

The first case-study looks at the early 1970s, when escalating mortgage rates, runaway house prices, boom and slump in the building industry, and seemingly endemic mortgage famine brought the societies to centre stage politically. Threats of more radical intervention from the then Labour government led to the establishment of more formal relations between the societies and government in the shape of a Joint Advisory Committee. This aimed to regulate the flow of mortgage funds with a view to stabilizing the housing market and controlling house prices.[4] The second case-study looks at the run-up to the new building society legislation in which the societies, through the BSA, developed a close, but in this case essentially informal, working relationship with government. In a context of consensus and correspondence of overall objectives, the societies, through the BSA, were, in corporatist terms, effectively incorporated into the policy-making process. The chapter first sets out the two case-studies. It then presents a more explicit analysis of the extent to which government–building society relations over these two periods can be characterized as forms of corporatist interest intermediation, as distinct from normal processes of consultation and lobbying typical of pressure group activity. Questions therefore revolve around the extent to which the BSA

[3] For a more detailed account of the two case-studies see Boddy and Lambert (1988).

[4] A fuller account of government–building society relations in the 1970s is contained in Boddy (1982). This includes a second case-study focusing on the 'support lending scheme', a scheme under which the societies were intended to compensate for reductions in local authority mortgage lending. This represents an additional example of co-operation in 'voluntary' arrangements in part to head off more direct intervention.

effectively integrated, regulated, and represented the interests of member societies, the degree to which the societies were accorded 'public status' and admitted into the policy process, and the extent of formal institutional relations.[5]

FORMAL CONFLICT: THE JOINT ADVISORY COMMITTEE

The early 1970s saw a rapid 'feast and famine' cycle in the supply of mortgage finance. During 1970 and 1971 in particular, building society investment rates were very competitive and money flooded in. Most of this intake was then lent for house purchase at a time when underlying demand for housing was strong. Building society lending substantially increased effective demand and fuelled house-price inflation. By 1973, however, the general level of interst rates had risen and societies' competitive strength was seriously eroded. As receipts fell, so did mortgage lending—exacerbated by the erosion in the real level of purchasing power due to the recent rise in house prices. Underlying demand for housing had in any case fallen due to the rise in interest rates and house prices. This sequence of events produced a series of problems. Rapid house-price inflation was followed by a sharp increase in interest rates which pushed up housing costs for recent purchasers and, together with higher house prices, priced others out of owner occupation. There followed a severe mortgage famine which, in turn, contributed to a major slump in the housebuilding industry. Government

[5] Methodologically, the research drew on semi-structured interviews and secondary, documentary sources. Interviews were conducted with senior personnel in a range of building societies, the BSA, Department of the Environment, Treasury, Committee of London and Scottish Clearing Banks, and other institutions. Most of those interviewed had been actively involved in the issues under discussion and were thus in a sense 'key actors' as well as sources of factual information. Documentary sources relating to the JAC included published and unpublished reports and reviews of its operations produced by the JAC itself and the BSA. Access to JAC minutes was approved by the BSA on condition of D.o.E. agreement. Access was refused by the D.o.E., which cited the thirty-year rule. Documentary material relating to the new legislation included a succession of BSA papers and commentaries, responses to the Green Paper from a wide range of organizations, and voluminous commentary in the specialist and general press, as well as the Green Paper, Bill, and parliamentary proceedings.

policy to support and extend owner occupation was undermined. More specifically, political sensitivity over mortgage rates, and house prices in particular, demanded some form of government response, and much of the blame was levelled at the building societies.

Government first intervened in April 1973, giving the societies a three-month bridging grant on the basis that they would hold mortgage rates to the prevailing 9.5 per cent. Then in October 1973, following discussions between BSA representatives and government officials, a Memorandum of Agreement between the Department of the Environment and the BSA was signed and the Joint Advisory Committee was established. The agreement committed the BSA to co-operation with government in supporting the growth of owner occupation and stabilizing the housing market and house prices. Government had, in effect, identified the level of building society lending as a potential lever of intervention in the housing market.

In 1974, an election year, the mortgage rate assumed increased political significance. A government loan of £500m. was granted to the societies again in return for holding down mortgage interest rates—the societies subsequently denied that this or the earlier bridging grant had any effect on their behaviour. More significantly, in 1975, following the election of a Labour government, the agreement to stabilize mortgage lending was formalized by the introduction of a lending guideline. This was to be an agreed monthly level of aggregate building society lending based on calculations by the JAC's Technical Sub-committee of the volume of lending deemed appropriate to maintain a healthy housing market and avoid excessive price inflation. In order to implement this, the BSA secured the agreement of the twenty largest societies to adjust their lending in line with the guideline.

It is essential to understand that these events took place at a time when much of the blame for chaos in the housing market was being laid with the societies and that there were very real threats of more direct intervention. The societies disputed their role in fuelling house-price inflation from the outset. They were also sceptical that regulating the level of building society lending could be effective in controlling prices or stabilizing the housing market. Political pressure, however, was intense. As one senior building society representative involved at the time put it:

no building society leader was in any doubt that failure to accept the JAC arrangement would lead to much worse consequences in terms of immediate legislation giving government powers of direction if not outright nationalisation in some form. The Memorandum of Agreement was therefore signed under duress . . . Nevertheless, the reality was that no outright opposition could be voiced in public—the BSA had to be seen to be voluntarily co-operating with the government in the public interest.[6]

The societies were reluctant to accept any form of control or interference but agreed to the arrangements essentially to head off more direct regulation. There was therefore, even at the outset, a measure of success for the societies in the JAC.

The JAC and its Technical Sub-committee met monthly from 1973 to 1979. The BSA was represented at a senior level, indicative of the level of importance attached to this forum. They met with senior civil servants and officials from the Treasury, the Bank of England, and the Registry of Friendly Societies. Although planning for a high and stable level of housebuilding was mentioned in the Memorandum, housebuilding representatives remained concerned that they were not included in the JAC.

Ostensibly a technical process, guideline lending levels were fixed through a process of negotiation and at times reflected straight bargaining between the societies and government. In practice, the guideline arrangements had little real effect on the societies. For much of the 1970s, receipts were such that lending was in fact below the level indicated by the guideline— the latter tended to be seen as a ceiling rather than a target to be attained, since raising investment rates to increase receipts would have conflicted with the desire to hold down mortgage rates. The first time the guideline arrangements really bit was for a short period in 1978 when societies reluctantly agreed to curb lending. This had little apparent effect on house prices, which continued to accelerate into 1979 despite rising interest rates and declining lending by the societies. This strengthened the BSA case against the guideline arrangements at a time of increasing disagreement over appropriate lending levels and more generally over the efficacy of the arrangements as a whole.

The guideline was reviewed by the JAC in 1980 and, with the BSA arguing its case strongly, government representatives were

[6] Private communication in response to a draft research report.

persuaded that regulation of building society lending was inappropriate as a mechanism for intervention in the housing market. Acceptance of this view had been reinforced by the election in 1979 of a Conservative government wedded to a 'hands off' approach to the housing market. Building society representatives at least, however, have argued that convincing D.o.E. civil servants of the technical case was the key factor. The guideline ceased to be relevant after 1978 and was formally abandoned in 1980. JAC meetings became less frequent and ceased altogether in early 1982.

From a government perspective, the formal JAC and guideline arrangements had little real impact on building society operations. Leaving aside the technical merits of the government case, effective control would have required stronger, mandatory arrangements and some form of bureaucratic regulation. Conversely, from a BSA perspective, the arrangements had the immediate benefit of heading off any more interventionist measures. More positively, the JAC also provided a forum through which the societies could, as they saw it, educate the government as to the operation of the mortgage and housing markets and gain experience of much closer working links with government.[7]

INFORMAL INCORPORATION: THE BUILDING SOCIETIES ACT 1986

The 1986 Building Societies Act was the first comprehensive revision of building society powers and their regulatory framework since the 1874 Building Societies Act. The impetus for the new legislation, which came initially via the BSA, was in particular the increased competition faced by societies in both savings and mortgage markets. It reflected a number of factors. There was growing competition from the banks in particular and other financial institutions for savings, but also increasingly for mortgage business, which with higher interest rates and the risks of overseas and corporate lending had become attractive to a wider range of lenders. The squeeze on building society interest rate margins as a result of the more competitive environment

---

[7] See n. 4 above.

made diversification into new activities attractive in order to generate income. Increased competition led to the abandonment of interest rates 'recommended' and subsequently 'advised' by the BSA and to growing competition between the societies themselves. There was some concern that, in the longer term, slower growth in owner occupation might constrain expansion based on traditional home loans, while increased involvement in housing associations and urban renewal was restricted by the existing legislative framework. Finally, there was some political concern over the accountability and control of the societies, resulting in part from the failure of the Grays Building Society in 1978. More generally, deregulation formed part of the government's wider strategy to encourage competition in the financial sector.

Following an internal working party report and considerable debate, the BSA published its proposals in early 1984 in the document *New Legislation for Building Societies* (BSA 1984). This anticipated the fact that new legislation had been promised by the government in the lifetime of the then current Parliament. This was clearly a carefully considered document aimed at selling the proposals both to BSA members and to MPs. It was this document that formed the main basis for discussion with government over changes in the legislative framework.

The effects of the government's monetary and economic policies had already brought increasing contact with the Treasury and the Bank in the early 1980s. With the prospect of new legislation, the Treasury came to be the main point of contact between the societies and government, rather than the Department of the Environment as in the 1970s. Formal arenas for discussion were not set up but there was an increasing level of informal contact with Treasury civil servants to discuss possible directions for change. The Treasury Green Paper (HM Treasury 1984), when published in July 1985, proposed most of the new powers requested in the BSA document. The BSA were informed in general terms about the contents of the Green Paper before publication. They were not closely involved in its detailed preparation. Nevertheless, the BSA document clearly formed an important basis for the government's proposals.

Once the policy objectives had been announced, the BSA was closely involved in the drafting of the Bill. There were frequent meetings with Treasury officers, draft clauses were sent to the BSA for comment, and the BSA provided the Treasury with seventy pages of detailed comment on the draft Bill—the extent of the BSA's prior knowledge of the Bill is indicated by the fact that they produced a detailed, clause-by-clause commentary on it only ten days after its publication. This commentary formed the basis, subsequently, for lobbying by the BSA during the committee stage of the Bill and for related discussion with civil servants. A senior member of the BSA secretariat attended all Committee sessions both to monitor the debate and to offer views on issues as they arose. The BSA provided a detailed explanation and comments on tabled amendments as these arose. It also made representations for its own amendments to be introduced via members on the Committee, who included its own Vice-Presidents.

The BSA was, then, the main channel of communication with government over the new legislation. The BSA's own view was that the legislation did not confer particular advantages on the societies and that it was therefore fit and proper for them to be closely involved in its preparation in an objective, technical sense. Nevertheless, the BSA did clearly use the relationship to push its own views as well as to comment on technical issues. It achieved some changes at the committee stage to procedures for mergers and the limits set on loans other than to owner occupiers. It failed at the time to win less onerous conditions which had to be met in order for a society to convert to company status—these were however subsequently relaxed, and in 1988 the Abbey National was the first society to seek its members' approval for conversion.

From the government's perspective, the societies' aims corresponded closely with its own policies of deregulation and increased competition. Increased involvement in rented housing, urban renewal, and other innovations in housing provision was also in line with housing policy aimed at squeezing the traditional local authority sector. BSA involvement in drafting the legislation was therefore of considerable benefit to the government. It could be confident that its proposals were workable in practice. The BSA also usefully integrated the views of member societies and could speak authoritatively on behalf of its members, facilitating the process of consultation for the government.

CORPORATIST INTEREST INTERMEDIATION

The remainder of the chapter analyses government–building society relations from the perspective of corporatist interest intermediation, focusing on these two contrasting case-studies. It first develops a framework for the analysis of corporatist interest intermediation. It then applies this to the case-study material.

Corporatist intermediation: an ideal type

Previous work offers a number of specific definitions of corporatist interest intermediation including Schmitter's much quoted version:

a system of interest representation in which the constituent units are organised into a limited number of singular, compulsory, non-competitive, hierarchically ordered and functionally differentiated categories, recognised or licensed (if not created) by the state and granted a deliberate representational monopoly within their respective categories in exchange for observing certain controls on their selection of leaders and articulation of demands and supports. (Schmitter 1974: 93)

Much of the corporatist debate has focused specifically on relations between government, organized labour, and the business sector. Panitch (1980: 173) talks of 'producer groups'. Schmitter's own definition, just quoted, refers to a *system* of interest representation. Two points should be noted. First, the building societies, although a major component of the financial system and housing market, are not directly involved in commodity production. They are not, in Panitch's sense, a socio-economic producer group. Nor do they relate, directly at least, to the capital–labour axis, or the tripartism on which much of the literature focuses. Second, the present study focuses on a single group of institutions and does not, in an immediate sense, set out to relate this to any wider 'system'. What is needed therefore is an essentially 'bipartite' definition of interest intermediation, potentially applicable to relations between government and different representative bodies. We are not concerned here with corporatism as a total societal form (mode of production) or a form of the state. More appropriate is something closer to the less ambitious conception of the SSRC Background Paper, which talks of 'corporatist arrangements, whereby organisations intermediate between the individual and the state receive certain benefits such as subsidies, monopoly rights or delegated powers of governance, in return for exercising some measure of disciplinary regulation over those whose interests they represent' (SSRC 1981). The difference here is the focus on individual *organizations*, the building societies, corporate bodies rather than individuals as such.

The diversity and lack of precision of existing definitions of corporatist interest mediation, and indeed of alternatives such as 'pressure group politics', is readily apparent. In part this is symptomatic of social and political theory in general. It also reflects the fact that different contributions to the corporatist literature have looked at different subject-matter, at different scales, from differing perspectives, and for different purposes. It is possible, however, to derive from the literature a number of 'defining characteristics' of corporatist interest mediation. These are drawn from those contributions to the debate which have something to say about interest mediation *per se*, at a general level, rather than focusing on tripartism, economic interests, or producer groups (Crouch 1979; Schmitter 1974; Offe 1981; Harrison 1984; Rhodes 1985). Together these characteristics imply a composite, 'ideal-typical' model of corporatist interest mediation. They represent a set of defining characteristics which could be used more generally to examine relations between government and a wide range of organized interests. To the extent that these various criteria can be identified in practice, the relations being examined can be said to be more or less 'corporatist' in character. This is analogous with the notion of corporatism as an 'axis of development' as used by Offe (1981). Relations between different organized interests and government can, as implied by Offe, be more or less corporatist.

Key defining characteristics of corporatist modes of interest mediation include representation, regulation, intermediation, institutional structure, integration, exclusion, and public status.

Representation refers to members' interests being aggregated into one representative organization which forms the main channel of communication with government, limits competition between members, and plays a prominent role in relation to decisions which affect those members. The representative organization may itself develop interests which are in a sense distinct from those of individual members.

Regulation: as well as representing members' interests the organization also regulates members' demands and has the ability to 'deliver' the membership, ensuring compliance with agreements reached with government. Implicit in this may be the existence of some form of sanction, pressure, or control to ensure compliance.

Intermediation: the representative organization has a monopoly or at least privileged position in negotiation and consultation. This implies that the organization is distinctive and separate both from its membership and from government—with, according to Rhodes (1985), its own appreciative system, perceptions, values, routines, and definitions of problems.

Institutional structure: there is a stable institutional structure, whether formal or informal, for bargaining and for the formulation and implementation of policy.

Integration: the representative organization brings together members' interests and promotes bargained compromise between members' interests and government. It may actively promote shared values, knowledge, and techniques in order to establish and maintain consensus—termed by Dunleavy (1981) 'ideological corporatism'.

Exclusion: the incorporation of selected interests implies the exclusion and marginalization of other interests.

Public status: organized interest groups are recognized by government and accorded 'public status' (Offe 1981: 136–7). Public status can be accorded in terms of (1) resources: the extent to which the resources of the organization are provided by government through e.g. subsidy, tax exemption, enforcement of membership, privileged access to mass communications, etc.; (2) representation: the extent to which the substantive area and/or potential membership is defined by government; (3) organization: the extent to which relations between members and between members and the representative organization are regulated by government; (4) procedure: the extent to which representative organizations assume a role in relation to legislation, the judicial system, policy planning, and implementation, or are granted the right of self-administration—as

Middlemas (1979: 371) puts it, 'admitted to the process of government'.

Some definitions of corporatist relations have stressed the role of formal, legally defined relations between government and organized interests. To quote Offe (1981: 137), on his notion of public status outlined above:

> by status we mean the specifically attributed, formal status of a group (as opposed to relations of informal cooperation between political and other segments of the elite, clientilistic relations, and status resulting from ad hoc tactical considerations of various groups or branches of the state apparatus); formal status based on legal statute and formally adopted procedural rules.

This would appear to be unduly limiting in that definitional characteristics as outlined above, while not embodied in legal statute, may nevertheless be identifiable in practice.

As already suggested, the boundaries between corporatist modes of interest mediation and other models of government–interest group relations are not clear cut. Corporatism, it has been suggested, is an axis of development. It is useful for definitional purposes, however, to distinguish some of the defining characteristics of the pluralist, pressure group model which offers an alternative ideal type. Key characteristics of pressure group politics are that: relations between groups are competitive; the state is seen either as another group or as a political market-place; the relative importance of different groups does not depend on their functional role (the centrality of capital and organized labour) but on resources and membership; groups press demands on government and lobby via Parliament and parties (weak lobbying) or direct to the Civil Service (strong lobbying); groups can exchange political support for gains in a bargaining process, although leaders have only weak organizational control and ability to 'deliver' the membership; this membership is essentially voluntary.

Pressure groups serve essentially to articulate demands and transmit them into the political process. They are not involved in defining interests, organizing consensus, making and implementing policy, or the 'process of government'. Their power is based on their membership and their ability to mobilize resources and publicity, rather than on the strategic importance of the group's resources to government (government does not 'need' pressure groups). And the competitive nature of pressure group politics contrasts with the (ostensibly) depoliticized and relatively invisible, consensual nature of corporatist interest intermediation.

Corporatist interest intermediation and the building societies

To what extent, then, can relations between government and the building societies, as mediated by the BSA, be defined as corporatist? Where on the axis of development of corporatist relations do the societies lie and how has this changed over time? A number of the key definitional characteristics of corporatist intermediation set out earlier are encapsulated in the notion of reciprocity and the relationship between representation and regulation. An *intermediary* body on the one hand *integrates* and *represents* members' interests; on the other, it *regulates* and *delivers* the membership in return for privileges and benefits granted by government—in return for *public status* or admission into the process of government, to the exclusion of others, the whole process operating within a stable *institutional structure*.

We can, therefore, look at relations between the government and building societies in terms of: (1) integration, representation, and intermediation; (2) regulation and delivery; (3) public status and admission to government; (4) institutional structure.

Integration, representation, and intermediation: the BSA is a strong trade association and forms the major channel of communication and negotiation between the societies and government. Membership is effectively complete and, with a number of specific exceptions related primarily to the former interest rate cartel, has been historically stable. Informal consultation between government and individual building society personnel does take place on a recurring though essentially irregular basis. Ministers on occasion will consult chairmen or senior executives of the largest societies. Government also, for example, consulted representatives from the smaller societies over the new legislation. Such contact is generally however supplementary and very much secondary to representation by the BSA.

Representation has been facilitated because the operations of the societies are relatively homogeneous even though they differ markedly in asset size. The interests of the smaller societies and, more significantly, their ability on an individual level to represent those interests, differ from those of the small number of major societies which dominate the assets of the industry as a whole. The BSA tends to represent all societies and certainly strengthens the representation of the smaller societies relative to their asset size, counterbalancing the otherwise overwhelming weight of the largest. This strengthens the effective integration of the industry. Even the largest societies readily acknowledge the effective role played by the BSA, most recently in relation to the new legislation but also for example in the debate over mortgage rationing and the JAC.

The demise of the recommended and subsequently advised interest rate system, the 'cartel', has altered the function and place of the BSA in relation to the membership. It was a key role for the BSA and possibly the major overt issue over which compliance was sought from or expected of the membership. It was the key recurrent item on the agenda of the BSA Council and the focus for political and public concern. Deviation from the advisory rate implied, under certain circumstances, resignation from the BSA. The demise of the cartel may therefore weaken the status of the BSA and the extent to which it integrates and represents members' interests. Increased competition between member societies and, in the wake of the new legislation, increasing divergence in their activities and interests (including for example conversion to company status) may also start to undermine the coherence of the BSA and its ability to integrate member interests. Thus far, however, the BSA remains a strongly representative, single voice with little if any challenge to its authority. This has been reinforced by its major role in relation to the new legislation, in which it is universally seen to have played a central and effective role. In part it seems it was able to perform this role effectively *because* there was little divergence of views or dissent within the industry. Actually *containing* dissent and controlling diverse interests does not appear to have been a major issue.

As an intermediary body, the BSA has attained a degree of separation from the industry as a whole. This is implied in its capacity to integrate the interests of different societies, most importantly perhaps different sizes of society. The BSA has to some extent sought to monopolize channels of communication and negotiation with government. Ostensibly at least it has done so in order most effectively to represent the collective interests and by implication the individual interests of the societies. The BSA remains, however, relatively closely tied to the membership. Financially, it is entirely resourced by member societies, and the Council, committees, and working parties are constituted from active building society personnel. Representatives of the largest societies do however tend to monopolize key positions within the BSA, constituting something of an élite.

Regulation and delivery: there is little evidence in the BSA's role of regulation, the ability to 'deliver' the membership or to ensure compliance with the terms of bargains struck with government. In a sense, this reflects the consensus between societies and government over the societies' functions and role in relation to the aims of government.

In the case of the JAC, the BSA did potentially have a regulatory function—it was to implement the overall guideline on the volume of mortgage lending, ensuring the movement as a whole complied. In practice, this occurred only for a brief period. Although sceptical and resistant, societies complied under the terms of the arrangement negotiated by the BSA. As already noted, the formal arrangements were however short-lived and the ability of the BSA to convince the membership of the benefits of compliance was not subjected to any extended test—this would have been implied had the JAC arrangements continued. And, again as noted earlier, the privilege or benefit obtained by societies from their 'bargain' with government was essentially negative—it diminished the threat, perceived by many in the industry, of more direct government intervention.

More generally, the BSA does not perform any real regulatory functions in relation to its membership, either formally or informally. This partly reflects the fact that the formal regulatory framework and the legal structure within which societies' operations are defined are administered externally by the Registry of Friendly Societies.

Public status and admission to government: the BSA is recognized by government as the representative body of the societies. It is granted semi-official status in this respect, though not in any sense formal, legal recognition. Attribution of public status can be examined in terms of the four dimensions identified earlier:

(*a*) *Resources*: the BSA is not resourced by government in any direct way by, for example, subsidy or tax exemptions (the regulatory functions of the Registry are in fact supported by a levy on the societies themselves). Its resources in terms of membership are not supported by any requirement by government for societies to be members, nor any inducement—it achieves virtually complete membership regardless of this. It has however come to establish good access to ministers and close informal links with government departments. This is illustrated in particular by the example of the new legislation. The JAC arrangements might be a counter-example. It can be argued, however, that these arrangements were made possible by the ability of the BSA to negotiate with government and to establish an alternative to more direct intervention. Moreover, the process and debate around the JAC and other issues at the time did much to forge the closer though less formal relations now observable between societies and government. The Association's resources in terms of knowledge and influence were stronger by the end of the 1970s as a result of the JAC process.

(*b*) *Representation*: the notion of 'representative status' does not appear to be very meaningful or applicable in the present context. The substantive issues on which the BSA represents the interests of its membership are effectively defined as a function of the statutory framework within which the societies operate. Within this context, the BSA represents member interests across the board. Similarly, the legal definition of building societies as corporate bodies defines the potential membership of the BSA. The substantive area of interest representation and the potential membership are in a sense defined by government, but only indirectly, as a by-product of the legal framework. They have not been defined by government as part of any explicit process of organizing or formalizing its relations with a particular interest group.

(*c*) *Organization*: relations between members and the BSA are essentially unaffected and unregulated by government. Relations between members are affected by the legally established rules and procedures affecting, for example, take-over and merger. This is currently very much a live issue in relation to the new legislation. Again, however, such regulation is not directly related to attempts by government to establish a particular form of relationship with the societies as an organized interest group.

(*d*) *Procedure*: in the case of the JAC, the BSA was opposed in principle to the details of the policy and sceptical of its efficacy. It was, nevertheless, closely involved in its planning and implementation. Moreover, its close involvement with government within the framework of the JAC enabled it to develop the arguments against lending guidelines and to win the case— effectively altering the detail of government policy. It was admitted into the policy process, but not in any sense as a reciprocal *quid pro quo*. It reflected the government's desire to control and influence the societies in a situation of conflict.

The BSA played a key role in the overall shape and the detail of the 1986 Act. The Treasury Green Paper reproduced in outline most of what the societies had been seeking. There was close contact and consultation between the Treasury and the BSA in drawing up the Bill and again, close contact through the committee stage. This appears to have represented considerably more than even 'strong lobbying' in the pressure group sense. In return for this privileged access, the government benefited from the expertise offered by the BSA. It could be confident that the legislation was workable in practice. And in terms of consultation, the existence of a single, unified, and expert voice representing and integrating the views and interests of the societies was seen as advantageous. The BSA seemed to be in a sense 'performing a service' for government, acting as expert consultant. This obviously reflects the significant degree of consensus between the BSA and government over the legislation. It also, however, allowed the BSA to make its case strongly and effectively where there were specific points of debate or disagreement.

The BSA was therefore, to some extent, 'admitted to the process of government' in terms of legislation, policy planning, and implementation (Middlemas 1979: 371). It has not, however, assumed any role in relation to the judicial system. Nor has it been granted (or indeed sought) rights in terms of the self-administration of self-regulation of member societies. The BSA certainly advises societies on issues of good practice, legality, and specific issues as they arise. It is very concerned to preserve the status and 'good name' of the societies. It is not clear whether the BSA in any sense 'polices' societies' practices and accounts independently of their own auditors and of the Registrar. In the case of a society in difficulties, the BSA has always in the past acted very rapidly to make arrangements for its take-over and to limit the repercussions on the reputation of the industry as a whole. These various activities of the BSA do not, however, constitute self-regulation in any formal or officially recognized and sanctioned sense. To the extent that they are informally acknowledged by the government and the Registrar, they may serve to keep more formal government regulation at arm's length and discourage imposition of a more overbearing formal, legal, regulatory framework. This would therefore represent an element of informal self-regulation.

In practice, the formal regulatory framework has come under close scrutiny in the process of legislative reform. This relates in part to the view that the Registrar, as things stood, was under-resourced, coupled with concern generated by the shortcomings of the Grays and the Alfreton societies and less dramatic difficulties experienced by some other societies. It also, however, reflects a concern to strengthen the framework to some extent, anticipating diversification in building society activity following the new Act. A Building Societies Commission has been established, headed initially by the existing Chief Registrar, but taking over from the Registrar sole responsibility in a formal sense for supervision of the societies.

Institutional structure: there is now no significant *formal* institutional structure within which the BSA and government relate. The more formal institutional structures of the JAC decayed in 1979. They have not been replaced by any analogous joint forum. The BSA meets with the government at ministerial level twice a year in a Mortgage Finance Committee, which simply maintains a minimal degree of contact. Formal institutional structures are, in some contributions to the academic debate, seen as symptomatic of closer, corporatist relations. In contrast to this the more formal arrangements of the JAC were essentially a product of the more *conflictual* relationship between government and the societies in the mid-1970s. Conflict generated rather than threatened more formal, overtly corporatist modes of interest intermediation. More formal relations were symptomatic of, if anything, the distance between the societies and government. Even then, however, conflicts over the volume of lending were confined within parameters which established a basic unity between government and the societies. This included a shared commitment to the continued expansion of home ownership and maintenance of stability in the housing market.

There was a shift during the 1970s from a degree of conflict and ambiguity in relations between government and the societies towards a relatively high level of consensus based on a coincidence of interests. Relations engendered by the JAC contributed significantly to the development of this consensus. As noted already it generated information and arguments which convinced the government of the case for winding up these more formal institutional structures.

As more formal institutional arrangements decayed, there was a growth of denser informal relations. An atmosphere of consensus has fostered an essentially informal but in many senses closer working relationship. This obviously relates to the distinctive policies and approaches of the post-1979 Conservative government, though reflecting, as already suggested, contact between the societies and the Civil Service through the 1970s. The 'hands off' approach of the government, as extended to the housing market, coincided with societies' own desire for autonomy of operation. And the provision in the new legislation for diversification coincided with societies' objectives of continued expansion and the need to compete effectively with, in particular, the banks, in the context of financial deregulation. The extent to which the societies have entered into government and gained 'procedural status' has evidently increased, then, although not in the sense of formal institutional structures. It is also worth noting that, in the process, links between the BSA and the Department of the Environment, built very much around housing concerns, have weakened considerably, reflecting the government's pulling back from active housing policy. This is less true of some individual societies pursuing specific housing initiatives. Relations with the Treasury, always important, have on the other hand been consolidated and much strengthened, in particular through contact over the new legislation.

REFERENCES

BODDY, M. (1979), *The Building Societies* (London: Macmillan).
—— (1982), 'The Public Implementation of Private Housing Policy: Relations between Government and the Building Societies in the 1970s', in S. Barrett and C. Fudge (eds.), *Policy and Action* (London: Methuen).
—— and LAMBERT, C. (1988), 'The government–building society connection: from mortgage regulation to the Big Bang', *Working Paper* 75, School for Advanced Urban Studies, University of Bristol.
BOLEAT, M. (1986), *The Building Society Industry* (2nd edn., London: Allen & Unwin).

Building Societies Association (1984), *New Legislation for Building Societies* (London: BSA).

CROUCH, C. (1979), *The Politics of Industrial Relations* (London: Fontana).

DUNLEAVY, P. (1981) 'Professions and policy change: notes towards a model of ideological corporatism', *Public Administration Bulletin* 36: 3–16.

HARRISON, M. (1984), 'Corporatism: A Review of some General Issues, with a Comment on Priorities for Theory Development and Research' (mimeo, University of Leeds).

HM Treasury (1984), *Building Societies: A New Framework*, Cmnd. 9316 (London: HMSO).

MIDDLEMAS, K. (1979), *Politics in Industrial Society* (London: Deutsch).

OFFE, C. (1981), 'The Attribution of Public Status to Interest Groups', in S. Berger (ed.), *Organizing Interests in Western Europe* (New York: Cambridge University Press).

PANITCH, L. (1980), 'Recent Theorizations of Corporatism: Reflections on a Growth Industry', *British Journal of Sociology*, 31/2: 159–87.

RHODES, M. (1985), 'Organised Interests and Industrial Crisis Management: Restructuring the Steel Industry in West Germany, Italy and France', in A. Cawson (ed.), *Organised Interests and the State: Studies in Meso-corporatism* (London, Beverly Hills: Sage), 192–220.

SCHMITTER, P. (1974), 'Still the Century of Corporatism?', *Review of Politics*, 36/1: 85–131.

Social Science Research Council (1981), *Final Report of the Corporatism and Accountability Research Panel.*

7. Agricultural Regulation and the Politics of Milk Production

Graham Cox, Philip Lowe, and Michael Winter

THE consideration of corporatism has generated a literature which is formidable in extent but often lacking in conceptual clarity. Considerable theoretic endeavour was devoted, initially, to the specification of the kinds of arrangements which might enable a system appropriately to be characterized as corporatist. Many writers, however, could only conclude their efforts by registering their disappointment with a concept which had seemed to promise so much. But even those sceptical about applying corporatist concepts to the representational structure of British politics were typically careful to make an exception of agriculture (Metcalfe and McQuillan 1979). We are conscious, therefore, that, in studying agriculture and, in particular, the dairy sector, we are examining relationships considered by common consent to be unproblematically corporatist in character.

We take 'corporatism' to refer to a distinctive form of interest intermediation involving interventionist action of an indirect nature whereby the state operates in conjunction with organizations that are based in the division of labour in society. What distinguishes corporatism, in this view, is the salience of producer groups and their capacity to regulate their own constituencies and reach bargained agreements with state agencies. There has, in more recent writing, been a welcome recognition of the proper limits of corporatist theorizing and a consensus has emerged which focuses attention on the significance of sectoral or meso-level arrangements (Grant 1985; Cawson 1985) and points to the importance of contrasts within, as well as between, sectors (Grant 1987). Indeed, in our previous work, we have sought to understand the very different worlds of

The authors would like to acknowledge the support of the ESRC in conducting the research for this chapter.

agricultural and environmental policy-making (Cox, Lowe, and Winter various) in terms of the distinctions between corporate and competitive spheres within late capitalism (Cawson 1982; Goldthorpe 1984). In this paper we concentrate our attention on the conditions relating to the emergence and persistence of strongly corporatist arrangements and, crucially, on the politics of their implementation. Our immediate focus is on the regulations associated with the introduction in April 1984 of milk quotas. Not only did these place a great stress upon the institutions and actors within the dairy sector in the first instance, but their imposition also had profound implications for the integrity of the agricultural policy community in general.

The quotas episode quickly gained a powerfully symbolic status within an increasingly beleaguered agricultural community. Quotas were seen as emblematic of the fundamental changes to which agriculture must necessarily adapt itself. They were, therefore, routinely referred to as constituting a 'watershed'. But while the opposition to them was not so extensive as might have been expected, the 'alternative land uses' debate which they helped to usher in quickly developed its own momentum and significance. The agricultural policy community has very much seized the initiative in the alternative uses debate to refurbish elements of the productionist ideology which has underpinned policy in the post-war period. Consideration of this debate illustrates how corporatist relationships and the private interest government which they entail need to be sustained by the promulgation of an appropriate ideology (Jessop 1982).

These relationships have persisted for some time. Quotas were, after all, necessitated by the extraordinary productionist success of earlier policies stretching over half a century. Fundamental to any understanding of corporatist relations in agriculture, therefore, is an appreciation of the processes which led to the state attributing a particular status to the key organized group within the industry, the National Farmers' Union. We have been concerned in our work to develop an analysis of both the emergence of the NFU and the extent to which it has been able to sustain the social cohesion of the interests which it represented. In terms of both the logic of membership and the logic of influence the NFU presents an extreme case because of its inclusive character and the extent of its policy participation in the post-war period. Challenges to the inclusive nature of the NFU have been few and far between and notably unsuccessful. But in view of the disruption which seemed likely in the wake of the imposition of quotas it was clearly important to understand the necessary and sufficient conditions for an effective challenge to the representational monopoly of the NFU. Accordingly, we present an analysis of the Farmers' Union of Wales; both because of its unique past success in this respect and because of the obvious significance of Wales as a potential site for opposition to quotas.

Our examination of the implications of quotas for agricultural self-regulation has revealed the inadequate knowledge of this aspect of corporatist arrangements in agriculture generally. Whereas the broad parameters of policy-making are relatively well understood, implementation and regulation have been largely ignored, especially at the local level. We have, therefore, also examined the development of a county NFU branch—that of Devon: the largest branch and in a county where dairying looms large in the local farming economy. Devon, moreover, has a history of periodically spirited resistance to central direction from NFU head office. It is, therefore, an appropriate county to select for comparative purposes in relation to our concern with challenges to the representational monopoly of the NFU.

The productionist success of recent agricultural policy has been due in no small part to the effectiveness of the advice which farmers have been able to receive from the Agricultural Development and Advisory Service. The comprehensive yet specific nature of ADAS support has helped nurture a strong relationship of trust with the farming community. Milk quotas, though, entailed a process of significant adjustment within the dairying sector in which ADAS advisers played a pivotal role at a time when the future character of the service was itself the subject of intense critical discussion. Clearly, a set of corporatist relationships as long standing and extensive as those which have characterized the dairy sector in Britain constitutes a significant resource upon which the state can draw in seeking to effect fundamental structural change. But such a resource cannot be drawn upon to an extent which, by generating widespread dissent, seriously compromises the existence of the resource itself, so mechanisms of policy promulgation assume a particular significance in relation to the politics of implementation. We, therefore, examine in some detail the role of ADAS as part of our overall concern with the implementation of milk quotas.

THE EMERGENCE OF AGRICULTURAL CORPORATISM[1]

If meso-corporatism is to flourish a high degree of sectoral unity manifested in a single, dominant representative organization is essential. For agriculture in late nineteenth-century Britain, however, this was far from the case. Not only were there political differences between tenant farmers, farm workers, and landlords, but even within these groupings there was little lasting agreement on the causes of, or solutions to, the problems besetting agriculture. The period was characterized by a number of political initiatives, mostly short-lived, and none capable of providing the basis for developments which might be characterized as corporatist. Indeed, these earlier groups were either too broad and inclusive or too narrowly defined by single issues or specific party-political allegiances.

The NFU has its origins in reactions to the failure of these intiatives and in the conservatism of the only organization which did survive, the Central Chamber of Agriculture. The immediate forerunner to the NFU was the Lincolnshire Farmers' Union founded in 1904. Three other parallel county groups were established in Cornwall, Devon, and Kent. In 1907, meanwhile, in a period of heightened activity in the politics of the land, both the National Union of Agricultural and Allied Workers (in East Anglia) and the Landholders' Central Association (in Lincolnshire) were formed. The spur to the formation of a national group came in August 1908, when a number of farmers in Shropshire opposed a move by the National Federation of Meat Traders' Associations to require a warranty of health with all cattle sold. A vigorous 'no warranty' campaign was set in motion, leading to the formation of a Shropshire union. In December 1908 the formal decision to establish a national union was taken in London. By 1910 the membership of the NFU was 15,000

[1] The material in this section is based on analysis of archival material held at the NFU headquarters library and the NFU Archive at the Institute of Agricultural History, University of Reading. A much longer version of this section with full footnotes to archival sources is available from the authors as an unpublished working paper.

and by 1918, 60,000, nearly one-third of the potential membership. It reached 100,000 in the early 1920s, and rose to its
highest level of 210,000 in 1953. Understanding the reasons for
the emergence of the NFU and its rapid growth is difficult in the
light of the relative paucity of interpretative material in this area.
We have found little evidence that the Union emerged primarily
as a response to farm worker trade unionism in the arable east as
claimed by Howard Newby (1987). Nor was it simply a response
by tenant farmers to the decline of landlordism (cf. Self and
Storing 1962). A more complex combination of factors appears
to have been at work. In particular, the Union has to be seen as a
response to a more interventionist state, including the promotion
of agricultural research and education, the increasing significance of a number of local government responsibilities with a
direct impact on farmers, food hygiene regulations, and
emergent rural development policies. All provided both opportunity and incentive for a representative farmers' organization
to engage with specific policy issues. In these early years,
therefore, the Union was much exercised at county level with
seeking to influence local government policies and spending on
issues such as road maintenance, adulteration of animal feeds,
and so forth. The importance of such local issues must not be
underestimated when accounting for the emergence of agricultural corporatism. The Union had established a relatively
high level of membership participation in local policy-making
and implementation prior to central government either requiring,
or facing demands for, the participation of a representative
organization in policy formulation.

Such developments, moreover, must be seen in the light of
emergent protectionist policies. For while the Union was
prepared to encourage indirect forms of protection, such as the
promotion of hygiene standards on imported food, it was more
ambivalent with regard to direct market intervention. This was
even the case after the First World War, when farming
prosperity had increased under a protectionist and highly
regulated policy framework. The usual reading of events during
the war years and immediately after is that the agricultural
interest was betrayed by government in the retreat from
protectionism in 1922. However, the farming interest was by no
means single-minded in its commitment to protection. There
was, nevertheless, general bitterness at the lack of trust which

government had displayed. Hence a toughness and an adaptability came to characterize the Union: a blend of particular usefulness in later dealings with a government more committed to both protection and initiatives characteristic of meso-corporatism.

For nearly ten years agricultural policy remained non-interventionist. But the Union was not idle. Its local organization improved and, nationally, it developed a central role in the dairy sector; namely its particular role in negotiating milk prices with the increasingly oligopolistic dairy manufacturers. Milk became a highly important agricultural commodity at this time under-pinned in 1933 by the introduction of a statutory marketing scheme. The advent of the Milk Marketing Board not only generated new confidence in production but also established the NFU at the centre of at least one aspect of agricultural policy, thereby forging a relationship which has persisted more effectively than any other such arrangement within British agriculture. Thus the genesis of the MMB provides a key example of the changing context of agricultural politics in the inter-war years and crucial indication of the NFU's corporatist role.

For, unlike the 1947 Agriculture Act, which emerged from the close working relationship between farmers and the state during the Second World War, the regulation of milk marketing came at a time when relations between government and the farmers were still only minimally developed. The initiative came primarily from government and the producers had, initially, to be cajoled into co-operation. The reasons for the 1929 Labour government's commitment to a compulsory milk marketing scheme have never been made entirely clear. One factor was the way in which government had been drawn into a series of inconclusive discussions with the industry, which convinced several leading civil servants of the need for action. Another was the government's involvement with the unsuccessful, voluntary Permanent Joint Milk Committee as a means of agreeing milk prices. These experiences convinced the government of the need to bring order to a market perceived to be of significant national importance in terms of health. As Winston Churchill was to put it in a broadcast some years later, 'There is no finer investment for any community than putting milk into babies.'

In choosing a sector of agriculture with great growth potential the government sought to find a means of supporting and sponsoring agricultural development without making a major long-term financial commitment. In contrast to the preoccupation with wheat for much of the late nineteenth and early twentieth centuries, the milk marketing scheme was a progressive project designed to facilitate further growth rather than promote a rearguard action to save 'traditional' British agriculture. Certainly the sector had very real problems, but for the farmers these were essentially problems of market organization rather than of inherent economic weakness.

The NFU's opposition to the compulsory scheme was transformed within six months of the passing of the 1931 Act to whole-hearted commitment. However, a few farmers remained opposed and a fierce campaign against the Board, assisted by Lord Beaverbrook at the *Daily Express*, led to an unsuccessful attempt to revoke the scheme in 1935, in which an 86.5 per cent vote in favour of the Board was registered. The Board, moreover, retained its key powers in the face of a series of reports on its activities. Most of these reports, for example that of the Cutforth Commission, were not critical of the underlying principle of a regulated market but sought consumer representation in the scheme. A persistent proposal, culminating in an abortive Bill in 1938, was for the formation of a Commission reflecting all interests to oversee the work of the Board. The Board fought a skilful campaign privately and publicly against the Bill and its failure illustrates the speed with which a meso-corporatist arrangement can become so firmly established that attempts to remould it fail.

However, it would be a mistake to exaggerate the strength of the Board in one crucial respect. The government retained control over wider agricultural policy issues, particularly terms of international trade, which influenced enormously the climate in which the Board operated. Even in the 1936–8 disputes the Board indicated a willingness to compromise if certain reforms regarding imports of dairy produce were acceded to. The Board knew its limits as well as its strength. It was also well aware of those areas where policy needed to be negotiated and those where it could take the initiative or be defensive itself. So the centralization of food control under wartime exigencies was not resisted. But even during these years, in contrast to other commodity marketing boards, the MMB remained intact, although some of its powers, particularly regarding pricing and a direct involvement in marketing, were transferred to the Ministry of Food.

Proposals similar to those of the Cutforth Commission resurfaced in the reports of the Lucas Committee (1947) and the Williams Committee (1948), but again failed to make headway. In spite of some antagonism from Labour back-benchers to the monopolistic characteristics of the Board, the post-war Labour government appeared reluctant to attack an organization which it had itself set in motion (Baker 1973). None the less, moves towards the deregulation of agriculture after the Conservatives assumed power in 1951, while guaranteeing a return to the Board's market powers of the pre-war years, did seek fresh ways of safeguarding the interests of the dairy trade: hence the formation in 1955 of the Joint Committee as an obligatory consultative body comprising members from the MMB and the Milk Distributive Council (renamed the Dairy Trade Federation in 1973), although this fell far short of the full and independent Commission proposed by Cutforth and Lucas.

More generally, the case of the MMB illustrates that formal corporatist arrangements may be state sponsored in the face of relative sectoral indifference, but once established they can be durable and vigorously defended by the private interests involved. Moreover, it is clear that the introduction of public and third-party accountability may be strongly resisted if such matters are neglected in the initial formulation of a corporatist scheme.

THE IMPACT OF MILK QUOTAS[2]

On 31 March 1984 the Council of Ministers approved the introduction of milk quotas throughout the European Community. They were first mooted publicly by the European Commission in 1978, and again in 1980 and 1981, but the Council of Ministers rejected the proposals. However, by mid-1983 it was apparent that all other efforts to control surpluses had failed, and the European Council instructed the Commission

[2] This section is based on interviews carried out with NFU, MMB, and MAFF officials, articles in the farming press, and government and parliamentary papers.

to produce new measures to limit agricultural spending. In Britain the Ministry of Agriculture and the Milk Marketing Board were, of course, aware of these developments, and discussions had been held on a number of key topics of quota administration, although the parties concerned did not, it seems, anticipate the speed with which change would occur.

In contrast to most unwelcome agricultural policy initiatives, therefore, neither the NFU nor the Board had the opportunity to prepare its membership. In consequence, in the immediate aftermath of the decision considerable dissatisfaction was expressed with the MMB and the NFU. Nevertheless, this did not develop into a full-scale challenge to the prevailing corporatist arrangements. In the event, the adaptation of producers to the quota regime, through adjustments in farm management techniques, ensured a relatively smooth passage to the new levels of production. Moreover the rapid development of quota trading independent of the holding to which it was allocated even allowed some farmers to continue to expand production using quota transferred from those (often smaller producers) giving up milk production. Thus the steady secular decline in the number of milk producers has continued in the post-quota years.

The MMB and NFU emerged remarkably unscathed from the episode for, in some ways, they were able to turn to their own advantage their apparent unreadiness for quotas. The speed of imposition could be blamed upon the EEC, and the decision was presented as a *fait accompli* that they had been steamrollered into accepting. The retrospective nature of the decision meant that implementation questions assumed immediate importance. And so, despite their bitterness, most farmers were more concerned to work out the details for their own business than to fight hopeless battles. The action groups set up to oppose quotas failed to attract significant or lasting support from either the Farmers' Union of Wales or traditionally militant NFU counties. Indeed there was a strong body of opinion in both Wales and the west of England that quotas provided a better form of control for the smaller family farm than price cuts.

Much of the dissatisfaction with the Board and Union manifested itself most forcefully in a campaign to reform the voting procedures for MMB members, so as to allow one vote per producer rather than voting rights determined by the number of cows owned by a producer. The campaign was successful but it proved a largely symbolic victory. The Ministry's acquiescence in this matter after fifty years' intransigence demonstrated an eagerness to allow energies to be diverted from the quota incident. Another source of possible opposition to quotas lay with other interests, such as ancillary industries and workers, those in milk manufacture and farm workers. But all these manifestly failed to organize politically, due to lack of incorporation in the policy process and historically weak political organization, and it was these groups which largely bore the brunt of the painful economic adjustments that quotas necessitated (Cox, Lowe, and Winter 1989).

The existing corporatist arrangements moulded the way in which quotas were implemented and consequent distributional effects. The assumption of responsibility by the Board reflected the existing bias in the regulation of milk policy in Britain. The corporatist management of milk quotas made possible the internalization of potentially damaging conflict in the case of smaller producers and producer-retailers and the marginalization of the interests of farm workers, workers in the supply sector, workers in dairy manufacture, and consumers. Thus the interests of the larger and progressive dairy farmer emerged at the forefront of discussions and the interests of other groups directly affected by quotas received scant attention. Nowhere was this more apparent than in the case of quota transfer. The interest of the larger milk producers in allowing quota transfer through a market mechanism was vigorously pursued within the Board. In following such a strategy the Board resolutely turned its back on any notion of the control of the reallocation of quota resting with a committee representative of the interests of smaller producers and new entrants and embraced, instead, a market solution.

The role of the MMB with regard to quota transfer clearly allowed shifts in policy from the original spirit of the regulations. The MMB is undoubtedly serving the interests of its own better-endowed members by allowing relatively free quota transfer. At the same time, although superficially allowing new purchases, it actually makes entry into the industry considerably harder than it might otherwise be, because the high market value of quota, which occasionally may even exceed the value of the land to which it is attached, is an added burden to new entrants. Moreover the market for quotas has severely limited the official Outgoers Scheme promoted by the European Commission, under which the payments offered do not begin to compete with market value for quota.

These conclusions regarding the impact of milk quotas should not, however, detract from other pressures which the MMB is facing, not from tensions within its own constituency, but from consumer interests and the interests of other EC member states. Nor should the wider context be ignored, for quotas remain a manifestation of a much wider agricultural crisis, as demonstrated in our overview of alternative land uses (see below). Moreover, although the industry's self-regulatory mechanisms have adapted well to quotas, the fundamental crisis of surpluses remains. Many dairy producers have diversified into other sectors not subject to quotas, so increasing other commodity surpluses. Nor is milk production itself yet fully in line with demand. Further cuts in quota and the extension of quotas or similar arrangements to other commodities will increase the problems facing the industry. The 'crisis of crisis management' (Offe 1984) will deepen.

THE MICRO-POLITICS OF IMPLEMENTATION: DEVON NFU AND ADAS[3]

The importance of the MMB with regard to the development of quota trading, especially its assumption of particular administrative responsibilities which allowed it to determine the details of transfer mechanisms, leads one to consider the wider implications of the Board's role in quota implementation and associated changes in inter-agency relations in the general implementation of agricultural policy. This exercise demands an overview of the development of MAFF's advisory service—previously the lead agency for promoting the development of the dairy sector—and the role of the NFU, particularly at the county level, and the MMB in policy implementation.

An examination of the post-war development of the advisory service in England and Wales shows a decline in the direct

---

[3] This section is based on a local study of the NFU and MAFF in Devon making use of interviews and archival sources.

regulatory functions of the Ministry up until quotas (Cox, Lowe, and Winter 1986*a*). Before 1958 the Ministry retained strongly interventionist powers regarding the promotion of food production and standards of good husbandry. These powers were vested in the County Agricultural Executive Committees (CAECs), which brought the NFU into a close, formalized, and sustained relationship with the Ministry. The CAECs were committees composed mainly of farmers, most of whom were appointed by the Ministry from the nominees of the NFU. The work of the Devon branch of the NFU was thus heavily orientated towards its partnership in regulation during the 1950s. Officers of the Ministry's National Agricultural Advisory Service (NAAS), although not directly employed by the CAECs, were formally attached to these committees. The partnership between NAAS and the CAECs was close and was characterized by a single-minded unity of purpose: agricultural productivity.

The role of the CAECs declined during the 1960s—they were abolished in 1972—as the emphasis of policy shifted from the promotion of maximum production to efficiency and cost-effectiveness and as many of their functions and powers were absorbed by the NAAS. Correspondingly the formalized contacts between county Ministry officials and Devon NFU became more attenuated. No longer was the Union required actively to assist in local policy implementation. The Ministry's advisory service became orientated to direct contact with the larger, technically progressive farmers, and in 1971 it was reorganized as the Agricultural Development and Advisory Service. It was also during the 1960s that the MMB developed a series of farm management consultancy services for its producers. Thus both the Ministry and the Board were content to focus attention on capable individual farmers willing to innovate, with scant regard for any wider remit regarding social and economic changes in rural communities. Moreover this role effectively bypassed the NFU at the local level. While Devon NFU continued to hold regular meetings with the Ministry, its centrality to policy implementation declined. Only on certain specific issues, where direct regulatory measures affecting all farmers were required, were local Union–Ministry relations of importance. These included hygiene standards in production, sheep dipping requirements, and so forth.

Corporatist relations between the NFU and the MAFF did,

of course, remain crucial nationally: especially through the annual review of prices. Thus the county branches increasingly found themselves with, on the one hand, a limited local regulatory function but, on the other, the expectation from headquarters that they would acquiesce in national policy decisions. It is no coincidence that the 1960s saw Devon NFU, with a number of other county branches, adopting an increasingly belligerent posture regarding both government agricultural policy and the role of the NFU in the determination of these policies. Britain's entry into the EEC and the shift of focus of much agricultural policy-making from London to Brussels exacerbated these tensions. Thus the plight of the smaller farmer, the impact of the cost–price squeeze, and the decline of livestock profits relative to either dairying or arable production all prompted the hostility of Devon NFU at a time when ADAS and the MMB continued with the quiet job of assisting the most favoured producers to improve their competitive advantage still further. Of the two agencies, the advisory role of ADAS, even in dairying, remained more significant than that of the Board for the simple reason that its advice was free.

The impact of quotas on the balance of inter-agency relations was almost immediate. The NFU, both locally and nationally, criticized the Ministry for inadequate warning and for advising farmers to increase milk production even during the days immediately before the decision to implement quotas. Although ADAS adapted its advice for the new circumstances, which was of undoubted benefit for many individual farmers, collective confidence in the service was shaken. Not surprisingly, Devon NFU supported the NFU nationally in urging the Ministry to delegate administrative responsibilities to the Board. Perceptions of the Ministry were damaged in a number of other ways. First, the local Ministry offices had very little information available with which to advise farmers. Thus, farmers telephoning the Ministry requesting advice on how quotas would be allocated, and how the system would work, were advised to phone the Board. Secondly, one element of the administration of quotas retained by the Ministry was the establishment of tribunals to adjudicate on farmers claiming special case treatment. Inevitably the work of the tribunals aroused contention. Neither the MMB nor the NFU was directly implicated in the work of the tribunals, although the Union did assist in nominating farmers for consideration by the Ministry. On the contrary, they helped individual farmers prepare cases to put to the tribunals. Thirdly, the implementation of quotas coincided with ADAS coming under increasing pressure from central government to become more commercially orientated, culminating in the introduction of charges for ADAS services under the 1986 Agriculture Act. In the milk sector, at least, the conditions were hardly auspicious for its new role. Not only had farmers' confidence in the service been undermined, but in performing its administrative duties with regard to quotas, the MMB had enhanced its reputation as an advisory agency.

Thus dairy quotas mark a shift in policy implementation from the promotion of production, with ADAS taking the lead role, to the regulation of production with the MMB playing the leading part. The implications for Devon NFU are somewhat less radical. Its relations with the Board have long been close, and have become more so as a result of quotas. Its importance in relation to the Ministry at county level has grown. It is committed to the extension of quotas to other commodities, in opposition to NFU policy, as the preferred alternative to price reductions. Moreover, its suggestions for the administration of quotas include a strong element of self-regulation in which the role of the county branch would be crucial.

ALTERNATIVE LAND USE

Since 1984 the terms of the debate about the farm crisis have shifted from food surpluses to a prospective land surplus. This was on the premiss that, if production controls such as milk quotas proved effective and were introduced for other staple commodities, some agricultural land would no longer be needed in production. The shift first occurred in agricultural circles; then in the farming press; and by 1986–7 it was reflected in the national press. Increasingly, policy options in response to the farm crisis were posed in terms of the need to promote farm diversification and alternative land uses (Cox, Lowe, and Winter 1989).

This debate was an important sequel to the implementation of quotas and was central to the subsequent reorientation of agricultural policy. Though most of the work on alternative crops and animal products was done by agricultural and environmental scientists (and on the future agricultural land budget by agricultural economists), the debate had distinct political and ideological determinants. The farm crisis and its solution could have been diagnosed quite differently, and to construe it in terms of the search for an encouragement of alternative land uses was to m⁻ke explicit or implicit choices that favoured certain interests (Lowe and Winter 1987). Economic analysis, for example, of a kind other than that emanating from the discipline of agricultural economics has tended to see the root of over-production in agriculture as lying in a surfeit not of land in production, but rather of other factors such as chemical inputs or machinery, or capital in general (Body 1982; Bowers and Cheshire 1983). To have tackled these over-supply problems, through either market or bureaucratic mechanisms, would have depressed landed capital and agribusiness interests.

Conversely, to incline policy choices and financial support to the redeployment of supposedly surplus land favours these interests. Thus recent policy initiatives and proposals have included grant schemes to make idle cereal land, reduce the stocking densities of beef herds, plant farm woodland, and support traditional farming practices in environmentally sensitive areas. There have also been efforts to relax planning constraints on the reuse of agricultural land and buildings.

Central to these developments has been the imperative for corporatist arrangements to be bolstered by a legitimatory ideology. Publicity about food surpluses had badly tarnished the farmers' projected image as efficient producers supported in the national interest and had drawn critical attention to their special privileges. The alternative land use debate, by shifting attention from food surpluses and their fundamental cause to questions of farm diversification and novel uses for rural land, has helped to reinstate a productionist and innovative image for the agricultural industry. Moreover, with the spectre of large-scale and un-managed land abandonment deployed as a warning against an uncared-for and derelict countryside, environmental policy for agriculture has come to be orchestrated in terms of the same agenda. In the process, pressures for fundamental reform of the agricultural support system have been dissipated. Indeed, we would argue that the manner in which the alternative land use debate has been orchestrated is itself an indication of the persistent power of constraint enjoyed by farming and landowning interests.

The question arises then of what happened to that broad coalition of forces which, in the early 1980s, seemed poised to play a key role in generating reforms in agricultural policy (Lowe *et al.* 1986). These forces included free marketeers, conservationists, and consumer and food poverty interests. A number of factors can be adduced to account for this failure to press home a thoroughgoing critique. In the first instance the neo-liberal appraisal of farm policy became marginalized within the Conservative Party as ministers realized the difficulties of reforming the CAP without jeopardizing the future of the European Community.

Electoral considerations, moreover, were felt to be significant by a government ultimately reluctant to pursue too severe a squeeze on Britain's farmers. Farmer and agricultural interests are still able to project an image of themselves as central to the well-being of the countryside, and a broader countryside vote is still considered a relevant constituency.

A third factor is that rural conservation interests, both voluntary and official, have typically regarded rural landowners as more their natural allies than consumer, food poverty, urban recreational, or development interests. In part this may reflect an incipient anti-urbanism in their outlook but, in addition, through many years of having to collaborate with farmers and landowners as the owners and controllers of the countryside, they have become conciliatory to their interests. They have therefore been reluctant to throw themselves behind radical reform of agricultural support. Undoubtedly, questions of political pragmatism have also been a consideration. Certainly, those groups, most notably Friends of the Earth, which have pressed for sweeping cuts in support prices and much stronger environmental controls seem to have had little impact on the course of events.

THE FARMERS' UNION OF WALES[4]

For much of the post-war period, the NFU has enjoyed a virtual monopoly on representing farmers' interests to government.

[4] Our understanding of the FUW is drawn from analysis of published papers and interviews with officials.

Observers have seen this and the unity within the farming lobby which it has been able to generate as central to the unique relationship the Union has enjoyed with the Ministry of Agriculture. Indeed, for a long time the Ministry actively fostered the Union's representational monopoly.

One group, though, did manage successfully to break away from the NFU and eventually to challenge its representational monopoly of the agricultural interest. This singular achievement by the Farmers' Union of Wales against what many consider to be the most strongly corporatist relationship in British politics invited analysis of its special circumstances and causes in the expectation that they would illuminate the processes through which dominant patterns of interest intermediation are maintained and revised.

The FUW was formed in 1955 in west Wales as a breakaway group dissatisfied with the attention given to the needs of Welsh hill farmers. Its first President and General Secretary had been the Chairman and General Secretary respectively of the Carmarthenshire branch of the NFU. A set of factors—social, economic, geographic, political, and cultural—coincided to give the breakaway group both a marked degree of internal cohesion and a strong sense of separateness. In mid- and west Wales there is a considerable concentration of small livestock farmers who were experiencing particular hardship at the time. In particular, they felt at a disadvantage within British agriculture compared with the larger arable farmers of the east of England who were perceived as dominant within the NFU. They were also predominantly Welsh speakers, and both their cultural distinctiveness and remoteness contributed to a distrust of London-based organizations.

Though the FUW quickly attracted support from many of the smaller hill farmers discontented at what they saw as the domination of the NFU by big farmers of the English lowlands, it had a considerable struggle to establish itself in its early years against the hostility of the NFU and the indifference of the Ministry of Agriculture. Its political tactics included public protests and campaigns to publicize the plight of small hill farmers, and efforts to win the backing of political and economic organizations in Wales as well as of Welsh MPs.

Indirectly, the rise of Welsh nationalism in the 1960s assisted and helped sustain the FUW's cause, although the critical breakthrough for the Union did not come until 1978, after many years of campaigning against the agricultural establishment. In that year, as part of the general effort to devolve to Scotland and Wales the administration of certain functions of central government, the Secretary of State for Wales assumed full responsibility for Welsh agriculture from the Minister of Agriculture. This led to the establishment of the Agriculture Department in the Welsh Office; and to the formal recognition of the Union by the Secretary of State, who agreed to consult it on all matters of agricultural policy. In other words, recognition for the FUW was integral to the effort to give political legitimacy to administrative devolution which in turn was part of a strategy to defuse the support for political nationalism.

Coincidentally, relations between the Minister of Agriculture and the leadership of the NFU were particularly sour. The NFU had become frustrated that the minority Labour government, concerned to hold down food prices, was not prepared to devalue the Green Pound to the extent of eliminating the gap between the green and market exchange rates. It therefore made the issue into a party-political one and used its links with the Conservative Party and the minor parties to engineer a parliamentary defeat for the government on the issue (Grant 1983). Government recognition of the FUW was in part an act of retaliation and was clearly meant as a rebuff to the NFU's leadership, though it also had a broader political rationale in relation to devolution.

We conclude that three major factors made possible the FUW's achievement and that while each was necessary none would, on its own, have been sufficient to splinter the agricultural interest. The first is internal sectional cleavage. The second is a distinct political and social culture. The third concerns the need of the state to legitimate its structures of authority.

Since 1978 the FUW has become closely involved in price review negotiations as well as frequent consultations with ministers and civil servants over all aspects of Welsh farming. It has also established a *modus vivendi* with the NFU. The former, bitter animosity has been replaced by a keen sense of rivalry. On occasions, such as the defence of the Milk Marketing Board following EEC entry, the two unions have even collaborated in their lobbying.

Significantly, in contrast to the NFU's opposition the FUW publicly supported the idea of milk quotas before their imposition, as both a more equitable and secure means of production control than squeezing prices and one more favourable to smaller farmers with restricted opportunities for alternative incomes. In the months following the imposition of quotas, the FUW studiously distanced itself from the opprobrium they attracted, and criticized the Ministry for the level at which production ceilings had been fixed. Nevertheless, the Union was careful to distinguish its objections to the details of the decision and the way it had been made from its approval of the general direction of policy. And, when the protests of *ad hoc* farmers' action groups threatened to get out of hand, the FUW, having extracted from the Ministry certain concessions for small producers in the allocation of quotas and the Outgoers Scheme, threw its authority behind the quota system.

The most recent twist in the evolving relationship between the NFU, the FUW, and the government came in January 1988 when, at the initiative of the Secretary of State for Wales Peter Walker (himself a former Agriculture Minister), and under his auspices, exploratory talks were held between the NFU and the FUW on the possibility of amalgamation. Walker had suggested that it would be better for farmers in Wales to speak with one voice, and leaders of the two unions had been told that separate meetings were squandering precious ministerial time and must end. The FUW's position was that an autonomous union for all Welsh farmers was needed, similar to the Scottish NFU, which would act in close association with the NFU as the representative of English farmers. The NFU in contrast, which has attempted to appease Welsh interests by strengthening its own Welsh Council and Welsh representation in London, stressed the importance of maintaining the unity of farmers across England and Wales. The most likely outcome is that the two unions will be forced to sit around the same table in negotiations and consultations with the Welsh Office while continuing to act independently at other times.

CONCLUSION

We turn finally to consider some very broad conclusions which we can draw from our work and which bear on the significance of milk quotas in relation to wider questions of agricultural and land use policy. Our principal concern will be with the issue of regulation, since this is central to any worthwhile deployment of the concept of corporatism (Williamson 1985) and we shall seek, in particular, to account for the evident readiness of farming and landowning interests to countenance controls in the sphere of production while refusing to concede that they may be appropriate in the sphere of countryside protection. We shall be concerned, in short, with what John Goldthorpe (1984) has termed strategic logics of action.

Our study of milk quotas shows just how extensively the existing corporatist arrangements within the dairy sector moulded the process of implementation. They made possible both the effective internalization of potentially damaging conflict stemming from the disaffection of smaller producers and producer-retailers and the marginalization of farm workers, workers in the supply sector, workers in dairy manufacture, and consumer interests. Structures must be seen not only as constraining but, equally significantly, as enabling (Giddens 1979), and our work shows how the 'resource' constituted by long-established corporatist institutions and arrangements made possible continued far-reaching structural change within the dairy sector without the political dislocation that might have been expected to accompany it. As we have seen, the protest groups which were formed in the immediate aftermath of quotas were, for the most part, ineffectual. The interests of larger producers have, in contrast, been protected.

The extent of the post-quota change should not be exaggerated though. For while the advent of quotas did, as we have argued, represent a fundamental discontinuity at the level of consciousness within the farming and landowning community, structural change had long been characteristic of the dairy sector in Britain through the post-war period. After peaking in 1950 the number of registered producers declined dramatically at a rate far faster than the reduction in the number of farmers in general and the number of registered milk producers in the UK fell, for instance, by 5,622 between 1980 and 1984. The decline continued after the imposition of quotas such that by 1987 the number was 46,740, whereas in 1984 it had been 50,265.

In the context of such change one of the main concerns in the immediate aftermath of quotas—a concern voiced by some officials in the MMB, the MAFF, and by academic agricultural economists—was the danger that a system of quotas attached to land would fossilize the existing pattern of production and prevent further rationalization of the agricultural structure. In view of the structural change that had already occurred in the dairy sector it might have been expected that such an argument would have held little sway; but it became, in fact, a very important consideration in working out the details of quota implementation. As we have suggested above, the interests of those, usually larger, milk producers wishing to expand production through gaining additional quota have been vigorously pursued within the Board. The mechanisms introduced to accomplish quota trading can, moreover, be readily understood in terms of the structures of constraint and logics of action which have characterized post-war agriculture and conservation policy.

In seeking to account for the evident readiness of the farming and landowning community to countenance controls of a particular kind within the sphere of production while refusing to concede that they may be appropriate in the sphere of countryside protection it is useful, heuristically, to make a distinction between 'zero-sum' and 'non-zero-sum' power situations.

In the circumstances of post-war agriculture, farming and landowning interests have inevitably seen the prospect of environmental controls as involving a loss of autonomy with no obvious compensating benefit for the individual farmer or landowner. Thus farmers on West Sedgemoor in the Somerset Levels claimed that the designation of a Site of Special Scientific Interest (SSSI) on the moor would leave them victims of 'conservation blight' because of the adverse impact on land values (Cox, Lowe, and Winter 1987*b*).

The situation is changing though. There is now less uncertainty than there was immediately following the passage of the 1981 Wildlife and Countryside Act (WCA) regarding probable payments under management agreements. In a context where land values are falling and the search for alternative sources of farm income is increasingly pressing, owning land which carries a designation can be seen as advantageous rather than, as formerly, entailing a form of penalty. If it changes character sufficiently, what may formerly have been seen as a 'zero-sum game' may hold out the prospect of compensating benefits for loss of autonomy. Whether the game can be defined in that way does, however, depend utterly on the provisions for compensation accompanying controls, the funds available for the negotiation of management agreements, and the extent to which declining agricultural profitability is or is not reflected in the value of such agreements. Though the very positive response to the Ministry's Environmentally Sensitive Areas scheme amongst a farming community much chastened by the advent of milk quotas indicates the extent to which the parameters for such calculations have been redrawn, the balance remains a fine one.

There is no ambiguity in the matter of controls over production however. Where significant structural change has to be effected over a relatively short time-span the individual advantage to be gained from accepting a degree of collective regulation is fairly evident. Thus, as we have argued, the introduction of quotas to cut back milk production did much to convince the NFU that the era in which all other aims were subordinated to that of increasing production was at an end and subsequently there have been calls for increased regulation in other commodity areas.

Regulation in the sphere of production can be seen as 'non-zero-sum', since it promises a predictable collective benefit. Clearly the degree of individual benefit will vary in relation to farm or estate structure, indebtedness, and a host of other factors. But at the very general level with which we are presently concerned, the 'zero-sum' 'non-zero-sum' distinction goes some way to accounting for the entirely rational disinclination of most farmers and landowners to accept environmental controls while acquiescing in, and even welcoming, controls in the sphere of production.

To understand why such tendencies are so powerfully accentuated, however, it is necessary to make a number of other distinctions which help to specify the nature of the forms taken by the relationship between the state, agriculture, and politics of land use in the countryside. In considering interests and their representation we have, in our previous work, drawn a contrast between corporate groupings whose identity stems from their distinctive place in the division of labour and sphere of production, and the pressure groups and voluntary associations—such as conservation groups—which, as groupings of individuals with a common interest, inhabit the very different competitive sphere of politics (Cox, Lowe, and Winter 1985*a*, 1986*b*).

The concept of corporatism is most usefully used in a restricted sense to refer to a distinctive style of interest intermediation. It implies interventionist action of an indirect nature whereby the state operates in conjunction with organizations which are based on the division of labour in society. It is crucially distinguished, therefore, by the salience of producer groups and their role in regulating their own constituencies reaching bargained agreements with state agencies. Corporatism is, however, only one of three modes of state intervention which may be identified (Cawson 1982). Where intervention is of a market kind, state activities are limited to those required for private markets to operate and for the mediation of conflicts between public and private interests; while a bureaucratic mode demands an extensive state and sets of authoritative command relationships which define the rights and duties of individuals and groups. Though analytically separable such modes are, of course, far from mutually exclusive in practice.

In considering the regulation of agriculture, then, we need to pay regard to both the nature of the regulatory instruments and the political structures within which they operate. The former, we would argue, can be located on a continuum ranging from permissive to controlling, while the latter—varying in the agencies or bodies vested with regulatory responsibility and the extent of their accountability—may range between the corporatist and the market, or pluralist. In terms of such a typology we can see that state intervention in agriculture and the countryside has been mixed, but with corporatist forms predominant. At times of national crisis, when there was a need for a rapid mobilization and expansion of agriculture (for example during wartime and during the period of post-war food scarcity), the corporatist relationship took a highly bureaucratic, or state-directed, form and County Agricultural Executive Committees remained 'controlling' in character up to 1958. But, typically, during the period between 1950 and 1980 when the pursuit of an incrementally expansionist agriculture was seen as a desirable feature of economic policy, permissive, rather than controlling, corporatist policies of production regulation prevailed. In retrospect we can see how this form of intervention, with its reliance on market mechanisms and incentives in the form of production and investment grants, ADAS services, and the like, suited the phase of policy which is now so clearly at an end.

Given the institutional context and recent history of agricultural policy, the preferred policy style of dominant interests within the farming and landowning community is clearly permissive corporatist, since it potentially maximizes both their economic security and their autonomy. Such regulation is however ill suited to a period when limiting rather than expanding output has become the object of agricultural policy. That strategy demands, at the least, controlling corporatist forms such as quotas or set-aside. There is, though, a more or less ready acceptance of such a shift even if it does represent a decisive break with a whole philosophy of agricultural production, because control does at least remain within the agricultural industry and because farmers are used to the temporary expedient of controls when necessary.

Least palatable to farming and landowning interests anxious to preserve their privileged status within a still relatively closed but increasingly beleaguered agricultural policy community would be regulation of a controlling pluralist kind, encompassing controls administered by non-agricultural authorities. Marginally less unacceptable are permissive pluralist arrangements and indeed, until the very recent past, such forms of environmental restraint were the only ones tolerated. Whereas the management agreement has come to be accepted in the environmental sphere, the present crisis and neo-liberal political ideas have encouraged an exploration of permissive pluralist mechanisms in relation to production as well, as grants are phased out and alternative—and as yet unsupported—uses for land are canvassed. An increasing reliance on free market mechanisms would, however, have damaging implications for the internal and external authority of the NFU in particular since they would undermine the corporatist relationship which has been characteristic of the kind of power it has enjoyed.

Under these pressures a number of factors are combining to transform the agenda of policy-making in agricultural and conservation politics. There is an increasing consciousness that agriculture is the most extensively supported sector of the economy and that the nature of that support has had considerable implications for the price and availability of food, nutritional standards, the welfare of rural communities, and the ecology of the countryside, to say nothing of international trading relationships. The corporatist bargain forged between state and agriculture in the light of the need for expanded food production in the immediate post-war period was clearly of mutual benefit to farmers and government alike. However, in a period of extensive readjustment involving the search for more diversified farm enterprises and ways of curbing over-production and protecting the environment, the relationship is being put under new strains. Indeed, in terms of the framework we are presenting it is evident that a hybrid set of arrangements is emerging which combines elements of both market and bureaucratic modes of state intervention.

At different stages in the development of agricultural policy, and partly as a result of the corporatist arrangements under which policy has been formulated, the NFU has accepted often quite extensive regulation. During the Second World War and the fifteen years that followed, the powers of the County Agricultural Executive Committees were readily accepted by the Union. Other examples include the constraints implicit in disease eradication campaigns, the quota controls on acreages to stabilize the potato market, and so forth. In these and other cases a characteristic feature of the NFU's readiness to embrace controls is that they should be vested in the government's agriculture departments. Its resistance to controls from other government departments is critically based on its perceived need to preserve the integrity of its own policy community (Cox, Lowe, and Winter 1986*b*).

Clearly, however, in line with its preference for 'permissive corporatism', controls—even those emanating from within the agricultural policy community—are not usually actively sought by the Union. Nor are they necessarily easy to 'sell' to a membership which has not always readily understood the subtle relationships assiduously cultivated by their representative organization. This helps us to understand the Union's public ambivalence towards the prospect of an extension of production controls; not wanting to be seen to be taking a lead but anxious nevertheless to shape the outcome. Moreover, controls are only acceptable if they are part of a wider bargain; in short, if they are a 'non-zero-sum' kind. Thus the post-war controls operated by the County Agricultural Executive Committees were accepted in return for the price guarantees of the 1947 Agriculture

Act. General environmental controls offer no such obvious advantages and have so far been strongly resisted.

The control of production in the face of surpluses is a more complex matter than price guarantees. Undoubtedly, the imposition of milk quotas came as a considerable shock to the Union which, although it had begun candidly to recognize the problem of surplus production, was still acting publicly as though ever-increasing levels of production would continue. The imposition of quotas has forced the Union to confront the issue of surplus production. Its initial fury over the sudden manner of their imposition has not prevented its acquiescence and active assistance in their implementation. The NFU, reluctant to compromise its 'insider' status, finds it difficult to declare an independent position or withdraw from a discussion when it is so enmeshed on a range of others.

In the four years since quotas were introduced it has become apparent that they present a more palatable solution than extensive price cuts. Moreover, given the reality of rolling surpluses as farmers switch to beef, sheep, and arable cropping, there are a number of ways in which direct control of over-production might cost the industry considerably less than the principal alternative, the 'permissive pluralism' of the free market. In Europe, too, the Commission is against such a solution, so on this matter at least the NFU is at present swimming with a powerful tide.

The lesson was gradually learned in relation to the prospective control of surplus grain. In the immediate aftermath of milk quotas the Union was vehemently opposed to quotas for cereals, suggesting instead a further period of moderate price restraint. However, it became increasingly clear that nothing short of a very sharp price reduction would reduce grain output and, at the same time, dairymen with milk quotas were demonstrating that margins could be maintained and even improved under quota. Pragmatically, the Union began to shift ground so that by early 1986 it was pressing its own Ministry—still committed to price restraint—to pursue some form of cereal quota.

The Union presented evidence to a Select Committee of the House of Lords during February 1986 in which it made out a case for flexi-quotas which would in fact involve compulsory set-aside or fallow as a proportion of each grower's arable area. As a quota system this would clearly fall short of the strict limitation on new entrants to the industry which now operates in the milk sector. The Union claims that unlike conventional quota it does not create a new capital asset or involve ownership problems and it stresses, moreover, the complex and costly administration that a comparable system would entail; though it admitted that such administrative arrangements would be required for the co-responsibility levy proposed by the European Commission. Though strongly opposed by the Union such a levy has been imposed and has, through the processing millers, in fact proved relatively easy to administer: set-aside would inevitably be a harder task. The Union is prepared to accept the regulation implied by a temporary set-aside policy (flexi-quota) to ease the immediate surplus problem and, indeed, would prefer any such scheme to be compulsory rather than the voluntary one which has been adopted.

The Union's commitment to compulsory set-aside has to be seen, of course, in the context of the various predictions concerning future land use and potential surpluses which received such wide coverage from 1986 onwards. By couching the problem of over-production in agriculture in terms of land surplus as opposed to capital surplus, the NFU and others have focused attention on new uses for land—of which set-aside is one—and diverted attention from market-led solutions which would cut farmers' incomes. The danger of non-compulsory set-aside is that the level of compensation might be set too low to attract sufficient farms. Its subsequent failure might then lead to price cutting as the only alternative solution, with potentially grave consequences for both farmers' incomes and land values. The Union's preparedness to countenance such regulation is accompanied by the hope that, in the long run, permanent quotas can be avoided by a combination of modest price restraint, the exploration of new markets for cereals (including industrial use), and the development of alternative crops.

But while it is clear from the tenor of the Union's arguments that it would be prepared to consider full production quotas should they ultimately prove necessary, there is no wish to go further down the controlling corporatist road than it has to. Indeed, one of the Union's fears is that full-scale cereal quotas would necessitate quotas in other commodities, leading to a highly regulated industry. The Union, as we have already indicated, fears fossilization of the existing farm structure and commodity mix. Its opposition to wholesale regulation is premissed on the need to sustain as favourable conditions for continued capital accumulation as possible. Clearly, a degree of regulation in conditions of extreme uncertainty and readjustment is conducive to the process; too much regulation would, however, be detrimental.

Such an interpretation of the Union's position is based partly on the understanding that its opinion leaders are dominated by a productionist large-farm mentality. Indeed it is borne out by the considerable emphasis now being placed upon the development of alternative crops and the pressure which the Union is exerting on the Ministry to support R & D in this area (Cox, Flynn, Lowe, and Winter 1988). It is also borne out by the much greater readiness of less well-placed sectors of the industry to accept regulation.

It might be expected that the smaller farming areas of the pastoral west, traditionally associated with a high degree of *petit bourgeois* individualism, would exhibit a strong disinclination to accept regulation by a central authority. But the FUW, unlike the NFU, publicly supported the idea of milk quotas before their imposition. Moreover, while the NFU leadership was moving reluctantly to its position on flexi-quotas for cereals early in 1986, Devon NFU—with the largest membership of any county NFU branch in the country—produced a policy paper (March 1986) arguing for a Central Agricultural Authority with producer and government representation to administer production controls on all commodities.

It is evident, then, that although the distribution of such a preparedness is mediated by farm size, structure, and other related factors, the farming and landowning community is more ready to countenance elements of regulation when the likely benefits are perceived as outweighing the likely uncertainties associated with the *laissez-faire* alternative. There are, of course, parallels between such arguments and the justifications for regulation in environmental matters, where the collective good to be secured is pursued on behalf not of a single industry but of the whole community. But with these different distributional implications, the position of the farming and landowning community switches to implacable opposition to controls based on the assertion of property rights.

REFERENCES

BAKER, S. (1973), *Milk to Market* (London: Heinemann).

BODY, R. (1982), *Agriculture: The Triumph and the Shame* (London: Maurice Temple Smith).

BOWERS, J., and CHESHIRE, P. (1983), *Agriculture, the Countryside and Land Use: An Economic Critique* (London: Methuen).

CAWSON, A. (1982), *Corporatism and Welfare* (London: Heinemann).

—— (1985), *Organised Interests and the State: Studies in Meso-Corporatism* (Beverly Hills, London: Sage).

COX, G., FLYNN, A., LOWE, P., and WINTER, M. (1988), *The Possibility for Alternative Uses of Agricultural Land in England and Wales* (Berlin: Wissenschaftszentrum).

—— LOWE, P., and WINTER, M. (1985a), 'Changing Directions in Agricultural Policy: Corporatist Arrangements in Production and Conservation Policies', *Sociologia ruralis*, 25/2: 130–53.

—— —— —— (1985b), 'Caught in the Act: The Agricultural Lobby and the Conservation Debate', *ECOS*, 6/1: 18–23.

—— —— —— (1986a), 'From State Direction to Self Regulation: The Historical Development of Corporatism in British Agriculture', *Policy and Politics*, 14/4: 475–90.

—— —— —— (1986b), 'Agriculture and Conservation in Britain: A Policy Community under Siege', in G. Cox, P. Lowe, and M. Winter (eds.), *Agriculture: People and Policies* (London: Allen & Unwin), 181–215.

—— —— —— (1987a), 'Farmers and State: A Crisis for Corporatism?', *Political Quarterly*, 58/1: 73–81.

—— —— —— (1987b), 'Landscape Protection and Nature Conservation', in P. Cloke (ed.), *Rural Planning: Policies into Action* (New York: Harper and Row).

—— —— —— (1989), 'The Farm Crisis in Britain', in D. Goodman and M. Redclift (eds.), *The International Farm Crisis* (London: Macmillan), 113–34.

Cutforth Commission (1936), *Milk: Report of the Reorganisation Commission for Great Britain* (MAFF Economics Series No. 44, London: HMSO).

GIDDENS, A. (1979), *Central Problems in Social Theory* (London: Macmillan).

GOLDTHORPE, J. G. (1984), *Order and Conflict in Contemporary Capitalism* (Oxford: Clarendon Press).

GRANT, W. (1983), 'The National Farmers' Union: The Classic Case of Incorporation?', in D. Marsh (ed.), *Pressure Politics* (London: Junction Books).

—— (ed.) (1985), *The Political Economy of Corporatism* (London: Macmillan).

—— (ed.) (1987), *Business Interests, Organisational Development and Private Interest Government* (New York: Walter de Gruyter).

JESSOP, B. (1982), *The Capitalist State* (Oxford: Martin Robertson).

LOWE, P., COX, G., MACEWEN, M., O'RIORDAN, T., and WINTER, M. (1986), *Countryside Conflicts* (Aldershot: Gower).

——and WINTER, M. (1987), 'Alternative Perspectives on the Alternative Land Use Debate', in N. R. Jenkins and M. Bell (eds.), *Farm Extensification* (Grange-over-Sands: Institute for Terrestrial Ecology), 1–17.

198   *Graham Cox, Philip Lowe, and Michael Winter*

Lucas Committee (1947), *Report of the Committee appointed to Review the Working of the Agricultural Marketing Acts* (MAFF Economics Series No. 48, London: HMSO).

METCALFE, L., and McQUILLAN, M. (1979), 'Corporatism or Industrial Democracy?', *Political Studies*, 27: 266–82.

NEWBY, H. (1987), *Country Life* (London: Weidenfeld & Nicolson).

OFFE, C. (1984), *Contradictions of the Welfare State* (London: Hutchinson).

SELF, P., and STORING, H. (1962), *The State and the Farmer* (London: Allen & Unwin).

Williams Committee (1948), *Report of the Committee on Milk Distribution*, Cmnd. 7414 (London: HMSO).

WILLIAMSON, P. (1985), *Varieties of Corporatism* (Cambridge: Cambridge University Press).

8. The MSC's Area Manpower Boards: The Role of Employer and Union Representatives

Roger King and Kris Schnack

IN May 1981, the then Manpower Services Commission published *A New Training Initiative: A Consultative Document*, which identified Britain's future training needs and established three objectives: the reform of skill training and the apprenticeship system; the establishment of a training scheme for young people; and planned increased opportunities for adults.

Over the next six months, the MSC received more than a thousand consultative papers from various organizations and individuals, to which it responded by issuing an 'Agenda for Action', which called for a youth training scheme to cover all school-leavers. The General Council of the Trades Union Congress endorsed these objectives as 'broadly in line with the TUC's policy of "Training for All"' (TUC 1982: 4). The Confederation of British Industry equally supported the 'Agenda for Action' which was 'substantially in line with CBI views' (CBI 1982: 1). At the same time, the government issued its White Paper on the New Training Initiative which concentrated on the youth policy issue and proposed a system of twelve-month apprenticeships for 300,000 unemployed minimum age school-leavers.

The Youth Training Scheme (YTS) differs from its predecessor, the Youth Opportunities Programme (YOP), in a number of fundamental respects. Instead of serving as a temporary crisis measure for the unemployed, YTS was designed as a permanent training scheme—whatever the level of youth unemployment. By offering twelve months' education, training, and work experience to all 16- and 17-year-olds, the scheme proposed to equip young men and women with a range of transferable skills and experience. Unlike YOP, nonemployed trainees could be covered by collective bargaining (including wages); and unions—through their representation on Area Manpower Boards—had the power to block schemes.

The comprehensiveness of the scheme was illustrated by the withdrawal of all other MSC grants for school-leavers, such as the first-year apprenticeship support and the Unified Vocational Preparation Scheme. Other youth training programmes were incorporated into YTS and by 1985/6 it accounted for nearly half of the total MSC budget at an expenditure of over £1 bn.

Much of the success of the proposed scheme was considered to be dependent on the MSC's local advisory machinery which—before YTS—was based on three networks of local committees—District Manpower Committees (DMCs), Committees for the Employment of Disabled People (CEDPs), and Special Programmes Area Boards. The latter in particular had been responsible for providing local assistance with regard to the delivery of the Youth Opportunities Programme, although the Boards had suffered from uneven distribution and relatively weak support.

Each Board was established to fulfil different needs but, in practice, much overlap occurred in terms of broad membership, function, and geographical coverage. The DMCs and the CEDPs were due to be reviewed before the beginning of 1983, but the introduction of YTS added a new element and gave impetus to a complete review of the MSC's local advisory machinery.

In its Report of April 1981, the Youth Task Group—a tripartite body set up by the MSC—considered an effective network of local advisory Boards to be essential in ensuring the successful implementation of YTS, and recommended that 50–60 Local Boards be established through the country with boundaries coinciding with those of the Local Education Authorities (LEAs):

The task of Local Boards would be to assess the quality and nature of opportunities required in their areas; to establish, support and supervise a network of managing agencies in their areas and, through them, to ensure that individual schemes meet criteria determined nationally; to mobilise local support to monitor and evaluate the progress of the scheme on the ground.

Membership of Local Boards should be adequately representative of employers, unions, local authorities, local education authorities, voluntary and youth organisations and the Careers Service. It would be a considerable advantage, wherever possible, for members of Local Boards to have direct experience of sponsorship of schemes (MSC 1982a: paras. 5–11, 5–12)

In terms of financial arrangements, the Task Group recommended that:

MSC funds should be allocated to Local Boards in relation to the forecasts of unemployed 16 year olds in the locality. Resources would be concentrated on areas of high youth unemployment, but in every area there would be adequate resources to cover the guarantee to unemployed 16 year olds. Local boards should draw up training plans for their areas designed to:

1) fulfil the guarantee for the unemployed;
2) offer as much support as they can for training in employment;
3) ensure that foundation training provision is properly integrated with longer term skill training arrangements. (MSC 1982a: para. 5–17).

The Task Group, however, decided to leave the final shape of the Local Boards to the MSC and the following month the MSC issued a 'Consultative Paper on the Future of MSC Local Advisory Machinery'.

The functions of the new 'Area Manpower Boards' as outlined in the Consultative Document marked a diminution from those recommended by the Youth Task Group and focused purely on advisory and support services. Little room was left for any executive function by the Area Manpower Boards and no mention of budgetary powers was included in the remit. The proposed functions of the new Boards were:

a) to advise on the planning and delivery of MSC employment and training services and programmes in the area;
b) to assist MSC in delivering and promoting the use of those services, and to encourage sponsors of all kinds throughout the area (employers, local authorities, voluntary organisations, etc.) to come forward with projects;
c) to promote links between MSC and local bodies whose activities influence manpower;
d) to advise on allocation of resources to particular kinds of youth training and other opportunities or to particular projects within guidelines established by Commission;
e) to be responsible for the approval of certain opportunities or projects within the area; and to assist in monitoring or assessing these;

f) to respond to requests for advice from the Commission, the Manpower Services Committees for Scotland and Wales (where appropriate) and the Regional Manpower Services Director; and
g) to assist in any other way the development and success of MSC's programmes and, in particular, to assist in securing the involvement and commitment of local interests. (MSC 1982*b*: 4)

The clear lack of executive powers for the proposed Area Manpower Boards received particular attention from one of the major respondents to the MSC's Consultative Document. The Electrical and Electronic Manufacturers' Training and Education Board argued that:

Only one of the proposed functions is executive: (c) 'to promote links between MSC and local bodies whose activities influence manpower' —but to what purpose? The only responsibility for decision-making proposed is to approve 'certain' projects, selected and agreed by others, presumably MSC staff.

　　With their 'advisory' functions, AMBs may be manipulated or ignored by the centrally controlled MSC bureaucracy in which, according to paragraph 16 of the Consultative Paper, will be invested the power to control the funds, access the training needs and the quality of training. (EEMTEB 1982: 1–2);

This view was echoed by the Ford Motor Company:

It is clear that 'toothless AMBs' will not gain the attention and commitment of the kind of industrial and commercial people who should be encouraged to man them. Equally, local boards must have the freedom and responsibility to identify and resolve their own problems with a minimum of top-down interference. They alone have the full range of alternatives open to them and have to live with the consequences. (Ford Motor Company 1982)

Similarly, the National Union of Teachers felt that: 'In every case the extent of the duty [in the remit] is qualified and this confuses the issue and leaves the function and accountability of the boards unclear between the area offices and the board itself' (NUT 1983: 24). In October 1982, the Commission considered the responses it had received to the Consultative Paper but made virtually no changes to the original proposals it had outlined in the Consultative Document. The number of Boards was set at 55, and each Board was to be composed of: an independent chairman (appointed by the Chairman of the MSC); five employer representatives (appointed after consultation with the CBI); five employee representatives (appointed after consultation with the TUC); one education service representative (normally a chief education officer); one representative of professional education interests (normally a college principal); one representative from a voluntary organization; one chairman of a Committee for the Employment of Disabled People; and two or three local authority representatives depending on the size and type of county covered (MSC 1982c: 3). In addition, all Area Manpower Boards could co-opt up to four additional non-voting members to represent other important interests. Principal careers officers would have the right of attendance when the Youth Training Scheme was being discussed.

Special responsibilities were ascribed to the Boards for the Youth Training Scheme. The AMBs were invited to:

—approve within agreed targets, budgets and policy guidelines, opportunities or projects for their area. AMBs will normally be expected to consider those which are novel, complex, unusually large or especially sensitive and to leave officials to consider routine projects on their behalf within the area plans approved by the AMB. Where projects extend beyond the boundaries of a single area, one AMB will take the lead on approvals but other AMBs with an interest will be kept informed. Approval of some very large projects covering a number of areas will be made centrally within guidelines approved by the Youth Training Board. AMBs will be kept fully informed of such approvals. The ultimate responsibility with MSC for the proper spending of public money rests with the Chairman of the MSC, who in turn is accountable to Ministers. Whilst this means that AMB decisions may be over-ridden it is expected that this would happen in practice very seldom. (MSC 1982c: 8, 9)

Many of the latter points proved to be contentious and a source of ongoing concern to Area Manpower Board members. In order to deal with 'some very large projects covering a number of areas' the MSC set up the Large Companies Unit, which was charged with negotiating schemes for private sector companies with several subsidiaries or plants, as well as for the nationalized industries and employers' training boards. Schemes negotiated nationally by the Large Companies Unit—which was staffed by MSC officials—accounted for one-third of all places offered by employers and were not subject to the approval or scrutiny of Area Manpower Boards. This led to resentment and concern amongst AMBs, as it was felt that LCU-approved schemes operating within their jurisdiction frequently failed to meet the standards applied to local schemes. Apart from appealing to their respective national organizations, AMB members were fairly powerless in this context. A 1985 postal survey of 280 trade union representatives on Area Manpower Boards indicated that 80.7 per cent felt they were not able to exercise effective control over LCU-approved schemes (Randall 1985).

The lack of executive functions had frequently reinforced the criticism of Area Manpower Boards as purely 'rubber stamping' bodies lending local respectability to MSC programmes. Boards were not consulted over a number of national policy decisions affecting local programmes and services such as the closure of Skill Centres and the phasing out of the Unified Vocational Preparation Scheme.

MSC could, and did, sometimes overrule decisions made by AMBs. A unanimous decision by Fife and Central AMB to reject a scheme proposed by Pitmans was subsequently overruled by MSC Chairman David Young. Similarly, a request by the Bradford, Calderdale and Kirklees Area Manpower Board for a representative of the Civil and Public Service Association to be invited to a Board meeting in order to present views on MSC proposals regarding the closure of Job Centres was opposed by MSC Head Office as 'not appropriate'.[1]

Area Manpower Boards were also warned by MSC about extending their activities into the realm of the political:

AMBs, as advisory bodies to the Commission, are requested to keep comments and business within the limits of scope of MSC activities and avoid being drawn into the consideration of matters which are properly the responsibility of the Department of Employment or other Government Departments and hence outside the AMBs' sphere of influence and scope for constructive action. (MSC 1982c: 8)

THE YORKSHIRE AND HUMBERSIDE AREA MANPOWER BOARDS

To examine the role of AMBs in practice, we draw on our research carried out in the Yorkshire and Humberside region.

---

[1] Interview notes.

Employer and trade union representatives on the region's five AMBs were nominated by the regional CBI and the regional TUC respectively. In what amounts to a *pro forma* process, the nominees were considered by MSC and a formal invitation was extended by the AMB chairman on behalf of the MSC Commissioner.

Many of the employer representatives we interviewed were unaware they had been nominated to the Board by the regional CBI. As one told us: 'At that time, I wasn't aware that the CBI had nominated me. I was approached by the regional director of the MSC who asked me if I would be interested in continuing from the Special Programmes Area Board.'[2] The process by which nominees are selected by the regional CBI is highly informal and to a large extent dependent on personal contacts and suggestions. In some cases, trade associations were approached by the regional CBI for possible nominees. For example, the CBI requested the National Farmers' Union to suggest a candidate, agricultural representation being considered necessary due to North Yorkshire's rural character. The calibre of nominees was questioned by a number of respondents, who felt that the CBI was not doing enough in getting interested and capable people to sit on the Area Manpower Boards. One AMB chairman, who is also a major employer in the region, felt that: 'There are problems with the CBI—they are not doing their job properly. The selection of nominees is lousy. They should interview appointees to determine their suitability.' Regional CBI faced some difficulties in finding employers with the time and interest required to serve on Area Manpower Boards. Whereas attending Area Manpower Board meetings may become an integral part of a union official's full-time occupation, in the case of employers such involvement is usually in addition to other regular responsibilities. The MSC secretary of one of the Area Manpower Boards observed that: 'It's not part of an employer's job. The employer reps are not well versed in committee work and contacts between them are very limited. Therefore they often don't know what's going on.' Unlike their employer counterparts, all trade unionists interviewed were aware that they had been selected regionally by the regional TUC executive, although the exact nature of this process

[2] The following quotes are, unless otherwise noted, based on interview notes.

remained unclear and was referred to by one unionist as 'one of those mysterious things'. Nevertheless, regional TUC attention generally focused on unions which would have the most contact with YTS and on individuals who were likely to become involved and stay involved. Some of the trade union representatives in the Yorkshire–Humberside region had been previously active on the Special Programmes Area Board or on the District Manpower Committee and continued on the Area Manpower Boards after the introduction of YTS. One senior trade unionist in the region felt, however, that the calibre of trade union representatives on the Area Manpower Boards was fairly low and that 'regional TUC are picking people who won't cause any problems—few of them are well-informed about the schemes and several are retired members'. Regional TUC was also concerned to avoid political controversy on the local boards. A request by the National Union of Mineworkers for a seat on the Leeds–Wakefield Area Manpower Board was regarded as a 'political move' and rejected.

None of the employer representatives we spoke to regarded themselves as accountable to either the regional or national CBI and a number were keen to stress their independence as 'free agents', which some felt gave them an advantage over their trade union counterparts: 'I don't see myself as representing their or any other interests. I will respond to circulars but, on the whole, contact is about once a year. I have attended CBI sponsored meetings but I couldn't say that I'm a regular.' This view was shared by the CBI's regional office in Leeds: 'The CBI cannot hold employers to any one line so we don't get involved in the day-to-day running of YTS. I would see our role as one of trying to set standards.'

This it did through irregular meetings organized for the employer representatives on the Area Manpower Boards or for managing agents in the region.

The trade union representatives in the region had a much stronger perception of accountability which most saw as being to the regional TUC. This perspective was underlined by the secretary of the regional TUC council: 'The representatives we select are first and foremost accountable to regional TUC through the procedure of a permanent consultative committee which meets once a month. It tries to co-ordinate the activities of all trade union representatives in the region.' Nevertheless, some respondents felt they were primarily accountable to their respective unions, while one perceived himself as accountable to 'young people'.

Apart from peer pressure, little discipline was exercised over employer representatives on the Area Manpower Boards. This is not a function which the CBI could or would wish to take on and problems were usually sorted out in a personal context.

The AMB Consultative Committee, organized by regional TUC to co-ordinate policy, also served to impose some degree of control over trade union representatives through an attendance requirement. There were no sanctions for non-attendance, but in the case of frequent non-attendance the executive would write a letter to the representative concerned. The executive could potentially ask a representative to resign but this had never been contemplated.

A further element of control was exercised through the requirement that trade union representatives on the Area Manpower Boards must be full-time officers. Lay officials were not considered to have the 'experience or the time that is necessary to devote to YTS'. Some union officials expressed their concern that 'some shop stewards would turn down a scheme on principle'.

Generally speaking, trade union representatives on the Area Manpower Boards tended to be far more active than their employer counterparts. A senior MSC official in the region felt that: 'Employers are the weak link. They do not stay at meetings, they don't understand the issues and are often ill-prepared— but there are exceptions.'

An employer representative on the South Yorkshire Area Manpower Board bemoaned the lack of preparedness and organization amongst his colleagues and commended the unions for having 'their act together'. A number of respondents considered a major stumbling block to be the sheer amount of pre-meeting paperwork (*circa* 130 pages).

There was also very little contact between employer representatives outside of the actual AMB meetings and, unlike their union counterparts, no separate discussions took place before Board meetings.

Trade union members tended to read the documentation provided by MSC with more care and thoroughness. One of the AMB secretaries in the region observed that the trade unionists took it very seriously, checking all the details, looking at employers, and also giving MSC 'a hard time—often rightly so'. Trade unionists also tend to be more supportive of each other and on some Boards (S. Yorks, Bradford–Calderdale–Kirklees) the trade unionists met separately before an AMB meeting to discuss the trade union policy and items on the agenda. Although their meetings allowed some degree of control and mutual influence, several trade union representatives emphasized that much depended on the individual personalities on each Board.

Employer representatives rarely discussed AMB-related issues with fellow-employers or executives at the workplace, although some would make a particular effort in this regard. Frequently, other employers were unaware of the role of Area Manpower Board members:

Some other employers, particularly those who are managing agents [of YTS schemes] view AMB representatives with some suspicion. They don't always understand why employer representatives might agree to vetoing a plan or agree to Health and Safety regulations. I had to convince some employers that this was not just another YOP.

Similarly, trade unionists had little contact with their membership over YTS related issues, and many felt that members were not really interested in the issue, except when one of their sons was likely to go on the scheme. None of the members we interviewed had any contact with the national level of the union movement and, at most, they received an occasional circular from their national headquarters.

Solidarity between employer and union representatives

One of the most interesting findings of our study is the great degree of affinity and solidarity which existed between the employer and trade union representatives on the Area Manpower Boards. None of our respondents spoke unfavourably of their counterparts on their respective Boards. One employer said: 'Relations with the trade unionists are very good. I think there is a great deal of consensus within the board and a respect for each other. These are the type of trade unionists who make up the majority of the trade union movement but are never reported on by the popular press.' Similar views were expressed by the trade union representatives on the Board: 'The CBI colleagues have been very helpful. They almost always support the unions if the case is well put and genuinely seem to want to assist employment efforts.' One senior trade unionist perceived a potentially negative aspect to this degree of cordiality: 'There's a danger of the boards becoming clubs with increasing familiarity between the reps. First name terms are standard practice now and a number have become good friends. But I have to say that those [employers] who attend regularly make a constructive contribution.' The high level of consensus on the Yorkshire–Humberside Area Manpower Boards was illustrated by the fact that votes were very rarely taken on issues that came before the Board. The chairman generally reached a decision following discussion between Board members.

Much concern existed on the Area Manpower Boards in Yorkshire and Humberside that the role of the Boards had been reduced to one of 'rubber-stamping YTS schemes'. This view was shared by a large number of trade union and employer representatives and was reflected in the submissions of some of the Boards in response to the MSC's document on the 'Review of Area Manpower Boards'.

The Board recognises the contribution made by Members to the successful launch and development of YTS and the Community Programme. However, it is concerned that it is often a rubber-stamping body lending local respectability to MSC programmes. This view is reinforced by recent policy decisions affecting local programmes and services which are made without consultation with AMBs or after hurried, superficial consultations. (South Yorkshire AMB 1985: 1)

This was supported by one of the chairmen (an employer) in the region: 'Eighty per cent of our time is spent just approving schemes (YTS and Community Programme). The bigger issues, such as unemployment in the region, are missed.' Dismay was also expressed at the lack of control which AMBs were able to exert over schemes approved by the Large Companies Unit. This view, shared by trade unionists and employers alike, was perhaps best expressed by one of the region's senior MSC officials in a particularly frank statement:

There are lots of problems with the LCU [Large Companies Unit]. It's politically motivated. It was originally set up by Ministers who made contact with major companies. Some, such as Marks and

Spencers and Sainsbury's are very good. Others, especially small and diverse chains, have long and bad lines of communication. They often don't know what they are supposed to be doing. The LCU presents many headaches as their schemes do not match local schemes. Of the thirteen 'below standard' monitoring reports we had last month, nine were LCU schemes which failed to meet standards.

The Area Manpower Boards can do nothing as the LCU is run by London region with its own programme teams. My staff can only assess them. LCU schemes shelter behind this fact. The CBI likes the LCU as they don't look too closely. Politically there is no question of it being abolished.

A number of respondents felt that the small business sector was being neglected by the Manpower Services Commission, even though it was providing the majority of placements in the Yorkshire and Humberside region. Most of the firms providing placements were members of the local chambers of commerce rather than the CBI and a number of suggestions were made to allow the chambers some representation on the Area Manpower Boards. As part of its submission to the 'Review of Area Manpower Boards', the South Yorkshire AMB suggested that consideration be given to: 'within the 5 employer places inviting representatives from Chambers of Commerce and/or Chambers of Trade whose members are very much involved with providing work placements on YTS' (South Yorkshire AMB 1985: 1). A similar recommendation was submitted by regional TUC to TUC headquarters recommending virtually the same changes.

Some of the issues we have described above point to a strong sense of regional identity which seemed common to all five Boards in the Yorkshire and Humberside region and which had undoubtedly assisted in breaking down the traditional divisions between capital and labour. This allowed a consensus style of politics to be adopted by the Area Manpower Boards as employers and employees strove to find some solutions to the socio-economic difficulties facing the region. At the same time, a perception existed that their efforts were being hampered through insufficient consultation and a severe lack of executive functions—a view increasingly supported by the regional MSC officials serving the region.

Earlier in this paper we illustrated how the Youth Task Group's original proposals for the Area Manpower Boards were subsequently diluted by the MSC, notwithstanding the recommendations and submissions from various employers' associations and trade unions. In practice, the Area Manpower Boards found themselves restricted, not only in terms of the absence of executive functions, but also in terms of the consultative functions which they had been granted.

REFERENCES

CBI (1982), *CBI Education and Training Bulletin*, 12/2 (London, June).

Electrical and Electronic Manufacturers Training & Education Board (1982), *Discussion Document* (London: EETEB, 23 July).

Ford Motor Company (1982), Letter of 23 August 1982 (to the Secretary of the MSC).

MSC (1982a), *Youth Task Group Report* (London: HMSO, Apr.).

—— (1982b), *Consultative Paper on the Future of MSC Local Advisory Machinery* (London: HMSO, May).

—— (1982c), *Guide to the Work of the Area Manpower Boards* (London: HMSO).

NUT (1983), *Schools, the MSC and the YTS: A Union Guide* (London: NUT, May).

RANDALL, COLIN (1985), *The Trade Union Movement and the MSC* (Bristol: University of Bristol).

South Yorkshire AMB (1985), *Review of Area Manpower Boards* (Submission, 29 Mar.).

TUC (1982), *Circular* (London: TUC, 9 Dec.).

9. Tripartite Industrial Training Systems: A Comparative Study

Andrew Erridge and Michael Connolly

THIS chapter explores the networks for the design and implementation of policy on industrial training in three sectors, engineering, catering, and textiles, and in three countries, Northern Ireland, the Republic of Ireland, and the Netherlands. The focus will be on the nature of the relationships between the participants in the networks, including government departments, training agencies, employer and employee organizations, and educational interests. Various theorizations of such relationships will be drawn upon to provide a framework for analysing the networks. Each country will then be analysed in turn, the objective being to identify the extent to which recent developments in the area of vocational training and, within that, industrial training have been designed and implemented via tripartite bodies. This analysis will then lead to conclusions about the relative degree of meso-corporatism in each country, with any differences between sectors in this regard also being identified.

This reflects a shifting of the focus of study in the literature of corporatism away from overall national economic policy to the study of individual sectors. Following Wassenberg's (1982) distinction between 'macro, meso and micro' levels of analysis, Cawson (1985*a*) uses meso-corporatism to refer to individual sectors of the economy or trans-sectoral policy areas, of which industrial training is a good example. While research has produced little evidence of corporatism at the macro-level in Britain (Marsh and Grant 1977) the meso-level has proved more fruitful, and may assist in the establishment of corporatism from the 'bottom up' rather than the 'top down':

Corporatist arrangements do flourish in favourable circumstances at the meso level, and such arrangements may be able to make a greater contribution in the longer run to the task of evolving industrial adjustment policies which undertake the difficult but necessary task of promoting change and winning the support or at least the acquiescence of those affected. (Grant 1985: 11)

There has also been work at the regional and local level (Cawson 1985*b*; Simmie 1985), to which this chapter seeks to make a modest contribution in respect of Northern Ireland.

A major problem in empirical work on meso-corporatism is the difficulty of its definition and differentiation from other models such as pluralism. In this respect, the following definition of corporatism is helpful:

a process of interest intermediation which involves the negotiation of policy between state agencies and interest organisations arising from the division of labour in society, where the policy agreements are implemented through the collaboration of the interest organisations and their willingness and ability to secure the compliance of their members. The elements of negotiation and implementation are both essential to my understanding of corporatism. (Grant 1985: 4–5)

Thus there is a two-way process of interaction between interest organizations and state agencies, as well as between interest organizations and their membership: 'the operation of putatively representative organisations as intermediaries regulating their own membership and sharing in political authority by delegation' (Social Science Research Council 1981: 4). The reciprocal relationship between state and interest organizations distinguishes corporatism from pluralism: 'To my knowledge nowhere in the literature on interest groups written from a pluralist standpoint is stressed the reciprocity of the relationship between interest groups and the state' (Cawson 1985*a*: 9). A number of other points of contrast are frequently made. For example, Crouch stresses the importance of the interest organizations' intermediating role, their ability to discipline their members and represent their particular interests (Crouch 1983: 456–7). Cawson also identifies 'the process of closure (rather than competition) which can lead to monopoly interest representation'.

The relationship between tripartism and corporatism is one which has received much attention, and is very relevant in relation to industrial training. Marsh and Grant's (1977) four characteristics of 'tripartism' are almost synonymous with corporatism: three parties (TUC, CBI, and government) evolve commonly agreed policies; discussions are underpinned by consensus; élite leaders are able to ensure compliance by members; and all parties have similar degrees of influence. It is not therefore surprising with such demanding criteria that their analysis of macro-level industrial policy between 1962 and 1976 results in the conclusion that actual examples of 'tripartism' are few. A similar conclusion is reached using the same criteria in respect of the introduction of new technology (Richardson 1982).

In summarizing the above discussion, we will first distinguish between tripartite structures and the processes of interaction between participants. Structural elements incorporate the idea of a limited number of participants ('closure'), which is also a feature of tripartism. Key elements of corporatist processes identified above are:

1. close links between government and organized interests ('sharing in political authority');
2. the relationship between organized interests and their membership ('regulation'). The latter may be widened to embrace the relationship between organized interests and the 'clients' of the service being delivered, raising questions about the representatives of the organizations concerned, as well as the degree of compliance they are able to deliver. However, where the membership is not a substantial proportion of the clientele, that in itself may be indicative of a low level of corporatism;
3. the idea of 'consensus'. This has two elements: that of consensus between all parties identified by Marsh and Grant, but also the extent to which there is consensus between the organized interests themselves. The greater the degree of consensus between organized interests, the less opportunity for government to manage the network through 'divide and rule' tactics.

This may be an important variable, and our empirical analysis will lead us to speculate as to the relationship between the above variables, particularly whether there is a positive or negative relationship between the degree of influence of organized interests in their dealings with government and their ability both to achieve consensus amongst themselves and to regulate their membership.

Thus our framework is as follows:

1. Structures: the participants in the network and the bodies through which they interact and industrial training is delivered;
2. Processes: (*a*) the extent to which organized interests have a share in political authority through their influence on government policy on industrial training; (*b*) the ability of organized interests to represent and to regulate a substantial proportion of the clientele of industrial training; (*c*) the degree of consensus achieved between government and organized interests on the one hand, and between those interests themselves on the other.

Using this framework, we will attempt to determine the role of representatives of organized interests in the delivery of industrial training in each country, and particularly whether that role has been altered by recent developments such as changes in the nature of the apprenticeship and measures to combat youth unemployment.

NETHERLANDS

Structures

The lead government department for vocational training is Education and Science, which also has overall responsibility for all schools, whether general or vocational, public or private. The department's role is largely one of supervision and inspection rather than intervention. It does however approve apprenticeship programmes and regulate the general content of vocational training, whether it takes place in schools or in-company. In recent years the Minister of Social and Employment Affairs has developed an important role in relation to measures to counter unemployment which is impinging upon Education's dominant role.

The main employers' organizations are the KNOV (Royal Netherlands Organization for Entrepreneurs) for retailers and service industry mainly, and the VNO (Federation of Netherlands Industry) for manufacturing and large firms. The major employee organizations are the FNV (Netherlands Trade Union Federation), comprising socialist and Catholic unions, and the

CNV (Christian Trade Union Federation) for Protestant unions. Representatives of these organizations, together with smaller employer and employee bodies, meet together regularly in a number of national consultative committees. These include the Social-Economic Council (SER), which is consulted by government on most economic and social policy issues, the Foundation for Labour (SVA), which negotiates guidelines for wages and conditions of service at national level, and educational committees where policy on the school element of industrial training is largely determined.

As vocational schools provide the foundation for industrial training, and 44 per cent of secondary pupils are taught in such schools (Central Bureau of Statistics 1985), industry has objected for a number of years at its virtual exclusion from educational policy-making, which has largely been determined within a closed circle of religious and secular educational organizations which run the schools. It is only since 1985, following the reports of a Commission set up to look at the role of education in preparing young people for working life (Wagner Commission 1984), that employer and employee interests have gained seats on important educational policy committees, although they are still in a substantial minority.

At the sectoral level, supervision of industrial training is the responsibility of thirty-one sectoral training boards, which are private foundations covering over 400 occupations. They have a responsibility to promote training of apprentices and advise industry on the retraining of adults. The boards may also provide courses in specific skills, to retrain adult workers, or in management. Boards are consulted by firms on training problems and make recommendations on the organization, content, and supervision of courses. The boards are delegated under the Apprenticeship Law of 1968 to perform the following tasks: to compile complete practical programmes for apprentices; to set examinations; to assist in drawing up apprenticeship contracts; to ensure that the employer and the apprentice comply with the contract. Among the sectoral boards are those for hotel and catering (SVH), textiles (Betex), mechanical engineering (SOM), and electrical engineering (VEV).

Under the Apprenticeship Law, boards are composed of representatives of employers and employees, parent and educational organizations, although their other activities may be conducted under boards with differing composition according to the task performed. While there is no explicit government representation, the Department of Education must approve curricula and examination procedures. Employer representatives are nominated mainly by the KNOV and VNO from the major associations within each sector. Similarly most employee members are nominated by the FNV and CNV from major unions within each sector. Educational members are nominated by the GSB, which represents the heads and senior teachers of regional schools (BBOs), which provide the theoretical component of apprenticeship training. The GSB, together with the sectoral boards, is responsible for compiling the 'total programmes' or curricula for each of the apprenticeship programmes provided by the boards.

The boards established COLO, the Central Association of Training Boards, as a co-ordinating body, as a means of disseminating best practice amongst boards, and to provide a more focused means of bringing pressure to bear on government. The board consists of three employer and three employee representatives from national associations; two employer and two employee representatives from any section; and five school directors elected from any section. There is also a General Assembly which meets twice a year, with thirty-one representatives, one from each board.

In respect of apprenticeship training all the boards' expenses are met by the Ministry of Education, with the number of training staff employed directly related to the number of apprentices trained. Employers may also receive a subsidy of up to £2,000 from the Department of Social and Employment Affairs in respect of first-year apprentices taken on under the BVJ (Contribution Measure for Youth) scheme, which must be dispensed by fund committees comprising employers and employees. Most of the BVJ funds are channelled through existing training boards, though often by a separate committee, in order to exclude educationalists. In the engineering sector, however, more complex arrangements apply for channelling BVJ funds to industry, with the SOM having only a limited role for reasons discussed below.

Process

1. We have seen above that representatives of organized interests are closely associated with the development of policy on social and economic matters through national committees such as SER and SVA, although we also noted the imbalance in influence between educationalists and industry representatives on educational consultative committees. In respect of sectoral boards, organized interests have delegated authority to supervise apprentice contracts, compile curricula, and administer examinations leading to nationally recognized qualifications. Thus there is certainly a priori evidence of sharing in political authority through processes of consultation at national level and delegation of design and implementation of apprenticeship programmes at sectoral level.

Recent policy initiatives reinforce this view. Following the Wagner Commission's recommendations, and pressure from the sectoral boards via COLO, as well as employer and employee interests, apprenticeship training has been strengthened in recent years. While numbers of apprentices (excluding agriculture) declined from 76,000 in 1980 to 65,000 in 1984, they have since increased to 70,000 in 1985. The outcome of the Open Consultation process (Open Overleg Wagner) following the Wagner Reports is an agreement to double the annual intake of apprenticeships (COLO 1985), with a consequent increase in government funding. The upper age limit for apprentices, which used to be 27, has been removed. While employers are less happy with these developments than educationalists, as they are expected to find placements and ultimately jobs for the additional apprentices, it does suggest considerable commitment by government to the sectoral boards, and points to a willingness to share political authority with organized interests within the industrial training network.

This impression is reinforced when we consider the importance of apprenticeship training within the Dutch economy. Apprenticeships are central to industry's employment practices. They are based upon detailed modular programmes drawn up by training boards covering all of the thirty-one sectors, with examinations and recognized qualifications at each stage. This applies as much for chefs and waiters as it does for engineering apprentices. Apprenticeships are backed by legislation which places a legal requirement on employers to pay the apprentice a minimum wage, and both the practical and theoretical training is closely monitored by training board staff (the dual labour and training contract). Training programmes are flexible and cover a range of skills. For instance in the textiles industry there are a hundred modules from which apprentices can choose either a specialized or general training. Employment practices are geared towards taking on apprentice-trained staff and the incidence of substitution of untrained people or people with only limited training is low.

2. The membership of employer and employee organizations at both national and sectoral levels suggests that they may reasonably claim to represent a substantial proportion of the clientele of industrial training. The VNO has about 90 member associations representing over 9,000 companies, the majority of which are large companies employing more than 100 people. KNOV has about 10,000 individual small and medium-size company members employing about 600,000 people. This is out of a total working population of 5.3 million. These associations nominate most representatives to national committees and sectoral boards.

In respect of the latter, the largest employer association is the FME (Association of Mechanical and Electrical Industries), with a membership of some 1,000 companies employing 295,000 employees or 85 per cent of the engineering work-force. The FME provides members for several sectoral boards, including SOM (mechanical engineering) and VEV (electrical engineering). The main employer organizations in the hotel and catering sector are Horecanederland and Horecaf. Member firms of Horecaf are mainly large hotels, accounting for 25 per cent of turnover and 46.4 per cent of the labour force in the sector. Horecanederland has a membership of about 7,000 companies mainly comprising smaller hotels and restaurants. Between them they represent well over half the sector in terms of the work-force, and they, together with organizations representing fast-food restaurants and leisure companies, provide the employer members of the SVH, or hotel and catering training board. Similarly on the textiles board, Betex, most companies are represented through one of four employer organizations which meet in a co-ordinating body, Fenetextiel.

On the employee side, the FNV has about 950,000 members

and the CNV 300,000. The FNV is composed of eighteen affiliated unions, of which the largest are the civil servants union (Abvakabo) and the industrial sector union (Industriebond FNV), with 250,000 members each. Union membership varies from sector to sector, and is higher in engineering and textiles than in hotel and catering, where only a sixth of the work-force is unionized. Overall about a quarter of the total work-force are members of unions. The Industriebond FNV provides members for fifteen sectoral boards, including SOM, Betex, and VEV, and covers most craft workers, providing a good opportunity for co-ordination. The Protestant union, Industriebond CNV, provides a smaller number of members for these boards. In addition, Abvakabo provides members of the VEV. The main unions in hotel and catering are Horecabond FNV and Voedingsbond, representing between them about 16,660 employees. While in general unions are less representative of the work-force than employer associations, there is a higher level of membership amongst apprentice-trained staff, and there has been no challenge to the rights of unions to represent the work-force on sectoral training boards.

Co-ordination and regulation of employee and employer members are facilitated by a number of features. The national federations of employer and employee associations employ Education Secretaries, whose role is to co-ordinate policy on education and training matters. They attend national consultative committees, are members of COLO, and keep in regular contact with board members nominated by them. Employer members of SOM and VEV meet before board meetings under the auspices of the FME, and the Education Secretary and regional staff visit firms to identify views and give advice on training matters. Textiles employers meet up to six times a year in Fenetextiel to discuss wages and conditions of service, including training policy. The FNV has a co-ordinating group for apprenticeship training which meets four times a year, and includes officials from constituent unions who are members of training boards.

In respect of apprenticeships, representatives of employer and employee organizations have a regulatory role in that the training boards are responsible for monitoring the operation of the apprenticeship contract, and where a firm or apprentice is found not to be honouring the contract, the appropriate organization may take steps to resolve the problem. Firms not following the agreed policies of employer associations on training matters may be expelled if they refuse to toe the line. In general, therefore, though there is limited evidence of actual cases of disciplinary action against member companies, the degree of co-ordination and consultation within employer and employee associations suggests that the criterion of regulation is at least partially fulfilled.

Educational representatives are nominated by the GSB, the body representing executive boards of schools in the apprenticeship system. Members are expected to present a common view on policy issues.

3. While the degree of consensus between government and organized interests is not as great in the 1980s as it was up to the early 1970s (Peper and van Kooten 1984), there is still a high degree of common ground and any differences between government and organized interests are largely mediated through the national level committees mentioned above. However, differences exist within and between the organized interests themselves which perhaps challenge the impression of meso-corporatism sketched out above. Principal amongst these is the antagonism between educational and industrial interests mentioned above. At sectoral boards and on COLO, training staff generally ally with school interests to maximize the number of apprentices in order to qualify for more staff and government funding. Employers feel they have insufficient influence to match the contribution they are expected to make in terms of paying for placements and jobs. Employee organizations have to a certain extent supported employers in the engineering sector, where FME and Industriebond FNV have agreed to end the dual training and labour contract, and provide only training facilities and no guarantee of a job at the end of the apprenticeship. This has also led to a lower rate of pay for trainees than under the official apprenticeship system, which has also been accepted by unions. In doing so Industriebond have broken with the national policy of the FNV. However as FME and Industriebond FNV are respectively the largest employer and employee bodies, this development could presage a major change.

The agreement between FME and Industriebond FNV has also adversely affected SOM, the training board for the mechanical engineering sector. 70 per cent of the BVJ funds for this sector are passed on to industry through a central fund committee to regional committees, both of which are controlled by the employer and employee representatives. This is in order to neutralize the influence of educationalists on the training board and also to avoid the bureaucratic procedures of the SOM (Akkermans, van Dijk, and Hovels 1986). FME policy is to establish a series of regional training centres to develop the industry's training capacity independently of the schools. Thus there are two competing industrial training systems in engineering.

A further threat to the boards' monopoly of apprenticeship training comes from educationalists in the form of the KMBO (Short Middle Vocational Education). This was proposed by one of the major educational organizations, the ABB, which represents school boards of secular schools within the educational system, including most vocational schools. The KMBO was seen as a means of providing training for young people who were unable to obtain employment or an apprenticeship upon leaving school, and is almost completely school-based. Both industry and training boards are concerned that KMBO certificates will be seen as an alternative to the apprenticeship, even though there is only a limited provision for work experience. The outcome of the Open Consultation following the Wagner Reports has been inconclusive, with proposals to strengthen both the apprenticeship system and the KMBO, and a planned entry of 15,000 to KMBO courses. Though the apprenticeship system still predominates, the difficulty in finding agreement on a coherent system of industry training for young people is indicative of the divergent interest of industry and educationalists.

Summary

While in general the industrial training network in the Netherlands does exhibit elements of the meso-corporatist model outlined above, the evidence of lack of consensus amongst participants must pose questions about the likelihood of the system continuing as it is currently operating. Government clearly sees benefits in delegating industrial training to private foundations, and there is no evidence of a desire to exploit

divisions between organized interests. There is perhaps encouragement to move industry towards accepting training-only
as opposed to training-and-labour contracts, in order to
increase the number of places available for young (and older)
people who are unemployed. Thus the balance of influence
between organized interests may be shifting somewhat, with
boards losing their monopoly of apprentice training and industry
taking on a more direct involvement, but the overall shape of the
network remains meso-corporatist.

The evidence of conflict between organized interests demonstrated above may also have lessons in terms of the importance
of this variable. Where the principle of sharing in political
authority is accepted by government, and organized interests are
able to ensure that the service is delivered satisfactorily, and to
regulate their membership to that end, the need for consensus
between organized groups may not be as great as where the
network has to defend itself against a centralizing government
keen to manage the network, or even bypass it.

REPUBLIC OF IRELAND

Structures

The Department of Labour has overall responsibility for
manpower policy. Executive authority is delegated to an
executive agency. Until recently, this was An Comhairle Oiliuna
(AnCo), the Industrial Training Authority established under an
Act of 1967. Following a government White Paper AnCo was
merged with other manpower agencies to form FAS (Foras
Aiseanna Saothar, the Training and Employment Authority) in
January 1988. This discussion focuses mainly on the period
immediately before the reorganization.

The main decision-making body is the Council, which is
responsible to the Department for the planning and implementation of industrial training in general. In-company training
activities are the responsibility of Industrial Training Committees
(ITCs) covering seven sectors, including engineering and
textiles, which are currently under review. The ITCs are purely
advisory to the Council. ITCs supervise and monitor in-
company training, either apprenticeship or shorter courses, and

provide some training directly through a network of training centres, mainly for first-year apprentices, the majority of whom spend the first year off the job.

FAS is also responsible for implementing measures aimed at combating unemployment. Before the reorganization there was not a great deal of interaction between the Training Advisory (responsible for in-company training and the ITCs) and External Services Divisions of AnCo, and it remains to be seen whether there is any improvement following the recent changes. Currently FAS is pursuing a regionalization process which should result in better co-ordination at the regional level.

There are two complementary national employer associations with overlapping membership. The Confederation of Irish Industry (CII) is concerned with policy matters and is comprised mainly of employer associations. The Federated Union of Employers (FUE) is the employers' union, and negotiates wages and conditions of service on behalf of the individual companies which make up its membership. Before the reorganization, the CII and the FUE nominated two members jointly to the AnCo Council and equal numbers to each ITC from constituent companies or associations. In addition, major sectoral employer associations nominated a further three members to the Council. The national employee association is the Irish Congress of Trade Unions (ICTU), which nominated five members to the Council as well as all the union members of ITCs. Employer and employee representation on the FAS Council has been reduced to four each out of fourteen members, as opposed to five each out of fourteen previously. Thus both the Council and ITCs are composed of equal numbers of representatives of employers and employees, with a small number of educationalists and representatives of government appointed by the Department of Labour.

In addition to FAS there are a number of important national bodies in the economic sphere of which employer and employee associations are members. Principal among these is the National Economic and Social Council (NESC), which like the Dutch Social-Economic Council is consulted on most important economic and social issues. Other tripartite bodies are the National Prices Commission, the National Enterprise Agency, Sectoral Development and Consultative Committees, and Manpower Consultative Committees. Thus tripartite structures are a prominent feature of the Republic's economic policy processes.

Funding of ITCs is by a levy/grant system under which companies whose training programme rates sufficiently high to meet certain criteria are exempt from paying up to 90 per cent of the levy, the remaining 10 per cent going to pay the administrative costs of ITCs. Levy income in 1988 was Ir£21m. Additional sums in the form of Domestic Industry and New Industry Grants were channelled through AnCo's Training Advisory Service to companies by the Industrial Development Agency (IDA). In 1985 these amounted to Ir£11.5m. and Ir£20m. respectively, up to 55 per cent of which was provided by the European Social Fund. However, the ITCs tended not to be involved in the allocation of these grants, limiting themselves to deciding on the allocation of the funds remaining after remission of the levy.

A separate body, the Council for Education, Recruitment and Training (CERT), is responsible for training in the hotel and catering industry. It was established by the industry in 1963, though it was soon adopted by the Department of Labour as an executive agency. Its membership consists of employers and a lesser number of educationalists, representatives of unions, the Departments of Labour and Education, Bord Failte (Tourist Board), and, recently, some political appointees. Employer and employee members are nominated by the main employer associations and unions in the sector. CERT performs a somewhat wider role than ITCs, and, unlike them, is the final decision-making body for training in the sector. In the 1986 White Paper, it was proposed that CERT form part of the new training agency, but following vigorous lobbying by the industry, and a change of government in March 1987, it retained its separate identity. Ironically, its former administrative head became the Chief Executive of FAS.

CERT is funded mainly by the Department of Labour, with 55 per cent from the European Social Fund. In addition hoteliers pay a small registration fee to Bord Failte which goes to CERT. There is some pressure on employers currently to contribute more to training to place them on an equal footing with employers in manufacturing industry.

It is too soon to assess whether the new structure introduced in January 1988 will prove more effective than their predecessors.

In examining processes below we will examine the reasons why reform was considered necessary.

Processes

1. The above description of industrial training structures suggests that representatives of employers and employees have a major influence on policy and its implementation. The importance of these structures has been enhanced in recent years, with increasing amounts of money being channelled through AnCo and other tripartite bodies. In real terms, expenditure on all areas of training has grown rapidly in the 1980s, though the increase was most marked in AnCo's Training Centres, used mainly for first-year apprentices and courses for the young unemployed. In 1986 a reduction in ESF funding led to a parallel fall in AnCo's expenditure reflecting the Republic's dependence on this source (see Fig. 9.1).

The main focus of AnCo's expenditure was on short-term, mainly socially orientated programmes, first-year apprentices, and redundant post-first-year apprentices. In respect of the latter groups, AnCo was clearly substituting for employers' unwillingness to take on a sufficient number of apprentices. Numbers of first-year apprentices in 1985 were 3,453, lower than the 1979 level of 4,218, while 35,294 non-apprentices received training, 5,567 of whom were on community-based programmes.

The above figures illustrate the importance of industrial training in terms of public expenditure, and a willingness to delegate its execution to tripartite bodies. Nevertheless, a recent report by the NESC identified problems of co-ordination and confusion over responsibility for the policy function between the Department of Labour and the executive agencies:

When overall policy direction does not emanate from the sponsoring department it is inevitable that the executive agencies take on the policy function by default. However, since executive agencies are only interested in their own sphere of activities there is a danger that policy becomes unbalanced. Another consequence of a lack of policy direction is a lack of coherence in the executive area. (NESC 1985: 17–18)

The report recommended that the department take a stronger role, and that: 'all the existing agencies be reconstituted into one

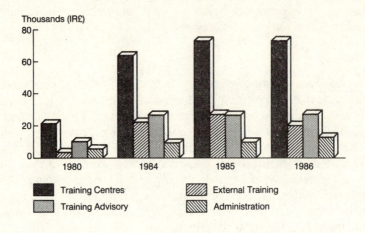

Thousands (IR£)

Training Centres | External Training
Training Advisory | Administration

	AnCo Expenditure IR£million			
	1980	1984	1985	1986
Training Centres	21.4	63.6	72.8	72.9
External Training	3.6	22.2	26.9	20.2
Training Advisory	10.3	26.7	26.4	27.0
Administration	5.8	9.3	9.9	12.8

Source: Public Expenditure Estimates

FIG. 9.1. *Republic of Ireland: AnCo expenditure (Ir£000)*

executive body—a State Manpower Agency—and that all policy activities previously exercised by these bodies be taken over by the Department of Labour' (NESC 1985: 278). The White Paper endorsed these recommendations, proposing to amalgamate AnCo, CERT, the National Manpower Service, and the Youth Employment Agency into a new tripartite National Manpower Authority, and to strengthen the Department of Labour's policy and co-ordinating role.

A further area of criticism relates to the apprenticeship system. A New Apprenticeship System was launched in 1976 involving standard curricula and a system of testing and certification. Although some of its elements have been introduced, the NESC Report commented that: 'its implementation is far from complete and is unlikely to be completed for some time yet ... revisions to this form of training will be out of date before they are completed' (NESC 1985: 109). This applies in particular to the curricula covering thirty apprenticeships which have been drawn up over a number of years by committees of educationalists and representatives of both sides of industry. The NESC Report is critical of employers, trade unions, and educational authorities for their inability to see beyond 'the pressures and exigencies of the current situation', and calls for them to adopt a longer-term perspective. The White Paper criticizes the current system as costly, inflexible, and inefficient, but refrains from direct criticism of employers and employees. It calls on the new agency to develop a system based on standards rather than time served, to ensure a balance between supply and demand, and to reduce the cost to the state while maintaining quality (Department of Labour 1986: 30).

Financial mechanisms are also under scrutiny. There is widespread dissatisfaction amongst employers with the levy/grant system, which they regard as generating a considerable amount of paperwork in relation to the relatively small funds involved. The NESC Report argued that it had outlived its initial usefulness in encouraging companies to invest in training, and recommended a new system integrating the various forms of state funding, including the Domestic and New Industry Grants. However, the White Paper proposes to keep the levy/grant system, while targeting all training funds more selectively by means of company development plans and identifying key skills areas, a process in which FAS will take the lead.

While the above developments indicate that industrial training is in a state of flux in the Republic, the role of organized interests in executive bodies is to be retained, despite the criticism of them outlined above. Political channels in the Republic are fairly open to both employers and unions regardless of the political party in power. Representatives of these interests use political contacts to persuade ministers and officials to take account of their views. The representative of a major employer association put this point very succinctly: 'we can change the detail of policy through the boards, but we can change the policy itself through political channels.' In respect of industrial training, government has been reluctant to force organized interests to accept radical changes of policy which would threaten their interests, as has happened in the United Kingdom. The search for accommodation through consultation and delegation to organized interests has resulted in a failure to take positive steps to meet the training needs of industry.

2. The national employer associations, the FUE and CII, have an overlapping membership of over 3,500 companies employing 250,000 people, or about 50 per cent of the private sector work-force. In engineering membership is nearer to 60 per cent in terms of numbers of employees. Important sectoral federations are the Society of the Irish Motor Industry, the Engineering Industry Association, and the Construction Industry Federation. Most employer representatives to the AnCo Council and sectoral ITCs were nominated by these bodies. The main associations represented on CERT are the Irish Hotels Federation, with a membership of 450 out of 650 hotels, but 80 per cent of beds, the Restaurants Association of Ireland, and the Vintners Federation of Ireland. Coverage of bars and restaurants is less extensive than for hotels, and urban establishments are better represented than rural.

Seventy-two trade unions accounting for over 90 per cent of trade union membership in Ireland are affiliated to the Irish Congress of Trade Unions (ICTU). ICTU nominates members directly to the Council and from constituent unions to ITCs. The largest single union is the Irish Transport and General Workers' (ITGWU) with 150,000 members or 12 per cent of the work-force, but 80 per cent in textiles and 60 per cent in engineering. ITGWU nominates both union members of CERT, eight out of ten members of the Textile ITC (the others are from the Federated Workers' Union of Ireland), and one member of the Engineering ITC. Other general unions, the FWUI and the Amalgamated Transport and General Workers' Union (ATGWU), provide a further two members, and the other seven members are from craft unions.

There is some evidence of tension between general and craft unions in the engineering sector, in that the former have expanded at the latter's expense in recent years as the number of trained craftsmen in the industry has fallen, and many of those who remain have joined the stronger general unions. Of the craft unions, the sheet metal workers (NUSMWI) and National Engineering and Electrical Trades Unions (NEETU) have lost members to the general unions and the Electrical Trades Union

(ETU), while many technicians have joined TASS. The ability of the smaller craft unions to represent their members is also limited by a lack of full-time officials, unlike the richer general unions. However, each union is allocated one place on the Engineering ITC rather than membership determining numbers of seats. As the general unions tend to be more progressive on changing work practices, the continuing high level of representation of some craft unions is a block on changes necessary to introduce more flexible working practices and multi-craft apprenticeships.

There is little evidence that employer or employee associations are able, or willing, to regulate their membership. Any co-ordination of employer members is informal, though the FUE would call meetings of employer members or circulate members when new or controversial issues arose. Sectoral associations appear to be more active in monitoring employer members. Members representing the Engineering Industry Association report back to their Council every two months, and Irish Hotels Federation nominees on CERT put forward policy agreed by its Manpower Committee. There are few sanctions any employer organization can impose on employers who exploit trainees, short of expulsion, and there were no examples of such action. However, a leading officer of one employer association said that in cases of repeated exploitation of trainees the Department of Labour would be informed, and the employer would no longer be able to take on trainees.

Union members are co-ordinated to an even lesser degree. The only issue on which ICTU called members together was over the length of time an apprentice should serve. Although members generally follow Congress policy, they are at liberty to pursue their own policies. Members may report back to their union branches, but there is no organized mechanism for ensuring that the membership is consulted or informed about developments.

There are however areas where employers have statutory responsibilities. Companies within a designation covered by an ITC are legally bound to pay the levy or seek exemption once the enabling Order has come into force. They must also complete standard forms in order to qualify for exemption or grants. Apprenticeships are generally subject to tighter legal controls than other forms of training, but the NESC report commented: 'even in the case of statutory apprenticeships, some of the codes and regulations are little more than voluntary guidelines and there has been a rather indifferent attitude in regard to their implementation' (NESC 1985: 107). In any case, policing of these obligations is not a matter for the organized interests, but for the Department of Labour.

Educational members of ITCs are Inspectors of Education and act as a link between the formal education system and AnCo training activities. They work closely with AnCo staff on the certification of apprentices, testing the school and Training Centre elements respectively. They are also involved with representatives of the other interests in drawing up the detailed curricula for apprenticeships under the overall direction of the Apprenticeship Curriculum Advisory Committee. Their role is to identify proposals which would have an impact on the educational system, to avoid overlap and duplication, and to act as channels of communication. However, they do not formally represent the school system or Vocational Education Committees (VECs), which manage vocational schools and colleges.

There is a member of the Irish Vocational Education Association (IVEA) on the Council of CERT, mainly because much of the training carried out in the hotel and catering sector takes place in catering colleges such as the Dublin College of Catering. All thirty-eight Vocational Education Committees are affiliated to the IVEA. Their representative on CERT is a former Chairman of Dublin VEC, and a member of the IVEA Council. He is not expected to canvass views nor to report back, nor are VECs required to follow IVEA policies.

3. The above discussion does suggest that industrial training in the Republic is underpinned by a considerable degree of consensus between government and organized interests. Politicians have been reluctant to disturb the generally co-operative relations with employers and unions by hastening the changes agreed in the New Apprenticeship Scheme. Possible conflict over funding has until very recently been avoided by the availability of European Social Fund money.

Differences between employers and unions on industrial training policy are not substantial. ITCs have developed a high degree of cohesion through their regular meetings, and employer and union representatives share a mutual respect. The only issue to have divided employers and unions is the attempt by the

Engineering ITC to abolish the levy/grant system, a proposal of which most employers were in favour. However the attempt was blocked when it came to the AnCo Council. Some imbalance of influence is apparent on CERT, and in the hotel and catering sector in general, reflected in the fact that there are only two union members as opposed to five employers on the Council. However, this may also be a reflection of the relatively low level of unionization in the sector, and any conflict arising from this imbalance is not apparent.

Potential for conflict exists between the formal education system and FAS over the extensive network of Regional Training Centres, which provide both apprentice and shorter training courses. The formal education system has been criticized for an emphasis on general as opposed to vocational orientated education, even in vocational schools. There are also a substantial number of early school-leavers who have no formal qualifications, and are consequently the main target group for social training programmes. Training centres are increasingly providing work experience and vocational training to remedy the perceived deficiencies of the educational system. The White Paper concluded that the primary responsibility for initial preparation of young people for work should lie with the Department of Education. This is another area where future change may bring potential conflict into the open, if either the education system or training bodies perceive themselves as losing control of their respective territories.

In this respect the influence of the professional training staff is paramount. Training managers are the driving force behind ITCs, and members largely respond to their initiatives. Before reorganization AnCo employed 2,080 staff in either administrative, research, or training capacities, having expanded rapidly in line with the scale of its activities. A significant reduction in staffing is however anticipated as a result of the reorganization. Some members of ITCs complained of the difficulty of obtaining detailed information from Training Managers, although on a personal and professional level they and their staff are respected for their energy and commitment. However, there have been cases of resolutions critical of ITC staff being altered before they reached the AnCo Council. Part-time members cannot hope to have the same degree of influence on the detail of training programmes as permanent officials, and the potential for an unaccountable bureaucracy to develop is thereby enhanced.

Summary

While overt conflict is not a feature of the industrial training network in the Republic, the consensus which is based upon organized interests having a major share of policy formulation as well as implementation through tripartite bodies has not effected the changes which were presaged as long ago as 1976 in the New Apprenticeship System. Short-term measures funded by the ESF have acted as a palliative while skill shortages have been allowed to increase. There is therefore evidence of meso-corporatism in the Republic, more so in the extent to which organized interests share in political authority and in the somewhat defensive consensus against radical change, than in the degree to which organized interests regulate their membership.

However, challenges to the status quo are emerging in the need for new sources of funds, in the move away from narrow craft apprentices reflected in the growth of general unions, and in the development of new skills in electronics and electrical engineering, where much of the training is carried out in institutions of higher education. Perhaps the strongest incentive for change is in the current severe economic problems facing the Republic, which may lead the government to challenge organized interests for the sake of economic recovery.

NORTHERN IRELAND

Structures

Since 1972 Northern Ireland has been subject to direct rule from Westminster, so that the scope for policy initiative is limited (Rose 1982). Policy tends to emanate from Whitehall, and in the area of vocational training the broad outline of structures and programmes reflect that in Britain in most important respects. This centralization constrains the degree of regional co-ordination, as specific policy initiatives tend to be related to Whitehall developments rather than to the attempt to construct a coherent policy for the province. However, different administrative structures operate in the province compared with the rest of the United Kingdom. Neither the Manpower Services Commission nor its successor, the Training Agency, covered Northern Ireland. Instead, overall responsibility for manpower policy, and within that vocational training, lies with the Department of Economic Development (DED), one of six Northern Ireland government departments.

Just as government departments in Northern Ireland are subordinate to Whitehall, organized interests of employers and employees are affiliated to national bodies. The main employers' body is the Confederation of British Industry through its regional office (CBI-NI). Policy is largely dictated by Head Office in London, though there is room for unofficial nuances on specific issues. Membership of CBI-NI comprises both individual firms and trade associations, such as the NI Engineering Employers' Association. A similar, though more complex, situation pertains for employee organizations. The main body is the Northern Ireland Committee of the Irish Congress of Trade Unions (NIC-ICTU), to which are affiliated major British unions, such as the Amalgamated Engineering Union (AEU), as well as Irish unions. In both cases unions may be constrained by national-level decisions, such as on the introduction of standards-based apprenticeships. Thus engineering unions, as well as employers, would be expected to abide by an agreement on apprenticeships reached between the Confederation of Shipbuilding and Engineering Unions (CSEU) and the Engineering Employers' Federation at UK national level. This clearly constrains the negotiation of agreements at regional level within the province. Furthermore, it demonstrates a difficulty of studying relations between government and organized interests at the regional or local level, in that participants are rarely free to come to an accommodation in the interests of the region or locality, which without the constraint of national policy they may be willing and able to do.

There are currently two elements to the industrial training structure in the province, namely the Northern Ireland Training Authority (NITA) and eight Industrial Training Boards (ITBs), including those for the hotel and catering, engineering, and textiles sectors. NITA provides administrative support for the boards, employs professional staff to provide training in sectors not covered by a board and, with the agreement of the boards, for training across sectors. It also has a particular responsibility for training in new technology and training techniques. The Authority is composed of a chairman appointed by the minister, the chairmen of the eight ITBs, three members with educational expertise, and one member from the Department of Finance and Personnel.

ITBs currently operate under arrangements which emerged from a review conducted in 1982 (Department of Manpower Services 1982). The impetus for this came from a similar review of ITBs in Britain, which emphasized the principle of voluntarism and led to a drastic reduction in the number of ITBs (Manpower Services Commission 1981). The outcome of the Northern Ireland review was different, with eight of the nine ITBs surviving, both because of the small number of firms in the province with a tradition of industrial training and because the boards were viewed favourably by participants, including the majority of employers.

The boards are responsible for training within specified sectors, and are composed of equal numbers of employer and employee representatives (nominated respectively by CBI-NI and NIC-ICTU), a small number of educationalists, and an independent chairman. In addition there are assessors from the DED and the Department of Education. ITBs are responsible for apprentice training and also sponsor a range of shorter skills, supervisory, and management courses either in-company, in Government Training Centres (GTCs), or in further education colleges.

Funding is by a levy/grant system, with firms paying a percentage of payroll to the board and those with training programmes satisfying certain criteria receiving remission of up to 85 per cent of levy. In addition firms may receive grants for certain kinds of training. Firms with payroll amounting to less than a specified minimum amount are exempt from the levy. Levy income in 1985/6 was £5.57m. supplemented by grants from the DED and the European Social Fund, as well as charges, to give an overall expenditure of £9.2m.

The Manpower Council is the consultative body which was set up in 1982 to advise the DED on manpower policy generally. It is composed of 5 representatives of employer and employee interests, nominated by CBI-NI and NIC-ICTU respectively, plus 5 independent members (educationalists and commercial trainers) and assessors from DED and the Department of Education (DENI). The Council has established 7 local manpower committees to oversee the implementation of the YTP, amongst other things, which the department only recognized in 1985, having operated through 13 local liaison committees previously.

These structures are currently under review. DED produced a consultative paper in April 1988 identifying problems of fragmentation, lack of co-ordination or leadership, lack of information about skill shortages, lack of training on new technology or using new training techniques, and a lack of cost-effectiveness (DED 1988). DED proposes a new single training authority embracing the training functions and responsibilities of DED, NITA, and the ITBs. Its status, whether an agency within government or outside, is left open. The department also proposes to examine the effectiveness of the levy system and alternatives to it. The following discussion illustrates some of the reasons why such a reform is thought necessary.

Processes

1. One measure of the extent to which organized interests have a share in political authority in this area is the relative importance of measures to combat youth unemployment, mainly the Youth Training Programme (YTP), and the training carried out by the ITBs. Whereas ITBs are tripartite bodies with executive functions similar to ITCs in the Republic, YTP schemes are designed and implemented largely in isolation from representatives of organized interests.

The pattern of expenditure over the years reflects a change of emphasis away from industrial training sponsored by ITBs towards measures to combat youth unemployment (see Fig. 9.2). In effect, total spending on YTP is much larger than the figures indicate, as a considerable proportion of expenditure on Government Training Centres (GTC) and other training or employment-creating schemes is accounted for by YTP trainees. GTCs are managed directly by the DED, and the short-term training they provide as part of the YTP now counts towards the apprenticeship, although members of ITBs are not convinced of its merits: 'The Board was not convinced that this was a satisfactory alternative to its first year off-the-job training programme, which had been used to train engineering apprentices

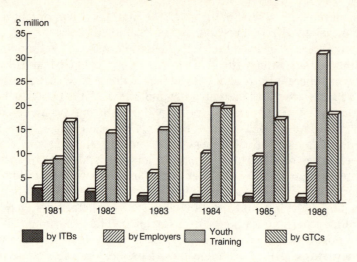

	Expenditure on Training (NI) £million					
	1981/2	1982/3	1983/4	1984/5	1985/6	1986/7
Youth Training	8.9	14.3	15.0	20.0	24.2	31.0
by GTCs	16.7	19.8	19.8	19.5	17.2	18.3
by Employers	8.0	6.8	6.1	10.2	9.6	7.6
by ITBs	2.9	2.2	1.3	1.0	1.3	1.3

Source: Appropriation Accounts 1981/2 to 1986/7

FIG. 9.2. *Northern Ireland: expenditure on training*

for many years, with appropriate amendments to suit changing circumstances' (Engineering ITB 1984: 6). By contrast, a significant change in financial arrangements regarding the ITBs occurred in 1982, in that administrative costs previously paid by the DED became the responsibility of the boards themselves. This decision prompted the following comment from the Engineering ITB: 'The Board still considers that this is an unwarranted, additional burden at a time when the industry is facing considerable financial pressure due to the continuing economic recession' (Engineering ITB 1984: 11). The grant from the DED to the Engineering ITB fell from £373,000 in 1981/2 to £210,000 in 1984/5, and reflected a move towards a more directive approach by supporting specific training programmes. These changes forced a reappraisal by boards of their activities, and led to a variety of cost-cutting and revenue-raising activities, such as making training staff redundant, increasing charges, or reducing the rate of remission. These developments contrast with the increased resources channelled through tripartite bodies in both the Netherlands and the Republic of Ireland. Ironically, one of the reasons cited by the Department for reviewing the funding of the ITBs is that: 'The income of some Boards severely limits their ability to respond to training needs' (DED 1988: 7).

A significant difference between the YTS in Britain and the YTP in Northern Ireland is the relatively limited involvement of employers in providing full-time training places. This is due mainly to the weak industrial structure in Northern Ireland and the limited number of large firms, and has led to an emphasis on training courses provided by community workshops and the network of GTCs, as well as courses provided in further education colleges. Although these courses do include periods of work experience, there is much less involvement of industry in a leadership role than in Britain, where: 'the aim of providing 70 per cent of trainee places within industry makes the scheme dependent to a degree on the compliance of both industrial capital and the trade unions, who still have the sectoral power to threaten the delivery of trans-sectoral policies' (Vickerstaff 1985: 63). This is less true of the YTP, and has consequences in terms of the ability of employers and unions to influence the nature of training programmes in general.

The involvement of organized interests in the planning and implementation of training programmes varies according to the provider. College courses have limited input from organizations representing employers and unions although individual employers or union officials may be asked to join an advisory board. Formal responsibility for approving college courses lies with the Department of Education's Inspectorate. Similarly, courses offered by the GTCs are designed by their own qualified staff, and approved at senior management level within the department's GTC division. Again there is no direct involvement of organizations representing employers and unions, although the content of apprentice-related courses is approved by the appropriate ITB. Employer-based schemes may be discussed within the collective bargaining machinery of individual firms in order to obtain the co-operation of union members, but depending on the degree of unionization even the absence of co-operation would not prevent the implementation of a training scheme.

There is more direct involvement by organized interests in relation to courses provided by the forty-four community workshops. These are run by management committees made up of representatives of community groups and may include union officials or local employers. However even here there are no formal links between such people as individuals and employer or employee associations at regional level.

While the Manpower Council has a formal consultative role in relation to the planning of places on the YTP, plans are only submitted at a late stage in the process after the DED has integrated plans from the various providers. Many members feel that the Council carries little weight, and its recommendations are unlikely to change departmental policy in any important respects. One union member gave a very negative view of the DED's attitude to the Council:

DED tends to ignore the views of the Council and resents any outside suggestions or objections regarding YTP. Disagreements on the Council are mainly due to differences of opinion between DED and the other members. Even where employer and union representatives agree—as with their proposal to scrap the Young Workers' Scheme—DED resists.

This feeling was echoed by an employer member, who described the attitude of officials on occasion as arrogant, and saw a danger in the 'political gap' in Northern Ireland—the absence of an effective elected body with executive powers—leading to civil servants feeling they run the system. He added: 'The DED was embarrassed at the setting up of the Manpower Council as it is outside their direct control. There was a proposal to set up GTC local committees to replace local manpower committees, but employers and employees co-operate well so there is no need to abolish them.'

Even in respect of the ITBs, members were concerned at the absence of a real say in policy-making. In respect of the review of the ITBs, one employer member of the Engineering ITB said: 'There was little discussion allowed on the consultative paper, and although there were critical responses it was rubber-stamped.' There is evidence then to suggest that the DED does not allow peak organizations a major say in the design and implementation of vocational training policy, merely a limited implementation role in respect of the ITBs. There is however some indication in the current proposals of a desire for a more co-operative approach, with the board of the new agency promised 'an effective say in its activities' (DED 1988: 10).

2. Nominations for board members are sought from major unions via NIC-ICTU in respect of employees and from major trade associations via CBI-NI in respect of employers. Firms representing about 70 per cent of the work-force in manufacturing, and about 30 per cent in service industries, are affiliated to CBI-NI. Union membership again varies according to sector, being higher in engineering and textiles than in hotel and catering.

Union nominations to the Engineering ITB are co-ordinated by the Confederation of Shipbuilding and Engineering Unions (CSEU), though once they are appointed there is no formal co-ordination of members. Those represented are the Amalgamated Engineering Union (AEU), General Municipal and Boilermakers (GMBATU), Transport and General (ATGWU), and TASS, the craft technicians' and supervisors' union. Though there are no electricians' representatives on the main board, a member of EETPU, the electricians' and plumbers' union, is on the Training and Development Committee. All the union members of the Textiles ITB are provided by the ATGWU. They also provide three members of the Catering ITB; in addition there are members from GMBATU, the Irish TGWU, and the Union of Shop, Distributive and Allied Workers (USDAW). Most of these unions do represent a reasonable proportion of workers in each sector, although there is one case of a union still being represented on a board despite its membership having shrunk to double figures. There is little attempt by board members to canvass the union membership's views on training matters, and board members tend to be reactive rather than proactive. There is also little attempt by NIC-ICTU to co-ordinate the various unions' policies or board members' positions before board meetings. Thus the representational role on the employee side seems fairly limited.

As for employers, sectoral trade associations, such as the Hotel and Caterers' Association, the Central Council of the

Irish Linen and Cotton Industry, and the Engineering Employers' Federation, are reasonably representative of firms in their respective sectors. Associations do seek to identify the views of member firms to a greater extent than unions. Employers in the hotel and catering and textiles sectors were consulted extensively on proposals to increase the levy following the DED decision to ask boards to pay their own operating costs. Attendance is generally higher than that of union members. Co-ordination by CBI-NI is limited to canvassing members' views on major issues such as the review of ITBs. Clearly the employers have more at stake than the unions in that they bear a major part of the cost of the boards' activities, and the evidence is that the main associations do represent and promote their member firms' views.

Even where organized interests can be said to represent their members, achievement of policy objectives is still dependent upon the ability of representatives to ensure that the membership supports their decisions and carries them into effect. Employees' participation in training programmes is entirely voluntary, and board members' approval of a training programme does not imply that places will be taken up. Conversely, on certain issues board members may discourage participation in programmes. One example is the introduction of courses in food preparation for bar staff, which unions regard as asking their members to perform two jobs without extra pay, and clearly linked to separate negotiations on wages. Another example is the GTC apprentice course, although here the objection is to it counting as part of the apprenticeship rather than to the course itself. Delivery of co-operation by union members is therefore not guaranteed and is dependent on the issue involved.

Similarly, employer associations have no internal mechanism for ensuring that training places will be taken up. However, in respect of matters concerning the levy or its remission, employer members' decisions, if approved by the DED, are enforced by statute, and employer associations are expected to canvass member firms to ensure their support. Firms are therefore legally bound to participate to the extent of paying the levy or seeking exemption. The premiss of the levy system and indeed the tripartite structure of boards is clearly that board members' decisions will receive the support of those they are supposed to represent. Nevertheless, provisions which allow firms to appeal to an industrial tribunal where either exemption from levy or full remission are not granted, and even to apply to have a board wound up (in the 1984 Industrial Training Order), point to a lack of confidence on the part of government in employer associations' ability to 'deliver'.

The ability of organized interests to regulate their membership is perhaps even less in respect of the YTP. One YTP scheme, Younghelp, was boycotted on the insistence of union members of the Manpower Council because they felt it was being used by some employers to exploit trainees. However, there is always a problem in getting all unions to follow a common line, and Younghelp still operates, with about 240 places in 1985/6. A leading engineering union official explained that the six-month GTC course would only be accepted as part of the apprenticeship if the difference in pay between the trainee allowance and the apprenticeship rate was made up retrospectively by employers, although he accepted that in practice this line was not always being followed.

The ability of NIC-ICTU or CBI-NI to deliver the co-operation or ensure the non-compliance of their membership is therefore limited, and partly explains their lack of influence. A leading ICTU official said: 'Attitudes to YTP vary from place to place in relation to both personality and interests. If YTP damages overtime or young people are paid low wages then a scheme may be blacked. However there is a problem in getting all unions to go along with a common line.' Union influence may also be limited in that many trainees are in sectors which are not highly unionized and, even where the unions are strong, may not wish to join. The same official also said: 'The CBI does not appear to be very well co-ordinated with employers, who do not necessarily follow "official" policy lines.' The voluntaristic nature of employer associations and the inability of CBI to ensure the support of members is well documented in respect of Britain (Grant and Marsh 1975). Individual unions or employer associations play a more active role in identifying cases of exploitation of trainees, but the sanctions they could impose are limited.

3. An important element in the ability of organized interests to influence government is the extent to which the different parties are able to agree common positions. We have seen that on the issue of the retention of ITBs participants were able to

agree a common position, with a favourable outcome. Consensus is aided on ITBs by close personal contacts between board members, not only on ITB business, but also through regular contact in the workplace. Other factors include the commonly perceived threat of economic recession, the small number of participants in the network, and the geographical isolation of the province. Thus union members would be reluctant to press hard for large increases in expenditure on training by employers, although both employers and unions do of course unite on arguing for public expenditure to be made available. Consensus is reinforced by what many members feel to be the negative response of government: 'The Manpower Council is still hampered by what one NIC representative described, very accurately, as the obstructionist tactics of the Department [DED] and their unwillingness to enter into genuine consultation' (NIC-ICTU 1986: 41).

Departmental assessors on ITBs act as channels of communication, explaining departmental policy initiatives and the details of grant eligibility. However, almost all board members interviewed felt that this was very much a one-way process of communication. The following comment is typical: 'DED is a typical government department, there is no way to change their views. The civil servant member abides by the rules. This inhibits the assessor's role—he. agrees that you are right but cannot do anything about it' (union member, Engineering ITB). However, the consensus between employer and employee members of the industrial training network has not resulted in a corresponding enhancement of their role in policy-making or implementation.

Summary

There is therefore little evidence of meso-corporatism in the vocational training network in Northern Ireland. In respect of the YTP, organized interests play a role limited to consultation through NIC-ICTU, CBI-NI, and the Manpower Council, although individual employers or union members may be involved to a greater extent in the running of schemes. While the tripartite structure of ITBs may give rise to expectations of a more influential role for organized interests, the evidence suggests that this is not the case in respect of their role *vis-à-vis* either their members or government. We have seen that DED is regarded by representatives of interest groups as directive and unresponsive, and crucial decisions which set the agenda for the network as a whole are clearly not negotiable. One explanation for this may be the Northern Ireland administration's subordinate constitutional position.

In Northern Ireland, as in the United Kingdom generally, the constraints on public expenditure and priority given to combating youth unemployment have led to the deregulation and financial restriction of industrial training at a time of increasing skill shortages, as new technology changes the nature and range of skills required. While high youth unemployment has led to a long-overdue attempt to resolve the impasse over craft apprenticeships and the role of the education system in preparing young people for working life, this has largely been imposed on uncooperative groups which had previously been able to obstruct change. The combination of centrally directed policies and a constitutionally subordinate administration in the province is a severe constraint on the development of consensus between NI departments and organized interests in the province to the detriment of the design and implementation of effective vocational and industrial training policies for the province.

CONCLUSIONS

Our examination of industrial training in three countries indicates substantial variations. While there is evidence of meso-corporatism in the Netherlands and the Republic of Ireland, the former has resulted in more positive outcomes. Northern Ireland is characterized by centralized policy-making and a limited role for representatives of organized interests.

If we consider the elements of the meso-corporatist framework, we find a different relationship between the variables in each country, illustrated in Table 9.1.

The incidence of tripartite structures in the more meso-corporatist systems is higher than in Northern Ireland, and organized interests have a greater share in political authority. However the other variables show a less consistent pattern. Organized interests' ability to represent and regulate their membership is nowhere high, though greater in the Netherlands

Table 9.1. Meso-corporatism in the Netherlands, Republic of Ireland, and Northern Ireland

	Tripartite structures	Political authority	Processes: representation/ regulation	Consensus
Netherlands	High	High	Medium	Medium
Republic of Ireland	High	High	Low	High
Northern Ireland	Medium	Low	Low	High

than in the other systems. Employer and employee organizations are better co-ordinated, and it provides the only example of the organization of educational interests. In the Republic, it appears that organized interests have a share in political authority almost by default, while in Northern Ireland the weakness of organized interests has been exploited by government to force through policies and programmes which they are unable to resist.

Consensus between organized interests is paradoxically high in Northern Ireland, born of the difficult political and economic situation in the province, and based on a strong regional identity. This may be generated as much by resentment at the lack of real consultation as by any positive agreement on policies for industrial training. There is however a substantive consensus on the need for more real skills training, with the skills content of YTP not highly regarded, and on the view that parity with schemes operating in Britain is not appropriate. This relates in particular to rates of pay for trainees, and to the need for a higher level of skills training, as there is a lower level of skills available in the province than in Britain. There is also resentment at the way that developments in youth training have bypassed tripartite ITBs, with members believing they could contribute far more to the diagnosis and remedy of industrial training failings were they given the opportunity. Thus there are elements of positive consensus, which has not resulted in a share in political authority.

Consensus is also relatively high in the Republic of Ireland, corresponding to the evidence of meso-corporatism there. However, we have identified major differences between organized interests in the Netherlands, which revolve around the role of educationalists and industry in training young people for work. Government is attempting through the Open Consultation following the Wagner Reports to resolve these differences, and is clearly committed to a continuing delegation of industrial training to organized interests. However there is no dispute there about the nature of the apprenticeship system, as there is in the Republic of Ireland and Northern Ireland. Here traditional time-serving is slowly being replaced by standards-based apprenticeships, with unions fighting a rearguard action to wrest concessions in return for changing work practices. In the United Kingdom, government is trying to force through such changes, often by policies to which both sides of industry object, while in the Republic government has so far allowed organized interests to reach a slow accommodation. Thus the high degree of consensus has led in neither country to an effective industrial training system, nor in Northern Ireland to a share in political authority.

Were we to require as evidence of meso-corporatism a high rating on all four criteria, it is unlikely that many policy areas in Western societies would qualify. On the other hand, arguing that a system may be meso-corporatist while not satisfying all the criteria may weaken the concept. We could argue on the above evidence that some criteria are more important than others, such as the existence of tripartite structures and sharing in political authority. However, as mentioned in the introduction, most writers on corporatism also require the regulation criterion, and consensus either underpins or is a product of corporatist arrangements.

Attempts to theorize about political models such as pluralism and corporatism do however suffer from a major drawback in respect of the difficulty of empirically determining whether the criteria which theoretically constitute the model actually are present. In respect of the criteria selected here, evidence is highly subjective. Nevertheless, were agreement at least possible on the criteria, then successive research projects might result in a more accepted and accurate assessment of the conditions which satisfy their fulfilment. This chapter represents a modest step, however faltering, in that direction.

REFERENCES

AKKERMANS, M., VAN DIJK, C., and HOVELS, B. (1986), *Neo-Corporatism and Vocational Education in the Netherlands* (Interim Report for the European Centre for the Development of Vocational Training, Berlin).

CAWSON, A. (ed.) (1985*a*), *Organised Interests and the State: Studies in Meso-Corporatism* (Beverly Hills, London: Sage).

—— (1985*b*), 'Corporatism and Local Politics', in Grant 1985: 126–47.

Central Bureau of Statistics (1985), *Education Statistics* (The Hague).

COLO (1985), *Perspective on the Work Programme of COLO 1985–1987* (The Hague).

CROUCH, C. (1983), 'Pluralism and the New Corporatism: A Rejoinder', *Political Studies*, 31: 452–60.

Department of Economic Development (1988), *The Organisation of Training in Northern Ireland* (Belfast).

Department of Labour (1986), *Manpower Policy* (Dublin).

Department of Manpower Services (1982), *Training for the Future: Proposals for the Industrial Training Boards and the Northern Ireland Training Executive* (Belfast).

Engineering Industry Training Board (1984), *Annual Report 1982–3* (Belfast).

GRANT, W. (ed.) (1985), *The Political Economy of Corporatism* (London: Macmillan).

—— and MARSH, D. (1975), 'The Politics of the CBI: 1974 and After', *Government and Opposition*, 10/1: 90–104.

Manpower Services Commission (1981), *A Framework for the Future: A Sector by Sector Review of Industrial and Commercial Training*.

MARSH, D., and GRANT, W. (1977), 'Tripartism: Reality or Myth?', *Government and Opposition*, 12/2: 194–211.

National Economic and Social Council (1985), *Manpower Policy in Ireland* (Dublin).

Northern Ireland Committee of the Irish Congress of Trade Unions (1986), *Annual Report 1985–86* (Belfast).

PEPER, B., and VAN KOOTEN, G. (1984), 'The Netherlands: From an Ordered Harmonic to a Bargaining Relationship', in S. Barkin (ed.), *Worker Militancy and its Consequences* (New York: Praeger).

RICHARDSON, J. J. (1982), 'Tripartism and the New Technology', *Policy and Politics*, 10/3: 343–61.

ROSE, R. (1982), *Understanding the United Kingdom: The Territorial Dimension in Government* (London: Longman).

SAUNDERS, P. (1985), 'Corporatism and Urban Service Provision', in Grant 1985: 148–73.

SIMMIE, J. (1985), 'Corporatism and Planning', in Grant 1985: 174–201.

Social Science Research Council (1981), *Final Report of the Corporatism and Accountability Research Panel*.

VICKERSTAFF, S. (1985), 'Industrial Training in Britain: The Dilemmas of a Neo-corporatist Policy', in Cawson 1985*a*: 45–64.

Wagner Commission (1984), *Education and Youth* (The Hague).

WASSENBERG, A. F. P. (1982), 'Neo-Corporatism and the Quest for Control', in G. Lehmbruch and P. C. Schmitter (eds.), *Patterns of Corporatist Policy-Making* (London: Sage): 83–108.

10. Cleavage and Concertation: The Limits of a Corporatist Analysis of the Scottish Political Economy

Chris Moore and Simon Booth

THE most significant development within corporatist theory since the rebirth of neo-corporatism in the 1970s has been a move away from grand systems theory (Schmitter and Lehmbruch 1979) towards analysis of constituent elements of the political economy (Cawson 1982, 1986). This has involved an examination of relationships between interest organizations and state agencies at the level of policy sectors and regional space. Our research set out to assess the interaction between these two intermediate levels of sector and space within the Scottish political economy, to see how far corporatist relationships existed at the sub-system level within a region of the UK with a unique set of institutional relationships and identity.

The chapter begins by briefly emphasizing the importance of a differentiated analysis of the modern political economy. We then set out some distinctive elements of the Scottish pattern of politics. Then a critical examination of competing major conceptualizations of Scotland as a political arena is made, arguing that none of them satisfactorily adopts a sufficiently complex and differentiated model which can explain developments in key sectors. Three critical elements which we suggest make Scotland distinctive within the UK polity are then outlined. We go on to identify ways in which the significance of these elements can be measured in a manner which could provide the basis for future comparative research.

The way in which empirical testing of these factors can be achieved is outlined by a brief examination of key policy issues within the Scottish economy. The key question is how far the economic decline and structural transition of the Scottish economy has forced cross-class and status group alliances to defend or promote a 'Scottish interest'. We examine this by highlighting the fate of two major collective campaigns in the recent past—the Ravenscraig steel campaign and the Scottish economic summit. This enables us to see how far sectional interests identify with regional space in conflict with their wider UK group or class loyalties. In contrast, we also look at strategic economic development by analysing the scope of a distinctive institutional arrangement in the form of the Scottish Development Agency to act with other interests to shape the regeneration of the Scottish economy.

In conclusion, we argue that the corporatist analysis is at best a partial explanation for the distinctive pattern of the Scottish political economy. However, the combination of territorial and sectoral dynamics can provide a means for generating distinctive Scottish policy outcomes which are not found in England. There are relatively autonomous areas for interest bargaining and negotiation with the Scottish Office and its satellite agencies. In the light of a third victory for the Thatcher Conservative Party the room for manœuvre at the Scottish level may be further limited but it has not disappeared. The poor electoral performance of the Conservatives in Scotland in 1987 raised questions about legitimacy and accountability of the state. Paradoxically, the strength of Conservatism at the UK level and its weakness in Scotland may create opportunities for bargaining in order to maintain political and social stability. Or it may lead central government to dismiss the claims of Scotland for different treatment. Indeed, Scotland may become a laboratory for increased Thatcherite experiments: for example it was the first part of the UK to implement the community charge. There is thus the potential for significant weakening of Scottish autonomy as much as for institutions for its defence. The outcome will depend significantly on the play of political forces and degree of consensus which can be generated at the Scottish level to preserve institutions of relative autonomy such as the Scottish Development Agency (SDA).

Why is sector significant in neo-corporatist theory? Firstly, corporatist theory cannot be satisfactorily applied at the systems level without becoming too abstract and generalized to provide a meaningful mode of analysis of the modern political economy. Secondly, relationships within the political economy between organized interests and the public sector occur not simply at peak national levels. Indeed, at these levels corporatist arrangements may be largely symbolic. Key decisions and resolution of conflict occur at a sector level. Bargains can be struck around common interests while the peak level becomes an arena for playing out class and group conflicts (Wassenberg 1982). Thirdly, the sector level of bargaining and decision-making may allow for agreement to be reached on necessary changes and transition because it is removed from the peak level of symbolic conflict (Grant 1985). On the other hand, it may allow for opportunities for sectional interests to come together to defend their interest at a sector level against the centre. Fourthly, a sector-based analysis allows for examination of the key policy arenas, especially in the economy, at the level where most decisions are made and implemented, that is at the level of industrial sectors and enterprises (Young and Lowe 1974).

Our research has analysed relationships at the meso-level of the UK political economy in terms of sector and space. While the overwhelming focus of the meso-corporatist model has been on sectoral differentiation, the significance of territory has been ignored in the past. Though accepting that the UK is a relatively highly centralized political state, we would agree with Rose, who has argued that it is not territorially uniform (Rose 1982). The comparative regional dimension is an important arena of study for a meso-level analysis. Its significance will vary with the degree of territorial identity, the strength of the institutional network, and the set of distinctive and relatively autonomous interests within the region. Undoubtedly, within the UK, Scotland provides a unique testing ground for an analysis of the importance of spatial politics given the combination of a separate political institutional network with a degree of decision-making autonomy and resources to implement policies; a strong socio-cultural identity with an undercurrent of nationalism; and a distinctive associative order and pattern of interest representation.

At the same time the significance of this spatial dynamic is uneven. We would simply be repeating the mistakes of the earlier neo-corporatist writers if we argued that Scotland represented the 'most corporatist part of the UK': firstly, because it would elevate the concept of corporatism into a distinctive political system; secondly, it would over-emphasize the autonomy of the Scottish political interest. It is much more accurate to argue in terms of a differentiated analysis which identifies different interests and relationships across policy sectors. The spatial dynamic can then be placed within this wider context.

HOW DISTINCTIVE IS SCOTLAND?

Scotland is different from the English regions in its patterns of government and decision-making. These differences are reflected in, and maintained by, three factors: a sense of national *identity*; a set of relatively autonomous *institutions*; and a pattern of *interest* representation and intermediation. It is important to emphasize that these factors do not mean that Scotland constitutes a separate political system, as some writers have tried to argue (Kellas 1983). At the same time these arrangements amount to more than an administrative sub-system controlled from the centre. The autonomy of decision-making is relative. It changes over time and with issues. This is why a dynamic and sufficiently differentiated analysis is essential to understanding the political process in Scotland.

The standard works on Scottish politics put forward inadequate conceptualizations which have limited explanatory value. There are three main models which need to be considered.

Kellas (1983) argues that the combination of distinctive national identity, institutions, socio-cultural patterns, and political behaviour make Scotland a *system*. But he then goes on to say that this is subordinate to the wider British political system. The argument is at best ambiguous, given the acknowledged limitations on an independent Scottish decision-making process. This leads Kellas to retreat from a coherent use of the term 'system' so that it begins to lose its distinctive properties as a defining concept. He undermines the very concept he uses to describe politics in Scotland, and ultimately the 'system' he puts forward is no more than a different pattern of political communication and a subsidiary administrative mechanism.

Rose (1982) argues that the UK is a multinational state with a unitary system of government. Scotland is a sub-system because of the degree of political, social, and economic integration with the rest of the UK. Its politics largely reflect the class-based and national (UK) orientation of other parts of the UK, and its economy is increasingly dominated by non-Scottish-owned and -controlled enterprises. Rose thus argues that Scottish policy-making is essentially concerned with administrative discretion in the implementation of central policies. This model is in our view inaccurate because it plays down any significant room for manœuvre in policy-making at the Scottish level as well as ignoring the power of sectional interests in certain policy communities. It fails to appreciate the distinctive relationships and interests within Scotland which make it qualitatively different from English regions. Decision-making outcomes are a product *not* simply of administrative arrangements, but of relationships between actors and a sense of identity which sees a distinctive interest operating at the Scottish level. The emergence of certain issues at the Scottish level can generate alliances which cut across UK-defined group or class interests and mobilize the political institutional network to make demands on the centre, for example the Ravenscraig steel campaign. Rose recognizes the continued salience of a distinctive *cultural* identity but dismisses its potential impact on policy-making. He focuses on structural and institutional forms without analysing their interaction with *socio-cultural* forces.

Keating and Midwinter (1983) argue that Scotland cannot be meaningfully defined as a political system since ultimate political and economic decision-making power lies outside Scotland. However, they reject the notion of sub-system because they argue that there is scope for relative decision-making autonomy in different policy areas. They thus characterize government and decision-making in Scotland as a series of policy networks operating at, and linking, different spatial levels—Scotland, UK, and EEC. Scotland possesses a set of distinctive policy networks with different degrees of decision-making autonomy depending on several factors, including the formal distribution of administrative, financial, and political authority for a policy issue, the political salience of that issue in Scotland, and the existence and strength of the Scottish interest network.

This third model seems to us to be the most fruitful way forward in analysing the pattern of Scottish politics. It takes into account the need for a differentiated analysis of the political economy. It is able to accommodate different degrees of decision-making autonomy at different levels, thereby avoiding the static characterization and generalizations of the systems and sub-systems models. It offers a much richer presentation of the complex relationship between politics and power in Scotland. It analyses Scottish politics in terms of institutions and relationships in the policy-making process.

What Keating and Midwinter fail to do is follow the logic of their own analysis when applying this approach to individual policy areas. In particular, they fail to employ a differentiated analysis in their discussion of the Scottish economy. They suggest that the existence of any distinctive institutional arrangements of interest networks has little impact on economic policy outcomes. Undoubtedly, at the macro-level of policy decisions that is so. Decisions on fiscal and exchange rate policy, broad public expenditure trends, and monetary policy are UK-wide policies. However, there is a meso-level of economic sectors and a micro-level of individual enterprises which are subject to the influence of distinctive Scottish institutions and policies, or what Young and Hood have called the 'secondary tier of industrial policy' (Young and Hood 1984). At this level the influence of Scottish patterns of decision-making and relationships between the public and private sectors does vary significantly in how far there is scope for relative autonomy.

Keating and Midwinter also fail to go beyond a largely descriptive basis to offer *measures* of what influences the Scottish policy networks. Such measures or indicators of the strength of these factors would provide not only a basis for understanding the scope for decision-making autonomy at the Scottish level, but also a basis for comparison with other parts of the UK.

Critical variables

We set out three critical variables which make up the distinguishing features of Scottish politics—identity, institutions, and interests—in Table 10.1. We also suggest indicators by which the strength of these variables could be measured and methodologies for research into them.

Identity: this is a socio-cultural variable concerning the degree to which people within the territorial space identify with it. The most recent survey of Scottish identity found that 70 per cent of the sample defined themselves as Scottish rather than British (Moreno 1986). National identity has always retained a strong appeal in Scotland, though its political significance as measured

Table 10.1. A theoretical framework for measuring the importance of territory

Variable	Indicators	Methodology
Identity	1. Strength of identity. 2. Level of consensus over values. 3. Autonomous socio-cultural institutions. 4. Level of regional interest felt by population.	1. Mass survey. 2. Élite interviews. 3. Analysis of social and cultural development through historical and sociological data.
Institutions	1. Strength of political institutional networks. 2. Amount of delegated responsibility for policy-making. 3. Amount of resources that are solely at discretion of regional bodies.	1. Political institutional analysis. 2. Constitutional arrangements. 3. Accounts and budgetary data.
Interests	1. Strength of public/private interest group networks. 2. Degree to which regional interest is protected and articulated by network.	1. Mapping of interest group and organizational network. 2. Semi-structured interviews of associational leadership. 3. Organizational analysis of membership, resources, controls, and relationships with UK-wide organizations.

by electoral support for the Scottish Nationalist Party or devolution has varied considerably (Brand 1978; Miller 1981; Drucker and Brown 1980). At its peak, for example, the SNP secured a maximum of 30 per cent of the Scottish vote in October 1974. This has continually fallen so that by 1987 the

SNP could secure the support of only 14 per cent of the Scottish electorate. While the electoral support for independence is thus variable, the growth of anti-Conservatism was evident at the 1987 election, when the Conservative Party managed to secure only 10 out of the 72 Scottish seats.

What makes the sense of identity potentially something more significant than regional loyalties found in England is the underlying nationalism mediated through a range of socio-cultural and political institutions. These include separate religious, education, and legal systems, a distinctive mass media, and the political institutional arrangements.

The limits on such an identity derive from two other patterns of identity. The first is class, which has acted as a centralizing force in political and economic representation in the UK. The other is local community, where people identify with non-class reference points, including ethnic origin and neighbourhood. In Scotland there are elements of this division between the Highlands and Lowlands and the distinctive identity of the Orkneys and Shetlands, which surfaced as an issue during the devolution debate in the 1970s.

In summary, the sense of Scottish identity is something of a stunted animal. It is more than the sense of regional loyalty to be found in England, but it falls short of the political identity of small European nation-states such as Norway, with which Scotland has been compared (Maxwell 1987).

Institutions: the second variable concerns the distinctive set of political *institutions* in Scotland. These allow for the articulation of the sense of national identity. At the centre of the network is the Scottish Office, which is a multi-functional government department. In contrast, administration in English regions is characterized by peripheral fragmentation (Hogwood and Keating 1982). They lack the political coherence, identity, and access which the Scottish Office and Secretary of State provide. While the political administration in Scotland must reflect the ideology and strategy of the centre as part of a unionist political system it also represents to the centre the particular interests of Scotland. It is a mediating point between the centre and periphery.

The importance of the Scottish Office as an administrative and policy-making institution has been enhanced by successive UK governments, partly in response to perceived 'threats' of disintegration through nationalism. In significant policy areas, including the economy, the Scottish Office has enlarged its autonomy through assuming new responsibilities and the creation of specific public agencies accountable to the Secretary of State.

The influence and strength of the Scottish Office will vary depending on political and personal factors. But its role was exaggerated by Malcolm Rifkind who, before becoming Secretary of State, referred to the office as being 'more like a premier than a minister' and to the Scottish Office as a 'mini-government' (Rifkind 1982). However, its very existence does suggest possible alternative relationships with the rest of the UK. As Miller has argued:

As a means of preventing political devolution the build-up of the Scottish Office has proved to be a Danegold. It stimulates rather than satisfies the appetite for self-government. It has made Scots government at once more Scottish and less subject to parliamentary control. A political top tier to this administrative machine appears ever more credible and more necessary. Yet the irony is that it owes so much of its growth to the actions of Unionists. (Miller 1981: 10)

Interest: finally, there is the pattern of *interest* representation and intermediation. The importance of interest groups operating at the Scottish level varies with both group and issue. The continued force of class politics and sectional loyalties defined at the UK level remains strong particularly in the economic arena. Both organized labour and capital in Scotland have a regional dimension but remain wedded to national UK class politics and interests. This tendency is increased by the nature of the Scottish economy, which is open and dominated in significant sectors by external (English and multinational) capital. For example, of the CBI's 1,300 members based in Scotland in 1983, only 400 were indigenous enterprises (Keating and Midwinter 1983). In key sectors of the economy like engineering, dependency on overseas firms for employment rises to 40 per cent (Young 1984).

However, it would be a mistake to assume that identification with a 'Scottish interest' is non-existent. The crisis of the Scottish economy in the old declining sectors has generated cross-class or cross-sectional alliances which have stretched the loyalty of traditional UK-wide identities. There are different fractions of capital operating in Scotland with different interests and degrees of identity with Scotland.

First comes multinational capital, with particular strengths in growth sectors like electronics or oil. The degree of identification of this interest with Scotland is a product of how its Scottish operation fits in with its global corporate strategy. Past studies have highlighted the consequences of this conflict between global interest and the Scottish interest (Hood and Young 1982). Recently the case of the Caterpillar plant near Glasgow confirmed that even when the Scottish operation is in itself profitable, this does not necessarily guarantee its future if corporate decision-makers find that it is more profitable to switch investment (Haworth 1987).

Second, there is Scottish finance capital, which has a distinctive identity but is increasingly international in its outlook. The financial institutions based in Scotland possess a degree of autonomy from English institutions which has made Edinburgh the most important financial centre in the UK outside London. North Sea oil provided new opportunities for Scottish finance capital to invest in the Scottish economy. New merchant banks were established to cater for the increased demand for investment. Scotland remains a major centre for the management of pension funds (Scott and Hughes 1980). The interests of finance capital based in Scotland, however, have become increasingly internationalized, so that, while Scotland remains an important decision-making centre, the search for expansion and greater returns on investment has meant strategies of external investment. This strategy was clearly seen in the bids for the Royal Bank of Scotland referred to the Monopolies and Mergers Commission in 1982. The overwhelming evidence of Scottish interests, including the Scottish Office, SDA, and Scottish Council, argued that any take-over would threaten the decision-making autonomy of the Bank with adverse impacts on the Scottish economy. Ironically, the Board of the Royal Bank itself favoured a link-up with Standard Chartered in order to penetrate international markets (Monopolies and Mergers Commission 1982).

The importance of having a Scottish-controlled financial base was highlighted in the Commission's survey of Scottish firms. Of 50 leading companies based in Scotland, 44 used Scottish banks as their primary banker. This linkage between Scottish financial institutions and Scottish industry was analysed extensively by Scott and Hughes, who found historically a high level of interlocking directorships through the banks (Scott and Hughes 1980). However, they observed that this had declined as the Scottish economy had become internationalized. Analysis of trends in investment by Scottish banks confirms the growing importance of overseas investment as against loans and advances to Scottish industry. Between 1978 and 1983 total advances by Scottish banks increased by 226 per cent. However, advances to manufacturing industry grew by only 165 per cent, while overseas investment increased by 337 per cent (Scottish Office 1986).

Thirdly, there is indigenous capital represented by smaller and medium-sized firms. In some sectors, for example electronics, this indigenous sector may become increasingly dependent on multinational capital. In other sectors, for example the woollen industry, there may be a strong sense of Scottish identity because of the nature of the product and markets.

Turning to the other major interest block, that of labour, we find similar divisions between the Scottish interest and the wider UK interests. The Scottish Trades Union Congress is an autonomous representative organization of labour in Scotland but the majority of its member unions are UK unions. There are varying degrees of internal devolution to the Scottish level, but the primary policy-making arena is at the centre. However, this does not mean that tensions and divisions are absent. Certain issues can generate a Scottish labour interest and identity which strains centralized loyalties. The fight to preserve the Ravenscraig steel plant was an example. The main steel union, the Iron and Steel Trades Confederation, had to balance the interests of its Welsh and Scottish regions, especially as BSC management could play off one area against another by promoting investment and modernization in one site rather than another. The Ravenscraig campaign assumed a broader Scottish identity above sectional or class identities, bringing local and regional trade unions into alliance with sections of Scottish capital and business organizations.

Keating and Midwinter (1983) argue that relationships between the state, capital, and labour in Scotland are generally closer and more informal, with the capacity to generate consensus over a 'Scottish interest'. Cross-class institutions like the Scottish Council, where all major interest groups are represented, provide a forum for articulating a Scottish view on issues like regional economic development and the threat of external take-overs and mergers.

We have shown that there exists at the Scottish level a complex pattern of differentiated interests, institutions, and identity which in the past has been largely ignored by researchers who concentrate on the UK level. Having identified the three critical variables in the pattern of territorial politics, we need to test their significance by empirical analysis. There are two approaches to such empirical testing. Firstly, we can examine key issues which have generated cross-class alliances around the notion of a Scottish interest. Secondly, we can analyse the scope for distinctive policy-making in critical policy arenas. The following sections test the significance of the three variables using both these approaches: (1) by tracing the development of two major campaigns in the Scottish economy; (2) by analysing the ways in which the Scottish Development Agency as the primary instrument of public intervention in the Scottish economy has sought to influence the market in different economic sections.

The filtering of issues in the Scottish political process

What is the impact of Scottish institutions and interests in defending or promoting a distinctive Scottish consensus? Undoubtedly, the critical issue of the 1980s for Scotland is the strength of the regional economy. While government ministers have pointed to the rise of new sectors of economic activity, especially electronics and services, there is concern over the crisis faced by older industries.

A consensus between different interests within Scotland has developed to protect and regenerate manufacturing industry. There are two reasons why such a consensus around safeguarding the traditional manufacturing base should be strong. Firstly, the continued job loss in these sectors outweighs any gains in the 'sunrise' sectors. Between 1979 and 1985 Scotland lost 171,000 manufacturing jobs, or 28 per cent of the manufacturing employment base. In contrast, the service sector has grown by only 50,000 jobs (STUC 1986). Those sectors identified as being catalysts for job growth have in fact remained stable. For example, the electronics sector in 1985 employed only 4,400 more people than it did in 1978 despite the major influx of multinational investment (Young 1987).

The second reason is that manufacturing industry is seen as essential to an *integrated* modern industrial economy. While interests may acknowledge the growth of the service sector as the main source of employment, it is argued that this in itself is not enough to provide adequate jobs, wealth, or a balanced economic future. This was highlighted in submissions by Strathclyde Regional Council to the Scottish Select Committee on the Steel Industry in 1982, where analysis showed the knock-on effects on the rest of the regional economy of any decision to shut down Ravenscraig (Scottish Select Committee 1982). More generally the STUC, in developing its own economic strategy, has strongly emphasized the important contribution of the manufacturing base and rejected what it claims is the 'fallacy . . . that a country like Scotland can survive economically . . . by depending largely on service industries' (STUC 1986).

We can distinguish two kinds of reaction to these issues. First, an *ad hoc* single-issue approach which is essentially reactive and defensive. Scotland, like other industrially depressed regions of the UK, has generated a number of such campaigns to try to safeguard manufacturing industries and enterprises such as Upper Clyde Shipbuilders, Ravenscraig, and, most recently, Caterpillar. Secondly, there have been attempts to move beyond this limited approach to develop strategic anticipatory campaigns. The convening of a Scottish economic summit and the subsequent creation of a standing commission in 1986 illustrate this approach.

The analysis of issues in terms of their propensity to assume a Scottish interest in relation to the rest of the UK is a product of the degree of cross-class or group consensus within Scotland, and of the configuration of institutional forces with sufficient autonomy to translate agreement at the Scottish level into positive outcomes. We can locate the steel campaign and the economic summit within these two variables in order to show their capacity to generate concertation and use meso-corporatist institutional arrangements. Fig. 10.1 provides a general framework for analysing how these issues were filtered through the Scottish political process.

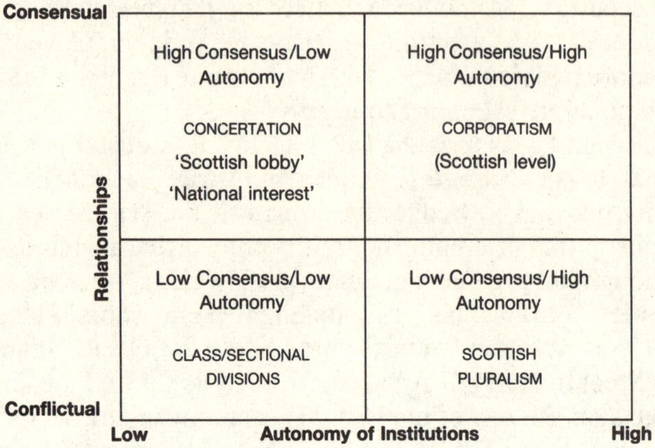

FIG 10.1. *Class, concertation, or corporatism: tracing the issues in the Scottish political economy*

The vertical axis measures the degree to which societal or sectoral relationships in the political economy can be characterized as conflictual or consensual. They will be conflictual where there is a high degree of class or group identification. In contrast, where there is agreement around a 'Scottish interest' in a particular sector, this will allow a high degree of consensus to develop.

The horizontal axis in the model represents the capacity for exerting political pressure and influencing outcomes through the institutional network. Concertation outside the formal institutional and political processes remains limited. It goes beyond pluralism in the sense that different interests unite around a collective interest rather than compete to maximize their own limited group interests, but it cannot be seen as corporatist unless this concertation is integrated into the decision-making institutions. Where there is a low level of integration, and where the institutions at the Scottish level *lack the capacity* for *autonomous decision-making* or bargaining, the possibilities for a distinctive corporatist relationship will be non-existent.

Single issue concertation: Ravenscraig

The threat to Ravenscraig by the British Steel Corporation in 1982 generated a high degree of consensus between different interests within Scotland. Evidence to the Select Committee by the Scottish Office, SDA, STUC, and local authorities was unambiguous in its support for the retention of an integrated steel operation. Only the CBI (Scotland) supported the overall strategy of the government in leaving the decision about the future of the plant to the commercial decisions of BSC management, and even then voiced concern over the political, social, and economic consequences of such a decision (Scottish Select Committee 1982). Strathclyde Regional Council was instrumental in bringing together various interests in the Standing Committee for the Defence of the Steel Industry, which included representatives from local government, trade unions, the Scottish Council, chambers of commerce, CBI, and Churches. This provided a co-ordinating forum for the campaign, widening out the commitment beyond the trade unions and labour movement. The Scottish Council argued in a series of policy statements for the retention of Ravenscraig as a fully integrated operation (Scottish Council 1982, 1985*a*, 1985*b*). Thus the Ravenscraig campaign began to move from an issue characterized by class and sectional divisions between the political and economic representation of capital and labour to a peak level (in Scottish terms) concertation.

An interesting aspect of the consensus in Scotland around the steel campaign was the division within the Conservative Party. Local Conservative MPs tended to support the case for Ravenscraig both in the Scottish Select Committee and outside Parliament. There were splits within the rank and file, with several prominent local activists resigning because they felt that the Conservative leadership in Scotland had not adequately pushed the case for Ravenscraig and was simply reflecting the government's policy. There was thus for some members of the Conservative Party in Scotland a growing crisis between their party political identity and a broader Scottish identity, and they felt that the Scottish interest was no longer best safeguarded through the Conservative political interest. In 1982, when the first threat to the future of Ravenscraig as an integrated steel plant was made by the BSC, the Scottish Office came firmly out in favour of the retention of the plant. George Younger, then Scottish Secretary, said in evidence to the Scottish Select Committee: 'If such a proposal [for closure] were to be made . . . as a matter of the highest priority all the energy that the Scottish Office could produce would be directed immediately to trying to prevent this happening at all' (Scottish Select Committee 1982: 26).

In 1985, when BSC decided to close the Gartcosh finishing plant which was part of the Ravenscraig complex, the Scottish Office changed its stance. In a public statement commenting on the decision, George Younger accepted BSC's case that there was no inherent linkage between the future of Gartcosh and the future of Ravenscraig (Scottish Office 1985). This went against the argument mounted by the Scottish Council and Steel Committee. What is significant is not the economic merits of the case but the fact that the Scottish Office had publicly accepted BSC's decision on this issue. This left the 'Scottish steel lobby' without any direct access to government. The campaign was reduced to trying to apply high-profile publicity as a form of pressure, a sign of its weakness in being excluded from the decision-making process. In the absence of an independently controlled Scottish steel corporation under Scottish Office sponsorship there was no chance of this issue being settled by some kind of corporatist bargain between the state, industry, and unions at the Scottish level. Indeed, if after 1988 Ravenscraig, under a newly privatized BSC, shuts down, we might see the reassertion of a traditional sectional interest representation on the longer-term future of the industry.

Thus the steel campaign, despite generating significant consensus amongst different interests, met with variable success in its objective of retaining an integrated steel plant in Scotland.

Multiple issue concertation: the economic summit

Moving beyond this kind of limited single issue presents different problems. In 1986 the STUC and Strathclyde Regional Council convened a cross-party conference on the Scottish economy. This was in reaction to a series of crises in the Scottish economy, including the threat to Ravenscraig. Initially, Strathclyde Region had called on the Secretary of State to convene such a conference. Not surprisingly, he refused and the Scottish Office declined to participate in the summit convened by the Region and STUC.

The objectives of the conference were to go beyond specific reaction to immediate crisis and to set an agenda for longer-range policy on the economy. In effect, it was a statement of discontent with existing government policy. Representatives included local authorities, political parties, Scottish Council, Churches, academics, chambers of commerce, and the CBI. An agreed statement was produced which argued for positive government intervention in the economy, support for specific sectors in crisis, policies for manufacturing industry and unemployment. A Standing Commission was set up, including a cross-section of those groups attending the conference. The purpose of this Commission was to guide the work of experts in studying various aspects of the Scottish economy. The Commission was likened to a select committee which would report back to a reconvened summit (Strathclyde Regional Council–STUC 1986). In the interim, the Commission has been co-ordinating a series of studies including work on investment, employment, and trade. Thus again we have an example of an issue beginning to generate cross-class or cross-sectional alliances which are institutionalized at a macro (Scottish) level in the form of a multi-party summit, and which develops into an instrument for analysing key economic issues at a sectoral or meso-level.

The major problems faced by this model of consensus and embryonic meso-corporatism arise over, firstly, the nature of consensus and, secondly, translating agreement into political action. The statement prepared for the summit was wide-ranging and generalized. It acknowledged that there would be different views amongst the participants about the health of the Scottish economy, and went on: 'It would be optimistic to assume that consensus can be achieved on all the details of a recovery programme' (Strathclyde Regional Council–STUC 1986: 9).

Consensus on broad principles and on the need for more government resources for Scotland were not too difficult to secure. Different groups could agree on the need for a larger share of the UK cake for Scotland. What was problematic was how far they could agree on the internal distribution of the slices, particularly where agreement on an alternative economic programme for Scotland was being addressed. As Keating and Midwinter have argued in relation to the Scottish Council, the reason why it can generate such a high degree of consensus is that it avoided antagonizing the sectional interests of any individual member. Consensus was largely based on the lowest common denominator of agreement (Keating and Midwinter 1983). Certainly the lessons of the past were not encouraging. In the early 1980s the STUC convened a similar cross-party summit on unemployment with a view to regular meetings, but the exercise failed to generate any long-term commitment (Kellas 1983).

The second problem was that, even assuming agreement was achieved over a range of highly specific policy proposals, how were these to be implemented against a hostile central government, unless the Scottish Office and satellite bodies like the SDA were prepared to take them up? The attitude of the Scottish Office to the summit was at best ambiguous. Initially, the Secretary of State was dismissive of the project. Subsequently, he toned down his criticisms to say that he was always prepared to listen to 'constructive proposals'. As in the Ravenscraig case, the tenuous integration between societal consensus and locus of political and economic power which essentially lies outside Scotland suggests that concertation cannot be translated readily into a form of Scottish corporatism at this macro policy level. Thus the fate of this initiative may be to produce advice in a policy vacuum and ultimately a loss of support between participants even if they can agree amongst themselves about policy prescriptions.

To summarize our analysis of the capacity of issues to generate agreement and assume a Scottish identity, we argue that the belief in England of an all-powerful Scottish lobby with undue influence over government is misleading. Both Ravenscraig and the economic summit generated significant cross-party consensus when measured by the participation of different interests in the various institutional fora. The steel campaign generated a high degree of concertation between 1982 and 1986. It was successful to the extent that the Secretary of State and Scottish Office supported publicly the case for retaining Ravenscraig. But it was unsuccessful in maintaining this political commitment over Gartcosh and the longer-term viability of the plant.

The economic summit similarly generated a level of consensus around the problems of the Scottish economy, including agreement over specific areas of concern. This consensus did generate a new institutional forum in the Standing Commission which might be taken as a very weak form of meso-corporatist arrangement. However, in the absence of Scottish Office participation, the chances of translating its prescriptions into policy were marginal.

Major changes in political and constitutional arrangements would be needed to turn concertation into something more than generalized consensus. Devolution or independence would certainly provide the potential for distinctive corporatist arrangements. In the absence of such radical change the opportunities for distinctive bargaining and policy-making can only be found in specific policy arenas where the institutional network possesses a degree of decision-making autonomy and can link into a Scottish interest and identity to translate policy into specific programmes.

THE 'TRIPLE ECONOMY'

On issues located at the macro-level of political decision-making the potential of the Scottish lobby essentially amounts to exerting concerted pressure. It is not strictly speaking corporatist because it lacks the *autonomous* institutional dynamic to translate societal consensus into policy outcomes. However, if we turn to a sectoral analysis of the Scottish economy we can identify *relatively* autonomous institutional and associative networks which come together in distinctive ways in order, from their perspective, to benefit the Scottish economy.

There may be costs associated with institutions and interests that undertake concerted action in the market. The major cost is where these arrangements act as a way of *insulating* a sector or industry from competition. Maintaining a sector like steel against changing international markets may have high economic costs, although there could be offsetting social benefits in preserving employment.

On the other hand there may be benefits to be derived from concertation. Institutional arrangements and bargains struck at the meso-level between public and private actors might provide in some sectors for temporary support to create new market opportunities. Cawson's work on teletext illustrates the positive outcomes of such arrangements at a sector level (Cawson 1987). Similar strategies can be seen in the development of particular sectors in Scotland, as we highlight later on.

The analysis of the relationships between state agencies and the market at the sector level in Scotland has led us to go beyond Cawson's dual economy thesis (Cawson 1982). Cawson argues that the developed capitalist economy can be seen in terms of either a corporatist or a market mode of interest intermediation and organized relationships. The corporatist mode occurs in the advanced organized large-scale enterprise sectors of the economy where the state historically actively intervenes in terms of macro- and meso-level economic and industrial policy. This generates institutionalized or structured links, including organized labour, as a partner in bargaining over economic and industrial policy. In contrast the market mode is found in those sectors of the economy still characterized by early competitive small-scale enterprises. State intervention in this sector is mainly indirect and restricted to providing a general framework for the market to function. Linkages between the state and interest organizations are minimal. Key arenas of bargaining, in particular labour–capital relations, tend to be mediated through the market.

However, our empirical analysis of sectors in Scotland found Cawson's model to be inadequate. It does not take into account the important dimensions of *spatial control* in different sectors of the Scottish economy, and the respective modes of inter-action between the public and private sectors. This led us to develop a new threefold classification, which is outlined in Table 10.2.

The Scottish economy is characterized in several key sectors by a high level of external ownership and control. The 'branch plant' economy is a well-observed feature of these sectors (Hood and Young 1982; Young 1984). The orientation of the dominant enterprises is global. Decision-making is located outside Scotland. In sectors dominated by major multinational corporate investment the development of a sector strategy by public agencies is based on attracting such enterprises into Scotland and seeking to maximize spin-off benefits for local companies in the form of technology and subcontracting. A dual dependency relationship develops. Firstly, public agencies, through offering packages of assistance and marketing, attempt to attract multinationals to locate in Scotland. Secondly, the presence of these firms is seen as providing economic benefits for indigenous enterprise.

Table 10.2 Models of intervention in the local economy

	Dependency mode	Concerted mode	Modified market mode
Market structure	Global competition Local monopoly	Managed market Oligopolistic	Pluralist Competitive
Dominant enterprise	Multinational	National	Local
Ownership	External	Indigenous (UK)	Indigenous (Scottish)
Intervention	Attracting	Concerted/ corporatist	Bilateral
	Servicing	Meso-level intervention	Micro-level intervention
	Indigenous sector develops as subcontractor	Partnership (sector working parties)	Clientelistic relationships

At the other extreme are sectors characterized by a high level of local control and competition. The market is made up of a large number of small to medium-sized firms. There is an absence of sectoral identity. Thus the relationship between the public and private actors assumes a bilateral mode. The public agency develops links with individual enterprises through provision of a range of services designed to make the firm more competitive. This type of relationship has been described in terms of 'micro-corporatism' (Cawson 1986). The interventionist strategies based on the concept of planning agreements by local authority enterprise boards is cited as an example of bargaining leading to concerted arrangements between management, labour, and the local state. However, as Cawson acknowledges, the capacity of local public agencies to influence the ways in which capital operates at the local level is limited. The concept of micro-corporatism must involve the enterprise acting as an *instrument* of *public policy* in exchange for targeted assistance with agreed objectives being set. The relationship between Ferranti and the government in the 1950s and 1960s during the initial attempts to create a Scottish electronics industry might be characterized in these terms as micro-corporatist (Hughes 1985). Others have described such relationships as 'sponsored pluralism' or 'clientelism' because they are bilateral agreements between state agencies and industry associations or firms based on consensus, rather than multipartite arrangements designed to manage conflicts of interest (Atkinson and Coleman 1985). We prefer the term 'modified market' because the long-term aim is to make selected firms more competitive in the market-place, but in the short to medium term this may involve discriminatory public support based on a bargaining relationship between the firm and state agency.

Finally, relationships between public agencies and industry can develop at the sector level. We have described this as a concerted mode of intervention in the market. The structure of the sector is characterized by a relatively small population of key firms under indigenous ownership and control. This provides the basis for concerted relationships to develop, based on bringing together various interests in a strategic forum in order to analyse problems and develop a policy for the sector. It is essential that there is some common identity or interest in existence or which can be generated by agency intervention.

Thus there are three critical variables underlying the modes of intervention in this model. Firstly, an *economic* variable which analyses the structure of the sector in terms of *enterprises, markets, ownership,* and *control.* Secondly, a *social* variable concerned with *values* within the sector and the degree to which these sustain a consensus which provides the basis for a Scottish interest. Thirdly, a *political* variable concerning the distribution of decision-making *power* and *governance* of the sector, in both the public sector and the private sector, which provides an associative order or network capable of promoting common values and providing a means of delivering public policy objectives. Table 10.3 provides a framework for understanding the way in which these variables can be identified and measured. The significance of these factors can be illustrated by using some examples.

Dependency sector

The development of a consensus at a sector level around some notion of a Scottish interest, and the creation of institutional fora to translate agreement into policy, are difficult in sectors which are international in their orientation and dominated by multinationals. The electronics sector in Scotland is the major example of the dependency strategy. It was the sector first identified by the SDA as an area in which Scotland could develop market growth in specific sub-sectors. The two objectives of the Agency's strategy for the sector were, firstly, to attract new inward investment, and, secondly, as a consequence of achieving this aim, to develop a strong indigenous sector. The Agency described its overall objective for the industry as securing a 'critical mass' state of development in which the industry would be self-generating in its growth.

The method of achieving this objective was the marketing and promotion of Scotland as a location for multinational investment. It was felt to be essential for the development of an indigenous sector that multinational investment was attracted to Scotland since local firms lacked the capital and technology to develop a major sector without such external infusion of investment. The danger was that the price of basing indigenous growth upon multinational investment was to perpetuate the dependency of the Scottish economy on decisions made outside Scotland on the basis of global corporate interests and not the interests of the Scottish economy.

The SDA's strategy has been successful in attracting inward investment. Since 1981 Scotland has benefited from over £1 billion of investment with a jobs potential of 15,000. Much of this investment has been by major US and Japanese electronics corporations. Electronics as a sector employs over 40,000 people in Scotland. However, recent analysis by the SDA itself reveals the market dependency on multinationals and the limited growth of an independent indigenous industry. The Agency's own survey of the industry in 1986 found that although 41 per cent of manufacturing companies in the sector were Scottish-owned, they accounted for only 8 per cent of employment. Scottish companies accounted for 5 per cent of turnover, while US corporations accounted for over 70 per cent. In addition there was a low level of export performance and lack of research and development by Scottish firms. Finally, only 12 per cent of the industry's inputs was being sourced from within Scotland (SDA 1986). This shows that multinational companies were making sourcing decisions which fitted in with their own corporate interests rather than any Scottish interest.

The problems of developing a strategy for the indigenous sector were thus constrained by two key factors. Firstly, the

Table 10.3. Measures and methods for analysing the critical variables in the Scottish economy

Variable	Analytical method	Criteria	Measures	Means
Economic (structural)	Economics	Degree of closure/ openness in the regional/ sectoral economy.	1. Levels of indigenous v. external ownership and control of the regional/sectoral economy. 2. Degree of cartelization, monopoly, competition.	Quantitative data on multinational and indigenous enterprise and sectoral/ regional economy. Input–output analysis. Import–export ratios. Census of industry/ enterprise—number of enterprises, size, ownership and control, significance in terms of employment, output, profitability, product. Company records and census of production.
Social (ideological)	Sociological	Degree of identity and consensus at the regional/ sectoral level.	1. Identification with regional/sectoral institutions and	Mass opinion surveys. Electoral voting patterns. Secondary analysis of

			organizations. 2. Evidence of socio-cultural autonomy. 3. Incidence of class conflict/harmony, e.g. number of strikes. 4. Sectoral cohesion. 5. Interaction between regional/sectoral leadership.	separate institutions, e.g. religious, educational, and cultural (language, media). Industrial relations records. Élite interviewing.
Political (institutional)	Institutional/ organizational	1. Degree of institutional/ organizational autonomy at the regional/sectoral level. 2. Capacity for effective decision-making.	1. Modes and levels of political/organizational accountability. 2. Sources of finance. 3. Delegated legislative or regulatory powers. 4. Level and independence of institutional/ organizational resources. 5. Degree of self-regulation.	Analysis of statutes and regulations. Accounts. Organizational analysis of sectoral associations and regional public institutions.

structure of the sector was heavily dominated by multinationals operating in global markets. Because of this major decision-making powers are located outside Scotland and thus there is a low level of identification with a Scottish interest. Secondly, the governance of the sector is clearly limited at the Scottish level by the presence of multinationals. The SDA for example has very little power or influence over these corporations. The most it can do is to bring together local managers in the sector in informal fora for discussion of topics of common interest.

The modified market sector

Sectors of the Scottish economy characterized by high levels of indigenous ownership and control do not necessarily generate a strong sense of identity, common interests, or developed governance through associational networks. Some sectors are fragmented in their markets, products, and types of enterprise. A prime example of this fragmented structure is the Scottish engineering sector. Young and Reeves (1984) argued that a major constraint in the development of a sectoral strategy for the industry was the lack of significant indigenous enterprises able to provide sectoral leadership and form the focus of strategic intervention by public agencies. The sector was in effect made up of several relatively autonomous sub-sectors catering for different markets. Ownership and control are divided equally between Scottish, UK, and overseas firms. There is no highly developed sense of identity or common interest between companies in Scotland. The associative order is geared towards sustaining sectoral unity on industrial relations and wages issues, rather than providing a means of developing a collective strategy for industrial development.

In such a highly fragmented sector, relationships between public agencies and the industry assume bilateral forms. This is clearly evident in the SDA's strategy for the sector in Scotland. It has developed a programme of corporate development which involves working with a company and its management to identify its strengths and weaknesses and develop its corporate objectives over the next three- to five-year period. The Agency then provides assistance to managers to help them improve their performance in the market.

It is clearly not a relationship based on a *free market* since it involves targeted public sector intervention and agreements between the public agency and the firm on the terms of that aid. It falls short of the corporatism identified in the industrial strategies of the 1970s based on sector-wide planning and consensus between the state, capital, and labour. The relationships and strategy are thus rooted in a market mode of intervention based on the individual enterprise. It is built on bilateral contacts between public agency and managers rather than multipartite fora or sectoral associations. In this sense, the relationship fits in with what Atkinson and Coleman have identified as 'clientelism' (Atkinson and Coleman 1985). Concertation is limited to the micro-level and relationships are essentially bilateral.

Concerted sectors

In sectors which combine a high degree of indigenous ownership and control with concentration of economic power, the opportunities for sector-level intervention are increased. The structural factors are favourable to meso-level intervention. In this situation the ideological and political factors become critical elements. This is well illustrated by the Scottish woollen industry.

The woollen sector in Scotland is subject to a high level of indigenous ownership and control. The products and markets are clearly identified. The SDA in its analysis of the sector saw it as providing an opportunity for developing a coherent strategy which could provide collective benefits to the industry above the capacity of individual enterprises in the market. The constraint was the fragmentation of interests and lack of associative order. Historically the industry had developed a number of sub-sectors with their own representative associations pursuing particularistic interests. The Agency offered a commitment to provide resources for the strengthening of the sector as a whole in return for agreement within the industry to come together. As a result, a new common organizational identity was created. Scottish Woollen Industries has fifty member firms representing 92 per cent of the sector in terms of companies, although only 65 per cent in terms of employment because two of the biggest employers (both branch plants) are not members. This institutional network provided not only a means of promoting a collective Scottish identity but also a means whereby the industry could play a role in the development and implementation of policies for the sector. A unified private sector organization had been created which became an instrument of public policy. An arena for striking collective bargains within the industry and with the public sector was established. This relationship corresponds to concepts of sector- or meso-level bargaining institutionalized in new formal arrangements involving the private sector and government. It has provided a means of delivering publicly funded programmes designed to promote collective benefits to the sector, for example generic marketing, training, and research development. Whether this is corporatism as traditionally understood in UK economic and industrial policy is debatable. What it is, however, is a modification of the market by collective action designed to enhance the competitiveness of selected enterprises within the market.

Summary

To summarize, the relationships between the SDA and the market in Scotland at a sectoral level need to be analysed through three variables. The structural or economic variable concerns the degree to which the sector is subject to indigenous or external forces in terms of ownership and control of enterprises and markets, and the degree to which it is concentrated or fragmented. Where the sector is dominated by multinationals the influence of Scottish level institutions and the identification of a Scottish interest is low. This results in a dependency mode of intervention by public agencies and in dependency relationships between the public and private sectors. Where the structure of the sector is subject to a greater level of indigenous ownership and control the ideological and political variables exert a more autonomous influence at the Scottish level. Depending on the structure of the sector, this can lead to one of two modes of intervention. Where the sector is fragmented structurally, and there is an absence of consensus over common interests and a weak associative order, public intervention assumes bilateral relationships with individual enterprises. Where the sector is more concentrated in terms of enterprise, markets, and products, and where this can be linked to a strong associative order, then a sense of identity around a common sectoral interest on certain issues of collective benefit may be generated. Public intervention can serve to help in this process by providing incentives for firms to co-operate and thereby help to instil a common identity and even create sector-level institutions which can deliver policy.

The relationships between the public and private sectors which develop in each case cannot satisfactorily be described by the term 'corporatist'. They assume different forms depending on the influence of these variables. The critical question is to what extent do they involve concerted modes of development which lie beyond what would commonly be understood as a liberal market approach or a state directed strategy?

CONCLUSION

The pull of centralized political accountability, the continued influence of UK-based political identity and sectional interests, and the open nature of the Scottish economy constrain the influence of Scottish institutions, identity, and interests. Forms of concertation can be seen concerning specific issues where sectional interests come to identify with a common interest defined spatially at the Scottish level over and above any UK identification. This tends to be spasmodic and where this does occur it is largely reactive and defensive, responding to perceived external threats. Where it tries to assume a broader, more strategic conception, it runs into the problem of antagonizing different interests and of class- or group-based conflicts. The issue-based concertation which we have identified is distinct from pluralism because it is based on collective identity and acknowledgement by different interests that they can benefit by sacrificing some of their own particularistic interests in order to advance a wider goal. Pluralism emphasizes group conflict and competition in pursuit of maximizing particular interests.

However, concertation is not synonymous with corporatism (Schmitter 1982). The latter possesses an institutional dynamic which transforms social consensus into a distinctive mode of bargained relationship between public and private interests in order to meet certain policy objectives. If corporatism is to have any meaning at the Scottish level we must be able to point to relatively autonomous public institutions of government and a strong associative order within the private sector. This network of relations must be able to generate a common set of values or consensus on certain issues and an identity of interests at a Scottish level separate from UK-defined interests. There must be sufficient political and economic autonomy at the Scottish level to translate consensus into policy outputs and to influence outcomes.

The capacity of Scottish institutions and interests to do this varies across economic sectors largely depending on structural factors, particularly location of ownership and control within the sector. There is room for manœuvre by political institutions and private associations and interests where these economic structural factors are favourable to Scottish influence.

Corporatism is too narrow a concept to characterize the complex range of relationships which we have found in different sectors of the Scottish economy between public agencies and private interests. It does not grasp some of the most important aspects of concertation. Bargains between the SDA and industry may take bilateral forms or may lead to sector-wide institutional arrangements which fuse interest representation with policy responsibility but lack the element of control, which is the classical defining criterion of neo-corporatism (Lehmbruch 1979; Cawson 1985). What is clear is that concerted forms of relationships can be distinguished from market or state bureau-cratic modes. There is a 'negotiated order' which operates at the Scottish level in some sectors of the economy.

In order to assess the significance of the relative autonomy we need to analyse on a sector basis the strength of the institutional infrastructure in both public and private sectors, and how these interests relate to each other and with a sense of identity at the Scottish level. The key limits operating at the Scottish level are partly political and partly economic. The political limits are apparent in the continued existence of class politics and centralized political accountability. The economic limits concern the external location of corporate and political decision-making power over the Scottish economy.

An approach which seeks to argue in terms of a 'Scottish corporatism' is in our view misplaced because it fails to grasp the importance of the key relationships. It leads therefore to a distorted picture of the Scottish political economy. A more fruitful approach is a differentiated analysis at the level of sectors and space linked to an analysis of the significance of Scottish institutions, interests, and identity. This provides a more complex but realistic model indicating the relative importance of the regional dimension in decision-making in Scotland. It shows that while in Thatcherite Britain the market model of decision-making and relations may dominate, there can exist within this paradigm a series of relatively autonomous relationships between elements of the state and selected interests based on bargained agreements designed to overcome market weaknesses or better to seize market opportunities. This was the official rationale for the continued existence of the SDA as an agency of public intervention in the market (Scottish Office 1987). The Agency has changed with the political and ideological climate. It continued to engage in bargaining with business interests and to seek forms of collective action within the market economy.

This negotiated order lies between market and state control and is based on a limited specific and less formalized consensus than classical corporatism. Scotland, because of its special institutions, identity, and interests, has provided an arena for such arrangements to develop.

REFERENCES

ATKINSON, M., and COLEMAN, W. (1985), 'Corporatism and Industrial Policy', in A. Cawson (ed.), *Organised Interests and the State: Studies in Meso-Corporatism* (London: Sage), 22–44.

BRAND, J. (1978), *The National Movement in Scotland* (London: Routledge & Kegan Paul).

CAWSON, A. (1982), *Corporatism and Welfare: Social Policy and State Intervention in Britain* (London: Heinemann).

—— (1985), 'Introduction: Varieties of Corporatism: The Importance of the Meso-level of Interest Intermediation', in A. Cawson (ed.), *Organised Interests and the State: Studies in Meso-Corporatism* (London: Sage), 1–21.

—— (1986), *Corporatism and Political Theory* (Oxford: Blackwell).

—— (1987), 'The Teletext Initiative in Britain: The Anatomy of Successful Neo-Corporatist Policy Making' (paper presented to the European Consortium for Political Research Workshop on Meso Corporatism, the Cutback State and the Politico-Industrial Crisis, Amsterdam, Apr.).

DRUCKER, H., and BROWN, G. (1980), *The Politics of Nationalism and Devolution* (London: Longman).

GRANT, W. (1985), 'Introduction', in W. Grant (ed.), *The Political Economy of Corporatism* (London: Macmillan), 1–35.

HAWORTH, N. (1987), 'Making Tracks: Caterpillar's Crawl from Scotland', *Quarterly Economic Commentary*, 23/4: 67–72 (Fraser of Allander Institute, Strathclyde Business School, Glasgow, May).

HOGWOOD, B., and KEATING, M. (1982), *Regional Government in England* (Edinburgh: Mainstream).

HOOD, N., and YOUNG, S. (1982), *Multinationals in Retreat: The Scottish Experience* (Edinburgh: Edinburgh University Press).

HUGHES, M. (1985), 'Debureaucratization and Private Interest Government: The British State and Economic Development Policy', in W. Streeck and P. Schmitter (eds.), *Private Interest Government: Beyond Market and State* (London, Beverly Hills: Sage), 87–104.

KEATING M., and MIDWINTER, A. (1983), *The Government of Scotland* (Edinburgh: Mainstream).

KELLAS, J. (1983), *The Scottish Political System* (Cambridge: Cambridge University Press).

LEHMBRUCH, G. (1979), 'Liberal Corporatism and Party Government', in P. Schmitter and G. Lehmbruch (eds.), *Trends Towards Corporatist Intermediation* (London: Sage), 53–62.

MAXWELL, S. (1987), 'Norway's Economic Lessons for Scotland', *Radical Scotland* , 25 (Feb./Mar.): 14–17.

MILLER, W. (1981), *The End of British Politics* (Oxford: Clarendon Press).

Monopolies and Mergers Commission (1982), *Report on Proposed Mergers of Hong Kong and Shanghai Bank, Standard Chartered and Royal Bank of Scotland*, Cmnd. 8472 (London: HMSO).

MORENO, L. (1986), 'Decentralisation in Britain and Spain: The Cases of Scotland and Catalonia' (Ph.D. thesis, Department of Politics, University of Edinburgh).

· RIFKIND, M. (1982), 'Reflections of a Scottish Office Minister', in H. Drucker and N. Drucker (eds.), *The Scottish Government Yearbook 1982* (Edinburgh: Paul Harris Publishing), 57–68.

ROSE, R. (1982), *Understanding the United Kingdom: The Territorial Dimensions in Government* (London: Longman).

SCHMITTER, P. (1982), 'Reflections on Where the Theory of Neo-corporatism has Gone and Where the Praxis of Neo-corporatism may be Going', in G. Lehmbruch and P. Schmitter (eds.), *Patterns of Corporatist Policy-Making* (London: Sage), 259–80.

—— and LEHMBRUGH, G. (1979), *Trends Towards Corporatist Intermediation* (London, Beverly Hills: Sage).

SCOTT, J., and HUGHES, M. (1980), *The Anatomy of Scottish Capital: Scottish Companies and Scottish Capital 1900–1979* (London: Croom Helm).

Scottish Council (1982), *A Medium Term Strategy for Steel* (Edinburgh: Scottish Council Development and Industry, 15 Nov.).

—— (1985a), *The Scottish Steel Industry*, Executive Paper No. 23 (85) (Edinburgh: Scottish Council Development and Industry, 28 Aug.).

—— (1985b), *The Future of The Scottish Steel Industry* (Edinburgh: Scottish Council Development and Industry, 19 Dec.).

Scottish Office (1985), *Statement by Mr. George Younger, MP, Secretary of State for Scotland, on the Plans Announced Today by the British Steel Corporation for the Period from 1985 until 1988* (Edinburgh: Scottish Office, 7 Aug.).

—— (1986), *Scottish Abstract of Statistics* (Edinburgh: Scottish Office), Table 15–14.

—— (1987), *Review of the Scottish Development Agency: Report of Review Group to the Secretary of State for Scotland* (Edinburgh: Scottish Office, Feb.).

Scottish Select Committee (1982), *The Steel Industry in Scotland: Report of the Scottish Affairs Select Committee, Session 1982–83* (House of Commons Paper No. 22, HMSO, Dec.).

SDA (1986), *The Scottish Electronics Industry Database 1986* (Glasgow: Scottish Development Agency).

Strathclyde Regional Council–STUC (1986), *Scotland's Economy: The Way Ahead* (statement from the Summit Conference convened by Strathclyde Regional Council and the Scottish Trades Union Congress, July).

STUC (1986), *Scotland: A Strategy for the Future* (Glasgow: Scottish Trades Union Congress).

WASSENBERG, A. F. P. (1982), 'Neo-Corporatism and the Quest for Control: The Cuckoo Game', in G. Lehmbruch and P. Schmitter (eds.), *Patterns of Corporatist Policy-Making* (London: Sage), 83–108.

YOUNG, A. (1987), 'Jobs Price we can't go on Paying', *Glasgow Herald*, 18 May.

YOUNG, S. (1982), 'The Foreign Owned Manufacturing Sector', in Hood and Young 1982.

—— and HOOD, N. (1982), 'Industrial Policy and the Scottish Economy', in Hood and Young 1982: 28–56.

—— and LOWE, A. (1974), *Intervention in the Mixed Economy* (London: Croom Helm).

—— and REEVES, A. (1982), 'The Engineering and Metals Sector', in Hood and Young 1982: 128–73.

List of Contributors

Martin Boddy teaches at the School of Advanced Urban Studies, University of Bristol. He is the author of *The Building Societies* (1979) and his main research interests are in housing, urban and regional change, and local government.

Simon Booth is senior lecturer in Management Studies in the Department of Economics, University of Reading. He is co-author with Chris Moore of *Managing Competition* (1989). Research interests include crisis management theory, urban policy, and the management of change and innovation.

Michael Connolly is Professor of Public Administration and Legal Studies, University of Ulster. His publications have been mainly concerned with local economic development in Northern Ireland. He is joint editor of *Public Money and Management* and is currently working on the nature of public management and policy-making in a divided society.

Graham Cox is lecturer in sociology at the University of Bath. He is co-author of *Countryside Conflicts: The Politics of Farming, Forestry and Conservation* (1986) and (with Philip Lowe and Michael Winter) of *The Voluntary Principle in Conservation: A Study of the Farming and Wildlife Advisory Group* (1989), and co-editor of *Agriculture: People and Policies*. His current research interests include the politics of land ownership and rural restructuring.

Colin Crouch is a fellow and tutor in politics at Trinity College, Oxford, and faculty lecturer in sociology at the University of Oxford. He is the author of *Class Conflict and the Industrial Relations Crisis* (1977), *The Politics of Industrial Relations* (1979 and 1982), and *Trade Unions: The Logic of Collective Action* (1982). He edited *The Resurgence of Class Conflict in Western Europe since 1968* (with A. Pizzorno, 1978), *State and Economy in Contemporary Capitalism* (1979), and *European Industrial Relations: The Challenge of Flexibility* (with G. Baglioni, 1990). He is joint editor of the *Political Quarterly*. Current research interests include the historical development of industrial relations systems in Western Europe.

Ronald Dore is currently Visiting Professor at Harvard University and also attached to the Centre for Japanese and Comparative Industrial Research, Imperial College, London. His books include *British Factory—Japanese Factory* (1973), *The Diploma Disease* (1977), *Taking Japan Seriously* (1985), *Flexible Rigidities* (1987). His main research interest is in Japanese social and economic development.

Andrew Erridge is senior lecturer in the Department of Public Administration, University of Ulster. He is the author of *The Politics of Industrial Training* (forthcoming) and his current research interests concern policy on vocational education and training in Britain and Northern Ireland.

Roger King is Director and Chief Executive of the Humberside College of Higher Education. He is the author of *Capital and Politics* (1983), *The Middle Class* (1981), and *Respectable Rebels: Middle Class Campaigns in Britain* (1979). He is currently preparing a book on 'The state in modern society'.

Martin Laffin is senior lecturer in the Graduate School of Management and Public Policy, University of Sydney. His publications include *Professionalism and Policy; The Local Government Professions in the Central–Local Government Relationship* (1986) and *Managing under Pressure: Industrial Relations in Local Government* (1989). Present research interests include corporatism in Australia and the problems of organizational change in the UK and Australian public sectors.

Christine Lambert is attached to the School of Advanced Urban Studies, University of Bristol. Her main research interests concern land policy, planning and development, and local government finance.

Norman Lewis is Professor of Public Law at the Centre for Criminological and Socio-legal Studies at the University of Sheffield. He has published and researched widely in the field of constitutional law and constitutional law reform. He is co-author (with Ian Harden) of *The Noble Lie: The British Constitution and the Rule of Law*, (1986). The present essay is part of a larger examination of corporatism and accountability shortly to be published with Harden and Patrick Birkinshaw as *The Hybrid Parts of the State*.

Philip Lowe is lecturer in countryside planning in the Bartlett School of Architecture and Planning, University College, London. He is the author (with Jane Goyder) of *Environmental Groups in Politics* (1983), a co-author of *Countryside Conflicts: The Politics of Farming, Forestry and Conservation* (1986), (with Graham Cox and Michael Winter) of *The Voluntary Principle in Conservation: A Study of the Farming and Wildlife Advisory Group* (1989), and (with Wolfgang Rudig) of *The Green Wave: Ecological Parties in Global Perspective* (1988). He is currently co-director of the ESRC-assisted project 'The Social and Economic Restructuring of Rural Britain'.

Chris Moore is lecturer in the Department of Organisation, Management and Employee Relations, University of Strathclyde. He is co-author with Simon Booth of *Managing Competition* (1989) and with J. J. Richardson of *Local Partnerships and the Unemployment Crisis* (1989), and co-editor with W. Lever of *The City in Transition* (1987). Research interests include urban politics and the political economy of regional industrial policy-making.

Michael Moran is a senior lecturer in the Department of Government at the University of Manchester. He has written on the politics of both labour and financial markets. His books include *The Politics of Banking* (1984) and *Politics and Society in Britain* (1985). He is completing a study of 'States and financial markets: the politics of the financial services revolution in the UK, USA, and Japan'.

Kris Schnack is a research executive with a market and social research consultancy in West Yorkshire.

Michael Winter is Director of the Centre for Rural Studies at the Royal Agricultural College, Cirencester. He is a co-author of *Countryside Conflicts: The Politics of Farming, Forestry and Conservation* (1986) and (with Philip Lowe and Graham Cox) of *The Voluntary Principle in Conservation: A Study of the Farming and Wildlife Advisory Group* (1989) and editor (with Mary Bouquet) of *Who from their Labour Rest? Conflict and Practice in Rural Tourism* (1987). Current research interests include religion in rural areas. He is UK co-ordinator of the EC's research programme on 'Farm Structures and Pluriactivity'.

Index